# Was It For This?

## Why Ireland Lost the Plot

John Waters

TRANSWORLD IRELAND

TRANSWORLD IRELAND
an imprint of The Random House Group Limited
20 Vauxhall Bridge Road, London SW1V 2SA
www.transworldbooks.co.uk

First published in 2012 by Transworld Ireland,
a division of Transworld Publishers

This book is a work of non-fiction. The author has stated to the publishers
that, except in such minor respects not affecting the substantial accuracy
of the work, the contents of this book are true.

A CIP catalogue record for this book
is available from the British Library.

ISBN 9781848271258

Addresses for Random House Group Ltd companies outside the UK
can be found at: www.randomhouse.co.uk
The Random House Group Ltd Reg. No. 954009

The Random House Group Limited supports the Forest Stewardship Council (FSC®),
the leading international forest-certification organization. Our books carrying the
FSC label are printed on FSC®-certified paper. FSC is the only forest-certification
scheme endorsed by the leading environmental organizations, including Greenpeace.
Our paper procurement policy can be found at
www.randomhouse.co.uk/environment

Typeset in 11/15pt Sabon by
Falcon Oast Graphic Art Ltd.
Printed and bound in Great Britain by
CPI Group (UK) Ltd, Croydon, CR0 4YY

2 4 6 8 10 9 7 5 3 1

MIX
Paper from
responsible sources
FSC® C016897
FSC
www.fsc.org

# Contents

For my daughter, Róisín Waters

# Introduction

# Stealing from the Future (and Pissing on the Past)

IN THIS SPRING OF 2012, IRISH SOCIETY REMAINS STUCK IN A FROZEN moment. There are many ways you might describe this situation, but for the moment let us stick to the most prosaic, the terms by which our condition is described to us on a moment-to-moment basis. Scuppered by relationships and a currency we were promised would represent our salvation, spancelled by our 'partners' who charge us exorbitant rates to lend us money as a solution to a problem arising from excessive borrowings, and screwed by two governments in succession which have treated us as though we have no say in any of it, we survey the bedraggled remnants of our sovereignty and wonder where it all went wrong.

A man from Mars, listening attentively to the continuing conversation, might before long gather the impression that current Irish misfortunes are rooted in the very recent past. In fact, this moment began to be generated in the early 1960s, when the prize of modernity was first scented.

This is a difficult argument to make in current conditions without being understood as antagonistic to the very idea of what is called progress. In many, many ways, the modernizing initiative was necessary and beneficial, lifting Ireland out of the doldrums of reaction and inertia and thrusting it forward into a new set of possibilities. But there were fundamental factors characterizing the Irish situation, which, by virtue of being unremarked, created a forward dynamic that was perhaps doomed from the start. For one thing, there was no sense of how a progress project might be rooted in indigenous resources and energies, or even that this might be a necessary or good thing. By the same token, there was no sense of a need for an idiosyncratic manifesto, which might have tailored the coming changes to Irish circumstances. Progress, then, came to be modelled on external precedents and paid for with a new set of dependencies, to wit: 'Europe', multinational industry and borrowing.

This modernity project appeared outwardly solid, but internally was stricken from the start because of its intrinsically dependent and its undemocratic nature. It was, to a large extent, an elitist programme, enforced from the top by what the broadcaster and journalist Eamon Dunphy had once named 'Official Ireland'. The main problem was that it lacked a positive concept of identity. It was a reaction to a reaction: an answering back to the previous and now deemed problematic ideologies of nationalism, traditionalism and Catholicism. It had no core except an artificial moralism constructed out of a repugnance for the older values and a demand that they be moved on from.

The old Ireland had been held together by a love of country and a secondary series of emotions which flowed directly from this core emotional cohesion. There was a deep attachment to land, to faith, to the music and language, even though these had been damaged in the years of interference from outside. Although the country continued to be poor, it had nonetheless remained rooted in a relationship with its own means and resources. There was a general sense that the means of survival would have to be located within. But the poverty was the only aspect of this that was to be remarked upon in the thrusting forward that began in the 1960s, as if the desire for Ireland to exist by its own lights and means was

2

itself the problem. As in many things, we began, implicitly, to believe the direct opposite: that progress and riches would in all probability be defined in, and delivered by, some new dependency, and that this would be, self-evidently, a good thing. To assert otherwise was to announce oneself as a reactionary, determined to drag us back into the dark and dismal past.

Thus, during the 1960s, 1970s and 1980s, a revolution occurred, which culminated in the period referred to as the Celtic Tiger. This revolution embraced several key elements, notably the adoption of 'liberal' and 'pluralist' values; the repudiation of tradition and its replacement with an unthinking consumerism; and the embracing of the European 'project'. This project was promoted on a daily basis in the Dublin media, which became, in effect, the cultural imperium of the new Ireland: the regime.

What is the truth about Ireland now? It is that the revolution has failed, that the project of Irish modernization has failed, indeed has led to outright disaster. For the moment, the consequences have been postponed: by more borrowings, this time under the supervision of the IMF, the EU and the ECB, colloquially known as 'the troika'. Underneath is nothing but a failure that has been normalized by stealing from the future. But because the imperium, the regime, continues to provide the diagnosis, this remains invisible and virtually unsayable. Instead, the daily diagnoses home in on technicalities and the search for plausible scapegoats, stoking public rage to the pitch of intellectual incoherence and despair.

My first book, *Jiving at the Crossroads*, which in a strange way I see as a kind of companion to the present volume, described what we might now identify as the mid-point in this revolution. But *Jiving at the Crossroads* was, I now feel, a somewhat naive book. The accusation I would level at my 1991 self is that I assumed that the worst the revolution could inflict on the old Ireland was disrespect. Now, it is clear that this was to be the least of the injuries. The various syndromes I tentatively sought to sketch out in that book afterwards developed an exponential acceleration, culminating in the Celtic Tiger.

The Celtic Tiger was the promise that nobody ever really imagined would come true. The objective had been to destroy the old Ireland by promising a new one that would, by virtue of its contrasting bounties and blessings, reveal the old one for the sham and failure it had been. But nobody thought this promise would be delivered to the extent that it was, or appeared for a time to have been. For a time, the progress project of the imperium became unquestionable. The problem was that this outcome was not a direct consequence of internal revolution, but a collateral benefit arising from the dynamics of the European project. To put it succinctly, we were enjoying the fruits not of our own self-created modernity but of the spin-offs of the investments of German pensioners doled out to Irish borrowers in the manner of Ecstasy at a rave.

Right now, Ireland is at the fullest extent of a cultural stretch it began in the early 1960s. The generation(s) that started that push are still in power, and have endeavoured to ensure that their objectives have remained largely undiluted by any significant input of new thinking. The younger generations have been maintained in a state of constructive alienation: pampered, indulged, empowered to shout abuse and obscenities from the ditch, but not to participate in any meaningful way. Thus, the young have bought into the normalized idea, and imagine that 'Ireland Inc' really exists, that it was a highly successful business that has latterly been brought down by incompetence and corruption.

There is corruption, right enough. But it is the corruption of thought: the promotion of a singular, flawed model of progress combined with the systematic exclusion of other options. And, strangest of all, the young whose futures have been snatched away by this project have been recruited as the willing defenders of the project that snatched those futures away, shouting abuse and ridicule in a manner harmonious with the very beliefs and initiatives that inflicted the damage.

For the moment, Ireland remains relatively prosperous and well fed. It is an illusion that may continue for a while more or collapse at any moment. Meanwhile, the political system is a sham manned by affable actors playing the parts of leaders and representatives. The kinds of politics, civic spirit or vision to be detected in the words of past generations of Irish leaders, who once spoke of a future based on a profound and dynamic sense of Ireland's destiny, are no longer to be found, and if they were would immediately become grounds for ridicule. Their absence is not consciously noted, but deeper down has left a void that seems to eat at the very substance of Irish identity, provoking a cynicism that accelerates the process of disintegration.

Nowadays, still, we take it for granted that Dublin is entitled to speak for Ireland, just as the city remains the principal seat of the Irish State. But Dublin remains only a small part of Ireland, and by far the least representative part, an administrative capital that has hardly covered itself in glory by the quality of its administration. Dublin may well be the 'brain' of Ireland, but this entity is by no means coterminous with the Irish mind, and our Dublin-based, supposedly 'national' media are not so much Dublin-centric as Anglo-centric, obsessed with exploring comparisons between Ireland and Britain and promoting British provincialism as the reality of Irish culture – except, that is, when they are extolling American values and aspirations as the ideal driving agents of 'national' desiring.

It may seem disproportionate and unfair to blame a city for the misfortunes of a nation, and of course it was not the buildings that inflicted the harm. Nonetheless, it is impossible to imagine that, if the capital of Ireland were Galway or Westport, Ireland would bear any resemblance to its present condition, which is largely a reflection of Dublin's confusing influence and control. Now, as in the past, it is Dublin as some culturally occupied entity, rather than as a living community, that we need to think about.

Whenever the events in Dublin 1916 are raised in the public discussion of today's Ireland, someone invariably tables a reminder that the Easter Rising had little or no support among the people of Dublin. And indeed, there was undoubtedly some vociferous opposition to the Rising, mainly from the wives of men fighting in the war against Germany, and therefore dependants of the British Crown. In his 1964 book, *The Easter Rebellion*, Max Caulfield noted that, as the rebel prisoners were marched away under arrest, they were attacked by working-class women, who pelted them with rotten vegetables and emptied chamber pots over them. In his eye-witness account, *The Insurrection in Dublin*, James Stephens wrote:

> Most of the female opinion I heard was not alone unfavourable but actively and viciously hostile to the rising. This was noticeable among the best-dressed classes of our population; the worst dressed, indeed the female dregs of Dublin life, expressed a like antagonism, and almost in similar language. The view expressed was 'I hope every man of them will be shot'.

Because of the odd cultural dynamics nowadays attending these discussions, such accounts are usually presented as reflecting badly on the rebels. There is another perspective: that they reflect the economic and cultural conditions of the time. Dublin in 1916 was a provincial city of the British Empire, bought in body, mind and spirit. It was in hardly any sense a capital city, but an outpost of British colonialism, more connected through governance, economics and culture to the 'mainland' than to the country at its back, and unmoored from the Irish nation by virtue of its complicity in the continuing occupation of Irish hearts, minds and territory.

With a deliberate, strategic obtuseness, our dominant conversations nowadays seek to depict the Rising as a failed attempt to take power in the capital. But in the minds of its key leaders this was simply the most literal and least potent dimension of their endeavour. The idea that there was a realistic chance of gaining power, especially following the non-arrival of promised troops and munitions from Germany, was about the last thing on anyone's mind. The point was to reclaim Dublin for the Irish nation by a gesture that would resonate for generations, to redeem Dublin of the sins of its acquiescence in the subjugation of Ireland. In a letter to his mother on the eve of his execution, Padraig Pearse wrote: 'We have preserved Ireland's honour and our own. People will say hard things of us now, but we shall be remembered by posterity and blessed by unborn generations.'

Back in 1994, my first play, *Long Black Coat*, was staged at Cleere's Theatre in Kilkenny. For reasons too complicated to go into, it was set in the vaguely distant future: approximately but not necessarily precisely 2020. Searching for devices to get this across without labouring the point, I had one of the characters wear an 'old' T-shirt, with a picture of Padraig Pearse and the legend '1916–2016'. I hoped this would suggest the possibility of a totally changed mind towards the past, denoting an Ireland in which the origins of Independent Ireland had ceased to represent a cultural problem.

It didn't work. The critics took the device as literally as critics invariably take everything and saw all kinds of allusions and allegories that weren't there. After a few performances, we deployed a woolly jumper.

Back then, the continuing conflict 'up North' was causing all kind of psycho-cultural reactions to ferment in the unconscious of the Republic, occasionally breaking ground in outbursts of name-calling. Three years before, the seventy-fifth anniversary of 1916 had been marked – or not marked – by a collective staring at shoes. In addition to the events organized by Sinn Féin, which claimed virtual total ownership of the event, there were just a few earnest but desultory commemorations, from which most people maintained an agnostic detachment. Fear of the power of our own history and mythology had become so great that we could not find words to think about ourselves out loud, never mind take any action that might dramatize a position.

That T-shirt anticipated a possible course of history in which the damage of a quarter-century of conflict had been undone – perhaps by the passage of two decades of peace-enabled thought. Nearly two decades later, and less than four years from the centenary, such a process of thinking has yet to begin. Despite more than a decade of relative harmony, the deeper questions about our sense of 1916 have not surfaced in the mainstream consciousness of Irish society.

The national sense of self is of the utmost importance, not merely in some airy-fairy sense relating to 'national identity', but centrally to the most practical questions concerning collective confidence and self-realization. It can very succinctly be argued that what has befallen us in recent years is the culmination of our refusal to take seriously what it says in what we used to call 'the Easter Proclamation'. Had we placed the common good rather than profit at the centre of our value-system, would we be in our present sorry mess? Had we honoured 'the right of the people of Ireland to the ownership of Ireland, and to the unfettered control of Irish destinies', could a few opportunistic speculators have cleaned us out? Had we retained a memory of why our forefathers had wanted us to be independent, would so many of those whom we trusted to carry out society's most sacred callings have dishonoured the Irish nation as they did and ultimately handed us over to a new set of masters?

The problems begin with a lack of self-knowledge, which derives from a refusal to look squarely at history. Too much of our engagement with our own history has been characterized by reaction rather than reason, and the processes relating thereto have been subject to a cultural double-bind that has prevented us discovering our true selves in the older, 'authentic' elements, the newer, imposed ones, or any combination of the two. For roughly the first fifty years of Independence, we sought to define ourselves in contradistinction to our former masters, striving to expunge all traces of the centuries of interference and abuse. In that period we became insular-minded and self-obsessed, pursuing notions of authenticity and self-sufficiency that had been rendered impossible by the cultural and psychological facts of history.

The half-centenary celebrations of the Rising, in 1966, seemed to mark, approximately, a change in this outlook. From the late 1960s onwards, we went in the opposite direction, seeking to draw our sense of Ireland from imported notions, new dependencies and a repudiation of most of what had been pursued in the early decades of Independence.

The fiftieth anniversary celebrations had certainly been unabashed and over the top. Easter Weekend had seen parades in most of the larger towns, replete with whatever militaristic trappings could be mustered. The leaders of 1916 were remembered as godlike figures. Everyone was a republican.

But, just as an idealized version of 1916 had been employed in the green-tinted post-Independence reconstruction, a caricatured notion of the 1966 commemorations was similarly utilized, from the early 1970s, to deconstruct the nationalist version of things, ostensibly in order to rationalize our cultural and political abandonment of Northern nationalists, but deeper down to justify the new path we had chosen on which our guiding star was to be material prosperity rather than things of the spirit.

Not knowing how to deal with the Provos' appropriation of history, we looked away. To convince ourselves that our idle by-standing was legitimate, we turned to rewriting the history. But even in this there was an ulterior motive: to disparage the past so as not to be bound by its passions or dreams. There was, of course, an understandable anxiety about giving comfort to the murderous thugs of the IRA. But the problem ran deeper: we did not trust the passions which the consciousness of 1916 threatened to awake in ourselves. The resulting conditions of forgetfulness and self-rejection made our present problems all but inevitable.

One of the legacies of the confused trajectory of events since '66 is that former simplistic notions of patriotism have been replaced with a vacuum. The very language political or cultural leaders might need to invoke in order to inspire a new generation of leaders or citizens is simply unusable in an age of irony, cynicism and contempt for anything remotely identifiable as 'tradition'. The heroes of yesteryear could gain no purchase on the culture of today's Ireland, because (a) everything they fought for is now taken for granted; and (b) the language they employed in sinking the foundations of an entirely different concept of Ireland is in-accessible to the tongues of present generations.

Padraig Pearse was clear that the battle they were fighting was not merely 'against' England, but a battle for what he called 'the national soul'. Such a concept could nowadays not be expressed without attracting a torrent of abuse and ridicule. The promises of true freedom articulated by the men and women of 1916 are so eloquent as unwittingly ironic prophecies of present-day failures that it is perhaps unsurprising that we cannot bear to look at them.

There was a week in May 2011, while I was beginning the writing of this book, when a confluence of events occurred that seemed to summon up these questions in ways that had not happened for quite a long time. One was the four-day visit of Queen Elizabeth II of England, back-referencing eight centuries of a relationship that had generally been fraught and suffocating from an Irish viewpoint. Another was the death aged eighty-five of Dr Garret FitzGerald, who had been Taoiseach for two periods in the 1980s and, right to the time of his death, as politician, statesman and commentator, a towering influence in the drift of national affairs and thinking in the previous four decades or so. The third event was the one-day visit by Barack Obama, President of the United States of America, in search of his ancestral roots in Moneygall, County Offaly.

By any objective set of criteria – and certainly by the terms in which they were expressed – you would surely have to say that our responses to the visits by Queen Elizabeth and President Obama were exaggerated, disproportionate and perhaps even slightly mad. Naturally, these events provoked much discussion, most of it of the navel-gazing kind. Dipping into the commentary from time to time during breaks from writing, what struck me was the uniformity, if not unanimity, that characterized public discussion of these events. The historic visit by Queen Elizabeth was evidence of our 'maturity as a nation'; it marked a new point of departure in our 'shared history'; it showed that we had 'finally transcended narrow nationalism' and 'grown up'.

The unspoken subtext was: we used to be a bunch of ignorant Catholic peasants and only for 'our nearest neighbours' taking us in hand, would have remained so. Virtue resided in being able to state this case more fluently or more forcefully than the previous speaker. Most striking about this discussion, though, was the way it seemed to slip out of time. In truth, there had, for a very long time, been no objection to or difficulty with the Queen of England coming to visit the Republic. Few of us, even those struggling to retain a healthy relationship with memory, felt any great urge to voice a quarrel with her. We knew about the complexity of our relationship with England, and didn't need to be lectured as though such characterizations amounted to an original analysis. And yet we now lived in a completely different Ireland, not one that had 'gone forward' but one that had slipped backwards, an Ireland that, were it to be completely truthful about its present situation, would be contemplating the facileness of its efforts to show itself to be 'modern' when it remained incapable of sustaining itself other than through burgling its children's hopes. In other words, perhaps what Ireland required was not further repudiations of 'narrow nationalism' but some sense of an integral and self-starting ethic, which would be capable of putting down roots in a truthful sense of its own history.

My problem was, is, that where I come from, Irish history is not some 'shared' experience with England or Britain. It is an obscene litany of thievery and abuse, inflicted on my people by outsiders who had no right to be here. It is something dark and terrible, a slow rape conducted with savagery and deliberation for several dark and bloody centuries. Our 'shared history' was not some jointly entered-into engagement that went wrong; it was a sustained exercise in radical interference, theft, racism and, frequently, ethnic cleansing.

Only when I read Queen Elizabeth's speech at the State dinner in her honour in Dublin Castle did I begin to understand the nature of my own feelings. Certain words and phrases grated on my sense of what was true. The Queen of England spoke about the 'painful legacy' affecting Ireland and Britain. She spoke about 'the complexity' and 'the weight' of 'our history'. She spoke, too, about the importance of 'being able to bow to the past but not being bound by it'. She said: 'It is a sad and regrettable reality that through history our two islands have experienced more than their fair share of heartache, turbulence and loss. The events have touched us all, many of us personally, and are a painful legacy. We can never forget those who have died or been injured, or their families.

'With the benefit of historical hindsight,' she said, 'we can all see things we wish had been done differently or not at all.'

In a certain present-centred sense, Queen Elizabeth's characterization of events was understandable and even tolerably accurate. The suffering, over the full run, had not been entirely one-sided. Queen Elizabeth herself had had to endure much personal pain on account of this history, including the callous and cowardly murder of her uncle, Lord Louis Mountbatten, off Mullaghmore, on the coast of Sligo, in 1979. Still, it needs to be remembered: looked at over the long run, what occurred was not a two-way crossing of wires, but an attempt by one side to plunder everything removable and destroy the remainder. I objected to the ruling monarch of the power that set out systematically to destroy my country for several centuries coming here and uttering weasel words, evasions, euphemism and circumlocutions designed to depict that experience as some kind of mutual misunderstanding. I would have liked to hear, somewhere about that speech, a sentence like, 'My people came to your country and inflicted great hurt and damage, and I am sorry for that.'

Superficially, what happened with the visit of President Obama seemed a straightforward example of celebrity euphoria. He came here at a time of national catastrophe with one arm as long as another, and yet left behind ecstatic discussion of the manifold benefits his visit had bestowed. I heard a vox pop on the radio on the morning after his departure, which, were it representative of anything, should surely make us worried about our collective balance and perspective. Almost everyone who was spoken to appeared to be in some state of euphoria, talking about the 'hope' that Obama had awoken in them and how greatly they had been affected by seeing him. This response, although somewhat different to that provoked by the visit of Queen Elizabeth the previous week, was similarly unspecific as to the nature or character of the 'hope' being discussed. But nobody seemed to notice this: the mere assertion of the 'hoping' was enough. Even more ominous was the thought that this 'hope' was imagined as arriving from outside, in the form of a matinee idol politician straight out of a Hollywood melodrama.

The hard truth, though, is that, considered as a political event, the US president's visit made absolutely no difference to anything except, perhaps, his own prospects of re-election in the year to come.

Hope is a strange word, much used in political discourse these days. Even though, at a surface level, man seems to feel that he is more advanced and intelligent than ever before, there is still this sense that hope is an urgent need, yet somehow adrift from the immediate material context, and therefore something he cannot generate at will for himself. The constant talk about hope implies that hope is absent, and yet nobody seems any longer to know where such hope might be located. Things go wrong in our economies, in our political systems, and these malfunctions seem to give rise to a diminution of human hoping, but the answers proffered are invariably either technical ones, arising from some new political stratagem, or arise from new personalities who promise hope as a tangible benefit in their campaign slogans.

This kind of hoping seems to have a shortening life expectancy. In the 1960s, a generation of politicians and cultural figures emerged in the Western world to totemize the idea of political hope for a whole human lifetime. The Kennedys, Martin Luther King, Elvis, the Beatles – all in their ways offered new hopes and expectations of a world in which freedom would be absolute, which seemed to accord with the deepest desires of those of us who were young in those times. But the lifetime these figures announced is now decisively at an end. All of the above, apart

14

from two members of the Beatles, are dead, although it is true that the magic of the 1960s idea continues to beguile the present generations with a sense of lost promise. Nowadays, too, we can observe our culture seeking to recreate those moments with new figures, but the plausibility of such personalities as harbingers of a renewed and more perfect world tends to be short-lived. They come and go, sometimes in a matter of months or weeks.

And yet, no matter how jaded or weary we become, at each new moment of change or uprising we become distracted again by the possibilities of a new beginning. And then it comes to nothing, or almost nothing, or is twisted by the reality of human nature, or the machinations of power as a force operating apparently of its own volition, holding human frailty in its grasp. We see the same process at work in the financial crisis afflicting Europe: our leaders clinging to an obsolete system, regardless of the pain it brings, because they cannot countenance starting again from the beginning.

Perhaps we speak about hope so much now because we have forgotten what it is, where it comes from. And this amnesia is accompanied by another, which erases from our minds the understanding that experience ought to leave behind: that hope in other human beings and what they can offer is contingent on things that cannot be measured in an economist's pie-chart. Hope is not some fragmented political resource, but an energy in the human heart that ultimately responds to the logic of a singular source. We, raised in a Christian civilization, know this source by a name: Christ. This word, name, was at the centre of all the dreaming of our ancestors, but nowadays is virtually beyond use in a civic context. Whatever we may think about this, we cannot surely argue that it is without consequences.

On the face of things, both Queen Elizabeth and President Obama came and left without leaving us any particular new reason for hoping. Nothing was changed in our economic circumstances when the two dignitaries left nor, to be fair, had

15

they promised any such thing. The Queen of England did not refer to the prevailing circumstances at all and Obama confined himself to generalized bluster, implying, at most, that the US would not leave Ireland swinging in the wind.

Indeed, if you paid close attention to the nuances, it was obvious that the chances of anything new emerging in the course of these visits was remote, because everything had been decided in advance. The meaning of every possible gesture or word was already scripted by those who told us what the visits signified. There was no facility for dissent; no possibility of deeper reflection.

There is always nowadays the risk that, when someone seeks to remember the dark facts of the past, it will be assumed that they are seeking to use these facts to accuse, or to obtain something, or to prolong resentment. Of course these agendas can be present – and problematically present – but this is not an excuse for self-imposed amnesia. The facts need to be remembered for their own sakes, and afterwards we can decide what to make of them, what to do with them, what they mean. Firstly there is the act of remembering itself, a sacred process that must not be trifled with. Such an idea is now almost impossible to communicate in a culture unable to distinguish between the capacity for memory and its potential for interpretation.

It is interesting to reflect that the main themes of both visits were qualities – hope and forgiveness – that were not long ago recognizable as religious ones. And yet, for the duration of both visits, as in pretty much all public events in Ireland nowadays, there was no sense of a religious/spiritual dimension in any of the discussion or coverage of the visits. It is not, I would say, that religion has been supplanted by sentimentality. Rather, it is that the secular discussion which hijacks and interprets everything in our culture now is tapping into the religious sense in human beings and appropriating it for ideological purposes, building a new language on top so as to imply that such qualities as hope and forgiveness are self-generating, self-standing and self-sustaining.

Garret FitzGerald, who died while the Queen of England was in the country, was rightly hailed as an extraordinary force in the recent life of Ireland, but again what was striking was the sameness of the constructions employed to characterize his contribution. He had 'led us into a new, liberal, pluralist' Ireland; he had helped us to 'break the hold of the Catholic Church'; he had pursued the 'liberal agenda' and his own 'constitutional crusade', designed to, as more than one contributor rather inevitably put it, 'drag Ireland kicking and screaming into the 20th century'.

I don't question any of this. What concerns me somewhat is the fact that we never seem to tire of saying certain things, even after they have ceased to be useful or germane. What astonishes me is that, even surrounded by the debris of our mistakes, the last thing we want to do is adopt a critical posture in relation to the thinking that led to the mess.

In the discussion of Dr FitzGerald's career, as in the coverage of Queen Elizabeth's visit, there was a strong sense of things being said for the purpose of self-reassurance rather than because of any firm conviction that they were especially relevant to the present moment. It was like listening to a digest reprise of all the discussion we had had for the previous thirty years, in which certain ideas about what Ireland needed to do or become were again elevated to the level of axioms and moral certitudes. The clear subtext of all this was that everything Dr FitzGerald proposed had been self-evidently good and had proved so in practice.

When you reflect deeply on the lives of great statesmen, what you tend to see in many instances is that their greatness was not contingent on a particular ideological outlook, but was grounded in a sense of guiding the public realm away from the dangerous tendency towards monolithic thought and behaviour into some kind of balance. Cometh the hour, cometh the man. Garret FitzGerald was indeed a giant, a man of great intellect, curiosity, passion and responsibility. He did not appear to be, as was certainly the case with many of his latter-day acolytes, an adherent to faddish ideas about modernity or liberalism for their own sakes. He seemed to see things in the round. He came to Irish life at a particular time, when certain obvious things needed to be addressed and dealt with. On these issues he led us in a certain direction, creating new realities, because that is what needed doing at that particular time.

Not all of these new realities are unambiguously good. Divorce, to take one random top-of-the-head example, had unleashed a new set of miseries on Irish society that, hidden behind the veil of a secret court system, have been left largely unventilated by the media, probably because such discussion might serve to undermine the continuing mood of self-congratulation concerning our new-found liberalism.

If you wanted to be provocative, you could assert that Garret FitzGerald changed Ireland in the following ways: (1) He appeared at a time when the youth population was expanding, and appropriated that energy to a necessarily blinkered and narrow purpose. (2) He reduced the public appetite for radical change and innovation to a narrowly focused programme concerning the treatment of private and sexual morality in the public arena. (3) He allowed a generation greatly disgruntled with the way things had been to move behind the wheel of power, while abandoning its radicalism and pursuing instead an imported model of change and progress. (4) He found a way of reinventing the civil war divide at a time when it might otherwise have been entering its death throes, insinuating himself as the moral alternative to the demonic spectre of Charles J. Haughey.

And in truth, FitzGerald had been an almost unmitigated failure as a politician. By the end of the 1982–87 Fine Gael/Labour coalition, the dream had begun to unravel and the sheen was wearing off FitzGerald's liberal halo. The expectations he had engendered with his rhetoric about a constitutional crusade against sectarianism and conservatism had foundered on the rocks of hard political reality. Many of those who had risen to his call were disillusioned by what was perceived to be his backtracking on abortion and his dissembling on other issues.

But, though its leader was, to an extent, becoming a marginal figure, one aspect of the revolution FitzGerald had heralded was already in train. The guard, at least, was changing. Over the next couple of decades, this revolutionary guard would gradually creep its way into virtually every corner of Irish public life and the institutions created for its management and operation. The media and the major professions, the civil service and institutions as diverse as health boards and universities, would gradually fall into the control of the post-Emergency generations, which would gain enormous, though to a large degree surreptitious power in Irish life. Perhaps the great single victory was the election to the presidency of Mary Robinson in 1990, which spoke of the overall project in a concrete and visible way, doing a great deal to mobilize and consolidate the outward appearance of revolutionary change, but very little to improve the quality of life as lived by the generality of people in the country Robinson contrived to lead.

And yet the illusion created by Garret FitzGerald has never really been shattered, and the agenda and ideological programme he established came to dominate the drama of Irish politics through the 1990s and beyond. The energies that might otherwise have been directed at taking charge of the society and making it coherent and self-sufficient were directed instead at chasing scapegoats and pursuing a pseudo-radicalism based on combating the ancient forces of reaction, which in truth were, like the famous Monty Python parrot, long since deceased.

It is inconceivable that, were he starting out today in public life, Dr Garret FitzGerald would be pursuing the same path he pursued in the 1970s and 1980s, or that, like those who sang his un-qualified praises in the days following his death, he would have been advancing analyses of Irish society that were by then a decade or more beyond their use-by dates. It is more likely that, coming along to the context set in place by the 'liberal agenda' and the 'constitutional crusade', a politician of FitzGerald's stature and ability would have turned his attention to proposing necessary refinements to the situation emerging from these devel-opments, adjusting and tweaking where imbalances had crept in.

It should have been possible to conduct respectful discussions about Dr FitzGerald's legacy that went further than pieties and clichés, that delved into the intricacies of Irish life and culture in a way that acknowledged his contribution without ignoring the inevitable limits of his initiatives. Equally, it should have been possible to welcome Queen Elizabeth without feeling the need to tweak our memory of our own history into an approximate harmony with the sentimentality her visit unleashed.

The most frustrating thing about all this relates not to the undemocratic suppression of particular voices but the fact that potentially fascinating avenues of exploration to do with our national condition, situation and direction are closed off by an ideological intolerance and moral censoriousness that constantly directs us all towards the 'correct' outlook. Those few days were extremely enlightening with regard not merely to the condition of dominant thinking in Irish society, but the way this is received by people who presumably might have considered other perspectives had these been made available. As on other occasions of national soul-searching or navel-gazing, I noticed, with some amusement, the way people I met in the street would speak in what sounded like verbatim regurgitations of newspaper editorials I had read earlier in the day, and lapsed into silence when I ventured in response that there might be other ways of looking at things.

# 1

# *The Emerald Tiger: What If?*

HOW DO YOU RECALL A DECADE IN NATIONAL OR SOCIAL LIFE? HOW do you verify your memory of things against those of other people? Can you be certain that your memories are definitive, or even accurate? There is that great maxim, which has now become a crushing cliché: the past is a foreign country. Cliché or not, it's true: we look backwards and, even from the same place as we once stood, regard a different reality that can only be approximately and unreliably accessed through memory.

If you ask me how the Celtic Tiger was for me, you immediately put me at a loss. I have no clear memory of a time called 'The Celtic Tiger'. I don't remember it in the way I remember, for example, the 1980s, or my twenties, or the period between Horslips' first album and their breaking up. I don't have the same kind of reference points as I have for my teens or my forties, or even, though I'm not a huge sports fan, for the Charlton era. Looking back, you might have some chance of defining the essence of a particular decade, like 'the Sixties' or the 1970s, but it wasn't like that. The Celtic Tiger was neither the Nineties nor the Noughties, but took a bite out of both that left the remainders of each like doleful twins cast adrift in time, creating a sense of a different possibility for a continuous reality in which the aberration of prosperity never came to pass. As time moves on, this alternative continuity seems to be causing a convergence in the popular consciousness to obliterate the patch of colour in between. Gradually, we are redacting the Celtic Tiger from our past.

I remember back in 1996 or 1997, talking to the painter Michael Cullen, and in a casual way letting drop the phrase 'Celtic Tiger', which by then had been in, I thought, general use for some time. He looked at me quizzically. What had I said? The Celtic what? When I repeated the phrase he latched on to it. He had never heard it. 'It's very good,' he enthused, and this was about the limit of Mick's enthusing about anything.

I wrote about his response for a catalogue for an exhibition he mounted round about then: 'It's the stripes that interest him . . . He thinks that, as an attempt to describe something supposedly unequivocally virtuous, the tiger, with its stripes bearing witness to the unavoidable reality of both life and colour, is an interesting admission of the society's unconscious awareness of its own intrinsic ambiguity.'

For his part, Mick just kept repeating the phrase 'Celtic Tiger' over and over, and was so tickled by its novelty that he later did a series of paintings in its honour, under the title 'Emerald Tiger': chaotic splurges of light and colour that seemed to seek some place beyond light and colour, splashes of optimism that seemed to see a different nation – more Mediterranean and exotic – to the one we inhabited. For a while, I seem to remember, 'Emerald Tiger' was in quite widespread use among international journalists as a way of referring to what was happening to Ireland's economic fortunes. Considering that alternative title now, it seems to hold out some promise of a different way of doing things, and perhaps some sense of the possibility of a different outcome. Somehow, the word 'emerald' seems softer, less strident and self-aggrandizing, though this may just be a trick of time and what-iffing. For his part, Mick was at pains to stress that he was not always the last to hear about things. 'It may sound ridiculous,' he told me in his soft understated way, 'but sometimes things have taken place after I've painted them.'

Of course, the term 'Celtic Tiger' was at first an ironic appellation rather than a reference to reality or real time, and this 'ironic' phase may have lasted longer than we remember. It was other people, mainly, who called it the Celtic Tiger in a way that implied admiration and envy. For our part, we assumed it was some kind of hoax, calculated to get our hopes up and dash them again. For a long time nobody really believed anything much had changed, and, by the time many of us began to realize that this was something out of the ordinary, it was almost over. It was like an intimate relationship that only became intense as it was ending, causing the grief to rise up all the more, and fuelling the sense of desperation to turn back the clock.

For a long time, the 'boom' was something that seemed to benefit other people. I remember for several years after people started talking about it, having this sense that I'd been doing much better before it started, and other people I spoke to seemed to feel much the same way. Perhaps this effect was a function of the 'traditional' Irish poor mouth approach to material matters. Nevertheless, I was writing about other people's Celtic Tiger by name from early 1997.

For me personally, things never really took off until about 2002, with the beginning of the huge influx from the former eastern bloc countries. From then on, I remember a different mood, a lightness about everything that seemed to vivify Irish society and invest it with a different personality. There was this sense of people having come to be with us, in our country with which we had this strange love–hate relationship, and seeming to think it a pleasant enough place. This caused us to perk up and act like we'd felt like this all along, which we had, intermittently, to ourselves.

I remember, too, day after day, reading positive-sounding

headlines in the newspapers. I remember a headline: 'The country is awash with money', and noting that it had no exclamation mark. I remember on the radio one morning jokingly saying, 'Sure we're all millionaires now' and not being attacked by anyone. I think all this must have been in the early years of the Noughties, when the irony coating on the term 'Celtic Tiger' began to wear off. It is odd to reflect, with the painful hindsight that has since arrived, that whatever solid basis there had been to the initial burst of prosperity was already dissolving into an artificial bubble sustained by inflated property prices.

I made a brief attempt, some time after the meltdown happened in 2008, to use newspaper archives as a way of going back in time, in order, mainly, to see what it had really been like. The exercise was exhausting and inconclusive. There are a lot of days in a decade – at least 3,652 – so it's difficult to get a sense of the times from reading things day to day. It's a kind of slow-exposure process that you think will add up to something meaningful, but it doesn't really. You get a vague sense of changing mood, different priorities, unfamiliar ethical outlooks, but nothing consistent or definitive.

There is plenty of topography to remind you that you are in a different country, but it is difficult to find your bearings. You notice, of course, the estate agents' blurbs and the accompanying puff pieces of the property supplements, nowadays sniffily dismissed as 'property pornography'. You notice that certain financial mechanisms that have since become anathematized were at one time regarded as unexceptionable. You might stumble, for example, on an advertising feature for some stockbroking company seeking investments under a soon-to-be-discontinued tax avoidance mechanism, warning in banner headlines that forthcoming Budget changes could mean that the scheme will soon be fully subscribed.

Sometimes you find something to provoke a wry smile. Dipping in as far back as 1996, I quickly came upon such an advert promoting a 'bed and breakfast' option, which involved selling shares and buying them back straight away at the same price. The advertorial explained: 'The net result of this is that your holding has not changed but the cost of your shares is deemed to have risen for tax purposes, so that when you sell your shares your taxable gain is reduced.' It is strange to observe something that has subsequently become so self-evidently dodgy being presented as thoroughly reasonable and upright.

One of the things you gather from this is that a society does not have a continuous personality, in the way that human beings tend to have: rather it lurches and shifts from one personality to another – a defence mechanism of amnesia, to shut out the way things were, being essential to the full investment in a new persona. The even stranger thing is that it is human beings, who themselves maintain more or less constant personalities, who cause this to happen. They 'participate' in the new collective personality, which is utterly different to the old one, while themselves seeming to be the same people they always were. Or perhaps this effect is just an illusion arising from the quantum of individual dishonesty that creeps into our collective conversation.

While it is interesting to go back and look at the evidence of a prior personality, the pickings from such cultural archaeology are slim overall. Anyone seeking new scapegoats among the scribes and chroniclers of the time will end up with a mixed bag of evidence that, when it comes to deeper understanding, adds up to more or less zero. The evidence is there, if you wanted to undertake an in-depth and lengthy analysis, but it is patchy, inconsistent and ultimately ambiguous.

For example, it is stated now that the media 'talked up' the boom, and this is naturally intended as a disapproving judgement. But what becomes obvious when you immerse yourself in this way in the past is that there is no sense of such a pattern. Certainly, at the commercial level of operation, the media were active in the whipping-up of public desires and aspirations, whether by un-critically talking up the property market or suppressing critical appraisals of what was happening in the economy. But there are ostensibly plausible reasons for both phenomena: on the one hand, there was, for most of the boom, a completely naturalistic sense that the property market was flourishing as a consequence of unprecedented factors influencing the broader economic picture; on the other hand, it is hard to see how the boom might have been reported other than in approximately the manner it was.

It is true that there were frequent manifestations of what in hind-sight appear to be positive-spin stories, but each of these in turn appears to have amounted to no more than a statement of the objective facts as they stood on the day. If you were to find fault with such journalism on the basis of stirring up some repressed longing in the Irish psyche, it is more in the cumulative that the dangers might be seen to reside, and this is a difficult quantity to pin down. Newspapers report news, and if the Economic and Social Research Institute says house prices are going up, then that's what gets reported. What else would? If this happens continuously over a period of years, it is bound to have a conditioning effect on public opinion, but it is difficult to identify any particular point or moment when it might have set off the alarms. In the economic sphere, what appears to be is at least as real as what is.

Perhaps some go-ahead entrepreneur might one day assemble a hologram of the Celtic Tiger from media of the time, and take people on guided tours of it, indicating, as they pass through the Tiger years at the speed of sound in a time-machine, the headlines about escalating growth and runaway house prices. Perhaps then, in such a speeded-up version, we might get some flavour of the change that took place. But when you look for the wood all you find is trees.

Take, for example, this headline: '70% growth in net financial wealth of households'. This might well be adduced as an example of the kind of nefarious media pot-stirring we 'recall' from the Tiger years. It appeared in *The Irish Times*, but not in 1999 or 2004. It dates from May 2011, nearly three years after the roof caved in, over a report that related mainly to reducing credit and the recovery in insurance and pension fund values. Factually, it was accurate, but by then we knew enough to understand that its meaning could be read in a positive or negative light. The result was that it neither made anyone feel much better or much worse. In isolation it had a neutral impact on confidence and well-being. A decade earlier, it would have been part of a pattern of stories which cumulatively contrived to get us high, high, high.

In May 1997, *The Economist*, one of the world's most prestigious economic periodicals, ran a cover-story about the Irish 'miracle' under the headline 'Europe's Shining Light'. There was no question-mark. 'On the face of it,' the article declared, 'this is one of the most remarkable economic transformations of recent times: from basket-case to "emerald tiger" in ten years.' The only hedging of bets was in the phrase we missed at the time but which now jumps out at us: 'on the face of it'.

At the time, very few Irish people believed that Ireland had become one of the world's wealthiest countries, and those who did believe it were divided between those who welcomed it and those who did not. There were cheerleaders and sceptics and those who vacillated between the two positions. It was all a matter of individual experience – shared, discussed, envied, emulated, added to and consolidated in repetition. Sceptical to begin with, we imagined the Celtic Tiger from a whiff on the wind and then came to believe in it to such an extent that, by the time the wind changed, we had come to see it as a concrete reality, which by now it had rather too literally become. 'Places don't change,' Mick Cullen had warned me, 'but your perception of them changes. There's nothing out there, in a sense, until you open your eyes and see it.'

*

In 1995 I had published a collection of essays called *Every Day Like Sunday?*, the title borrowed from the Morrissey song about the boredom and hopelessness associated with places from which the life has been drained, where every day is like Sunday, every day is 'silent and grey'.

The book reprised a theme of mine over the previous five years: the slow death of small towns, especially in the West, owing to the erosion of services and exclusion from developmental opportunities. The content was gloomy about the future. Rather melodramatically, I dedicated the book to my nieces and nephews, with the solemn hope that they might 'not leave without a fight'.

It is now my certain belief that the Celtic Tiger initiated its exploratory prowlings the morning after this book hit the shops. It was a year or so before anyone noticed, but, looking back, it is clear that, right under my nose, the portents were already beginning to turn good.

I am not naturally pessimistic. Within my own existence I tend to see the liquid element of the half-full glass, rather than the space suggesting that it's half empty. But, back then, anyone who expressed optimism about the future of the Irish economy would have seemed to be riding for a fall. We had just come through a slump unparalleled since the 1950s, narrowly avoiding foreclosure by the World Bank. Emigration had slowed down from its haemorrhaging of the 1980s, but was still a significant flow. Many rural towns and villages were indeed dying, with post offices, Garda stations and schools being 'rationalized', occasioning widespread fears about the disintegration of community life. The great economic catchphrase of the time declared the economy 'fundamentally sound', and indeed this phrase became the hook of the only joke in my book. In those days, to be a media pundit was to deal in doom and gloom, and it was difficult to be too pessimistic. Most of us took to our calling with a solemn zealotry. But, almost perceptibly, in the mid-1990s, everything started to change, and those of us who had led the keening over the corpse of the future were left stranded on the rocks as the tide swept into shore. Or so it seemed at the time.

We Irish have a natural streak of gloominess, largely connected with the weather. During a fine spell, there occurs a fundamental change in the national personality: we become happier but only in a certain qualified sense, as underneath the outward positivity is a clinch-knot of pessimism. It will never last, we decide; it's going to break again like last year when we got a couple of good weeks in May and then nothing until September when the kids were back in school. 'We've had our summer,' we tell each other after a wet day or two in early June. We don't trust the weather, because we've been left low and wet too often.

This pessimism, applied to economics, is hardly conducive to the kind of self-confidence required to create and maintain prosperity, even when the good times are manifestly rolling like never before. Our fate, weather-wise or economy-wise, is in the hands of external forces, of which we have no control and little understanding. Both subjects provoke much discussion but few accurate predictions. We find it best to err on the side of pessimism. Experience has taught us not to expect much, but we still get carried away at the merest sign of positive change. Just as a sudden burst of sun has us grilling ourselves like rashers in the certainty that clouds are not far beyond the horizon, the Tiger years spawned an unprecedented frenzy of conspicuous consumption which destroyed forever the myth of the frugal, ascetic Irish. We don't seem to have learned much in those years, but one thing we certainly discovered is that our past attachment to self-denial was just a way of accommodating ourselves to poverty: sour grapes disguised as virtue.

Not being used to prosperity, we remained suspicious of it for some time, nursing a sense that it had been delivered to the wrong address and would soon be taken away. The half-full/half-empty question split the Irish population in two during the Tiger years, roughly dividing those under forty from those over. The older cohort had a clear memory of the bad times and for a long time anticipated their imminent return. The younger generations went with the flow and were too busy partying to be bothered listening to their elders' prognostications of further doom and gloom. But because, for all kinds of complex reasons, the national conversation was chiefly dictated by commentators over forty, the dominant strain of commentary until well past the millennium was disbelieving of the phenomenon of Irish prosperity and sceptical of its chances of continuing for long.

Like most of the commentators now describing Irish reality, I belong to a generation which has monopolized Irish opinion-making for two decades. Those of us who belong to the generations that emerged from the 1960s and participated in what can loosely be called the counter-culture of the 1970s and 1980s had several things going for us: we didn't have to emigrate like every generation for 150 years; we had a strong sense of ownership of our culture and society; and we were determined to direct the energy of the 1960s to overturning the political and cultural monoliths of the past. Because the only point of speaking in public was to denounce the greyness, conservatism and failure of previous decades and generations, nearly all of this generation of pundits came at things from a vaguely leftist perspective. Thus, although we had been demanding change until our throats hurt, we missed the early signs of the Celtic Tiger because we were too busy denouncing. We were the Boys Who Cried 'Wolf!' and, when the wolf did not appear, we cried 'Wolf!' again and again, if only in the hope that, one of these days, the wolf would appear, as we had in the past been able to rely upon him to do.

It's an odd feature of Irish media that, whereas what you might call the engine and chassis of the vehicle is provided by solid economic commentary of an orthodox, market-centred nature, the bodywork is of an entirely different cast. Most of the media 'stars' are people who in the old days would have described themselves as socialists and who remain doggedly of a left-leaning disposition. Back in the 1980s, this left-leaning brand of journalist was the height of fashion. We all gave it a lash because it was so easy. All you had to do was adopt a pessimistic attitude, predict the worst possible outcome for any given aspect of public policy and, above all, accuse the government as often as possible of being wrong-headed and incompetent. Back then, the country was so lacking in direction or vision that it was impossible to be excessively pessimistic.

Not only was the Celtic Tiger neither expected nor predicted, but its arrival, and more especially its timing in the immediate aftermath of the collapse of communism in Eastern Europe, seemed to represent for the doomsters an accusation, suggesting they had been wrong about everything. For years they had been insisting upon the intrinsic unsustainability and amorality of the capitalist system and predicting the final meltdown of the Irish economy. Now, far from melting, the Irish economy was confounding every thing they said and believed, right in front of their eyes.

Things would have been lean had it not been for the tribunals, but Flood, Moriarty et al provided an opportunity to transmute the doomsters' ideological pique into a kind of postmodern fiscal Puritanism, allowing most of them to maintain a continuous high moral tone during a period when their portfolios of opinions were otherwise at risk of redundancy.

Thus, the nature of Irish journalism altered fundamentally in the Tiger years, manifesting a dearth of criticism of economic policy, or of issues of societal justice and fairness in a contemporaneous context. Gone were the old journalistic standbys like attacks on cutbacks in public spending, appeals on behalf of 'the less fortunate in society' and the angry polemic against incompetence in high places. A new tune was created: All Politicians Are Crooks And Shysters. Interestingly, this new score related frequently to the distant past and issues of an allegedly moral nature, avoiding other than passing and often tortuous reference to the contemporary management of the national affairs, which appeared so unassailable that the doomsters had no choice but to bite their pencils.

As time passed, most of us pundits developed an oddly schizophrenic attitude to the boom. On the one hand, we were somewhat discommoded to find ourselves so apparently wrong about everything; on the other, we were as open as the next man to making the best of it. Like most others, we watched the value of our homes increasing exponentially. We observed the transformation of the drab streets of our cities as a result of the influx of leggy Poles and Latvians. At first, such symptoms had a confusing effect. They pleased us and yet they served to remind us of how wrong we had been. For most commentators, it was not possible to switch horses overnight, although one or two did exactly that. Most of us, however, bided our time, began to make favourable noises about the new Ireland, while keeping our ideological powder dry. Gradually, we came out in favour of the transformation, at first gingerly and later with something approaching abandon. By the mid-Noughties, when the boom reached its zenith, most commentators had either become unabashed cheerleaders for prosperity or had lapsed into a sullen and bewildered silence. And thus another element of the national memory bank was disabled by a complex process of osmosis.

Despite all this, there were several moments over the span of the Celtic Tiger when it looked like plughole time might be nigh. At the end of 2002, for example, I wrote in *The Irish Times*:

> If I were to take a stab at predicting what 2003 will be like, I would venture that, the way things look today, it will be very like 1993. That was the year of the 'fundamentally sound' economy, that pre-Tiger platform of strengthening confidence and dissolving

pessimism. Now, alas, we are to visit that same moment on the return journey from prosperity, and how far we have to travel beyond it may depend on our own willingness to grasp the moment for ourselves. We can, if we choose, return all the way to 1986, when the Irish economy was a basket case and Ireland generally, in the words of the National Nanny, was 'banjaxed'.

It almost happened then, but somehow the whole thing was re-inflated and sent into even headier orbit. A few months later I took another tentative punt:

In the past five years of the Celtic Tiger, it has often been forgotten that prosperity has its victims as well as its victors. I refer not so much to that sector of the population which is factored out of prosperity, in relative terms at least, by virtue of being excluded from the economic mainstream, but rather to those, like myself, who had previously earned our livings in drawing attention to this but have had to keep our opinions to ourselves in recent times for fear of being labelled 'begrudgers'. One of the less obvious problems with prosperity is that attempts to question it acquire the appearance of vexatiousness . . . It has become almost impossible to question the moral basis of the Celtic Tiger version of modern Ireland. . . . This is first, of course, because the figures appear to be irrefutable, but secondly because there is now widespread agreement that nobody should be allowed seek to question or expose the nature of the illusion. Because the entire edifice depends on perception, any attempt to alter that perception is itself deeply threatening to the illusion. Because the consequences of the recovery have represented a total victory for the forces of modernization, there is an unwritten pact that nobody within the consensus will engage in the kind of uncomfortable shuffling that might lead to the boat being rocked. The strength of the Irish economy, like the success of the entire modernization project, has become an article of faith. Beliefs of one kind have been replaced by beliefs of an altogether different complexion, and these are reinforced on a daily basis by the high priests of modernization: the commentators, official and political spokespersons who describe reality. . . . And in the resulting babble no voice of dissent is able to make itself heard.

I find it fascinating now to look into such past ruminations and see both pessimism and a lack of total conviction about what was transpiring. This particular column seems to have predicted what would eventually come to pass, and yet it does so in a way that is tentative, ironic and somewhat ambivalent. It describes the general conditions well, but does not extend its analysis to make a prediction as to what may happen.

And, of course, very soon afterwards, the faltering economy was rebooted by fresh injections of borrowed money laundered in the property market. This pattern, occurring at frequent intervals, helps to explain why there was no widespread sense of scepticism about the unrolling of the apparent prosperity. Sooner or later, you got tired of scraping egg off your face. By the time the real crisis arrived, the Boys Who Cried 'Wolf!' had lost faith in their – our – own capacity to understand anything.

A handful of economic commentators did begin to make persistent and fairly ominous noises some time around the middle of the Noughties, but these were largely disregarded because, on the one hand, the necessity to continue believing was by then a widely understood and popularly accepted aspect of the psychology of the boom, and, on the other, even these prognostications of doom were rendered ambiguous by virtue of their being repeated virtually ad nauseam for several years without any sign of their coming true. The idea that there was a phalanx of begrudgers seeking to scuttle Ireland's prosperity was sufficiently persuasive of enough people to ensure that their interventions were read in the first instance as the kind of potentially self-fulfilling prophecies that were, for precisely that reason, better ignored.

Really, though, when you go right into it, to believe that anyone 'missed' anything – that with a little more vigilance we could have avoided the meltdown – is to misunderstand what was happening in the first place. It is to assume that what was happening was part of some coherent process that might have been sustainable had we let a little of the air out of it at the right time. This is bogus. The 'boom' was not a boom in any conventional or healthy sense, but a manifestation of unlimited human desire in economic terms. It was the inevitable outcome of a country with a history of privation and adversity being offered the opportunity to participate in an experience of prosperity such as other countries had long been taking for granted.

The conventional, consensual analysis of what has befallen us goes something like this: we used to be poor, then we got rich; then, arising from the incompetence and/or corruption of various agents, we became poor again. Hence, the past four years have seen the wiping out of perhaps twenty years of progress, prosperity and confidence-building. Now, cast shamefully back on the kindness of strangers, who insist on us repaying the vast amounts of money we owe to international banks and bond-holders, we have been cruelly required to face a new era of austerity, hardship and emigration.

There is a wholly different way of seeing things: that Ireland was never rich; that, because of a failure effectively to regenerate its economy following Independence from Britain, it lurched from crisis to stagnation and back again, until, in the 1960s, discovering a way of surviving that placed the least possible onus on indigenous efforts and instead sought literally to sell itself to the wider world. Since then, Irish membership of what is now the European Union, an industrial development policy geared towards attracting inward investment, an increasingly blasé approach to borrowing money, and a social partnership programme based on a deluded sense of indigenous earning power, created a false sense that the promise of self-realization had been attained. The true meaning of the present moment, then, is that these stratagems have run out of road, that a spectacular sleight-of-hand has been rumbled and that Ireland must go back to the drawing board.

What has occurred has really been the failure of the idea of Ireland posited by those who have sought to modernize the country on exclusively materialist principles since the 1960s. For half a century, Irish life has been dominated by a series of battles between traditionalists and modernizers on various decisive questions defining two opposing versions of reality. On the one hand, the traditionalists clung to an idea of a pious and God-fearing nation that eschewed materialism and valued itself by the principles of a simple faith and sought to shut out the menace of the modern world. On the other hand were those who insisted that, to become vibrant and prosperous, Ireland needed to turn its back on the simple verities of the past, to embrace modern values like pluralism, equality and freedom. This ideological struggle implied a moment of severance between past and future, which, having been insinuated into the culture, has rendered difficult a re-connection with tradition and the essential languages of patriotism and self-realization employed so effectively in the project of national liberation a century ago. This is why the leaders of 1916 and immediately afterwards now seem such remote figures: they stand marooned behind a cultural iron curtain, their words no longer resonant except as glimpses into an arcane world defined by its lack of sophistication and understanding, with their faintly ridiculous wittering about values and patriotism.

What afflicts Ireland is not really a failure of means but a failure of thought and words and self-understanding. Ireland is, after all, a country richly endowed with cultural gifts and natural resources. Its population is that of a small town in England or America and should be capable of sustaining itself without difficulty. Yet, for most of the nine decades since achieving its Independence, Ireland has struggled to maintain its population. In the 1930s, and again in the 1950s, it suffered massive depletion of its young adults, a pattern that had persisted since the Great Famines of the 1840s. There was a brief respite in the 1970s, arising from a momentary optimism inspired by a short-lived flowering of visionary competence courtesy of Seán Lemass's tenure as Taoiseach, from 1959 to 1966, but this was soon short-circuited by the in-fighting of his successors. Not unconnectedly, emigration resumed again in the 1980s and persisted until the apparently miraculous boom of the 1990s.

But these periods of what appeared like nascent prosperity have been misleading. The underlying truth is that Ireland has never sustained itself by its own resources, indeed has never respected its own resources, but has given them away for next to nothing. Irish fisheries are mainly exploited by Spanish fishermen. There are vast reserves of oil and gas off Irish coasts that politicians have for decades been contriving to dispose of in return for paltry recompense to the native population, to whom these resources rightfully belong. Irish agriculture comprises mainly beef and dairy farming, by far the least efficient use of land. If you drive around the fabled Irish countryside, you cannot avoid noticing that almost none of the land is cultivated. The Irish tourism industry is in the doldrums because of high costs and because we cannot decide which version of ourselves – traditionalist kitsch or cutting-edge modernity – to promote.

The two brief periods of resurgence of the Irish economy in the 1970s and 1990s were based mainly on borrowing and invited dependency. Since the 1960s, the driving economic model has back-boilered the development of indigenous resources in favour of doing deals with the outside world. Thus, Ireland's 12.5 per cent corporation tax – the lowest in the world – represents the main weapon in our armoury of self-sustenance.

Really, there have long been two Irish economies: the indigenous economy – underperforming, often barely functioning – and the highly efficient, hugely successful transnational industrial sector, producing computer components and pharmaceuticals, which, together with a thriving international financial sector, created a sense of Ireland as a healthy modern economy. This cuckoo-in-the-nest economy continues to break records, in spite of Ireland's now catastrophic economic situation, but the indigenous economy has long exhibited the symptoms of the mysterious condition identified in the odd diagnostics of economics as 'negative growth'.

At a deeper level, in what are conventionally understood as 'religious/spiritual' terms, Ireland's recent back story goes something like this: beset by an inadequate sense of God, camouflaged by an ostentatious piety, we had long wondered whether materialism might be the safest form of salvation; then, finally getting to give it a try, we discovered what everyone assumed we had known all along – that money doesn't buy happiness. And then the money vanished also, leaving us utterly bereft.

Ireland's 'tradition' of 'spirituality' has been much exaggerated. 'Faith' in Irish culture means, really, blind adherence to imposed prescriptions. There is little sense in contemporary Irish culture of a connection between what reality proposes and the idea of God or Providence. Mirroring the traditionalist/modernizer split, the culture has now divided into those who cling to simple pieties and those who reject any connection between Christianity and public culture, or indeed between transcendence and everyday existence. The public conversation is now avowedly agnostic, if not atheistic. The result is a sterile discussion, devoid of fundamental understandings, in which it is impossible to initiate any dialogue of starting over. Chastened by the raft of revelations about clerical abuse and its cover-up, the Irish Catholic Church contributes little or nothing to the public discussion of such matters.

The 'young people of Ireland', to whom Pope John Paul II professed his love in 1979, are now the adults who contemplate, like many Irish generations before them, the failure of their country to develop any collectively agreed fundamental understanding of itself. But these generations have never given any thought to the condition of their country: they didn't have to, until recently, and so far into the disaster zone they have in the main adopted the self-serving analyses of those who led Ireland on to the rocks, adding their tuppenceworth of spleen to the clamour of rage. As a result, their own children must soon start to consider options that may see another generation of Ireland's 'brightest and best' depart to, in the sorrowful words of Enda Kenny on his elevation to the position of Taoiseach in March 2011, 'build the future of another country'.

Ireland's problems – its inability to provide for its own people, or even to perceive the abundance of gifts it has been given and make good use of them, its constant searching for some new dependency to enter into – all these are symptoms of a historical experience that remains to be dealt with at a cultural level. Deep in Irish culture is a lack of self-belief, indeed a self-hatred, inculcated in the centuries of domination by our nearest neighbours, and still festering in the Irish mind like a recalcitrant virus that sleeps and sleeps and then, every so often, erupts once again. This has rendered it impossible for Ireland to retrace the line of its own destiny, to reimagine, after its long period of being dominated, how it might function in the world according to its own energies and ideas. The result is a society that lurches from extravagant self-regard to profound inferiority complex, which often seeks its answers in imitation of societies deemed more 'modern' or 'progressive'.

One of the least remarked-upon legacies of the Celtic Tiger is that its false prosperity served to suppress thought and discussion about what a coherent and successful version of Irish society might look and feel like. For more than a decade, it became impossible to argue with those who were able to lay claim to an unambiguous victory for a particular model of progress. By eliminating Irish attachments to tradition, nationalism, religiosity and singularity, the revolutionary generations of the post-Emergency period had succeeded in opening Ireland up to the outside world, and creating an economic model based on this openness. Few anticipated the extent of the vulnerability this would bring with it. The complacency of that period has recently been supplanted by an orgy of finger-pointing and recrimination. This too can be interpreted as a desire to evade the fundamental.

To go backwards in time in search of a moment when things began to go seriously awry, and thus to appear to downplay or avoid the issues which currently monopolize the continuing discussion in and about Ireland, is to risk seeming to exculpate those who are accused of offences of an ethical or even criminal nature in the years in which the country was 'awash with money'. To seek to go deeper, to opt out of the national venting exercise, is to risk attracting the attention of the bloggers and whine-line callers who see the present situation as an easy opportunity to engage in the two-minute-hate facility to which many of our media organizations have latterly reduced the idea of democratically focused journalism. Moreover, the very action of going deeper seems to suggest an ideological perspective, i.e. a deviation from what is 'obvious', a perverse attempt to rake up old questions when, really, all everyone else wants to talk about is what has happened to the wealth we were led to believe was ours as a natural entitlement.

But anyone who thinks seriously about what has been happening knows that there is a deeper-down explanation for where we now find ourselves. The circumstance in which the recent boom occurred arose not because of some sudden confluence of the energies and creativity of the Irish people, but because of certain choices we made arising from an interpretation of our capacities and potential. The Celtic Tiger was not the culmination of national efforts, but the outcome of a series of three-card tricks effected by our political classes going back to the mid-point of the last century, in which we, the people, readily acquiesced for reasons no less selfish or short-termist than those of our leaders.

In the early winter of 2010, as it was becoming clear that the International Monetary Fund was about to take over the reins of the national economy, the finance minister, Brian Lenihan, was heard to assert that, in the economic arena, Ireland's sovereignty had long been shared with other countries in the Euro zone. It was no big deal.

It was, of course, a spin, designed to take some of the sting out of this unprecedented moment. And it was also true: our joining the Euro back in 1999, and accepting the euro as a replacement for the punt in 2002, had indeed meant that we became, in effect, a small player in the federal economy of Europe. Lenihan's transparent but nevertheless comfortingly confusing ploy was fairly typical of the three-card-trickery that had long characterized Irish politicians-in-power approach to matters 'European': when seeking to persuade the electorate along a certain course, you always told them that this extra step would make no difference to Irish sovereignty/independence/values etc.; later on, when the time came to move them to a new stage in the process, you blandly remarked in passing that, of course, everyone had agreed to all this years ago.

Thus, the salami strategy of 'European' integration: one slice at a time and in the end you are truly sausaged. Lenihan was really doing no more than reminding the public of the manner in which they had agreed to being led to the present sorry impasse, while also being given the option of denying all knowledge of the series of decisions that had brought them there.

41

This was at the core of the Irish relationship with what was called 'Europe', our ostensibly enthusiastic membership of which arose from a series of sleights-of-hand, in which the electorate had been persuaded that it was a win–win deal with no price tag. By the time the statement dropped through the letterbox, it was too late to back out. Out of this tactic had developed in Ireland a surreal sense that 'Europe' was some kind of transnational philan-thropic organization, which rewarded our 'progressive' tendencies with unprecedented largesse. All we had to do was keep adopting the right measures, attitudes and positions, and the honey would keep on flowing. Any attempt to warn of possible downstream consequences, or even to point out that some element of trade-off might be expected in exchange for multi-billion sums of structural or cohesion funding, met with a response not unlike that of a baby whose dummy has been taken away.

An unwillingness to admit to the true basis of the booming times may have contained at least some of the seeds of the denial that fol-lowed its evaporation. Hence the otherwise inexplicable attitude of the Irish electorate to the treaties of Nice and Lisbon, both of which were rejected, Nice in 2001 and Lisbon seven years later. Looking back now, it is as though the electorate was seeking, above all, to issue elaborate repudiations of the idea that Irish prosperity had anything at all to do with reliance on the EU. Both treaties were eventually ratified when the powers-that-were refused to accept the first responses. This was condemned as 'undemocratic', but really it was just another reflection of the salami tactic: the electorate had forgotten eating previous slices of the sausage and needed to have its memory jogged. Because voters took literally the notion that they were each time being offered a democratic choice, they thought this gave them the right to say No. In fact, they had said Yes long ago, and so twice needed to be reminded of this long-standing answer.

Six, seven, eight years ago, dizzy with the idea of an economic and cultural transformation, we took the dramatic changes to our culture and public spaces for granted: as the promised flowering of European convergence. We didn't exactly understand what had happened, but we were not about to look its bounties in the mouth. Really, our opposition to Nice and Lisbon was the response of a people infected by a hubris generated by the very thing we were now seeking to reject. These were not thoughtful responses, but gut reactions, perhaps inspired by a growing subliminal sense that Ireland was no longer in charge of its own destiny. Simultaneously, however, we embraced what appeared to be the benefits of that which we struggled against.

It was between the treaties of Nice and Lisbon that the real damage was inflicted. For nearly a decade from 1999, interest rates – directed at German conditions – hovered below Ireland's rate of inflation, which meant that, in a certain warped sense, it was foolish not to be heavily indebted. With all the appropriate fiscal and financial levers long since surrendered, the nation's prudence went on automatic pilot as, with one side of our brains, we persuaded ourselves that, all things considered, we had been exceedingly smart to get ourselves hooked into this euro caper. With the other side of our brains, we continued to be sceptical, but this scepticism never came to anything except late-night muttering over pints and half-ones.

In preparation for the massive shifts in economic culture which were essential to our embracing of the euro, we had had to get our house in order. This meant sweeping State debt under the private carpet by transferring much of it to private mortgages. During Ireland's most recent previous economic crisis, in the 1980s, the big issue had been the national debt. The Maastricht criteria – in the small print of the eponymous EU treaty which we ratified in a referendum in June 1992 – involved requirements that national debt not exceed more than 60 per cent of GDP, and that governments not borrow more than 3 per cent of spending needs. Ireland met these criteria, more or less – largely by diverting borrowing from the public to the personal arena, using stamp duty charged in the purchase of property to cream off revenues from the housing bubble. This meant that citizens would continue to pay for years on their mortgages the cost of State services incurred perhaps a decade or more in the past.

Many such barely registered factors of the shifting underlying economic realities were part of the narrative that led us to where we ended up. Although they have since been subject to wall-to-wall parsing and analysis by pundits and experts, at the time they were downplayed, not least because all of our newspapers and other media organizations were involved in cheerleading for Irish participation in European Monetary Union. In truth, our fate was sealed not in September 2008, or even on 1 January 2002, but on 18 June 1992, the day we voted for the Maastricht Treaty, which prepared the ground for the introduction of the euro.

Listening to the radio in the months after the arrival of the IMF into Dublin, with the single currency tottering as it came under pressure in Greece, Spain and Italy, you might be forgiven for thinking that everyone in Ireland had foreseen the problem with the euro and had accordingly voted against it in the referendum of 1992. It is interesting to reflect on what this process reveals about how a whole people can come, over the course of years or months, to arrive at a view of the past that is utterly at variance with the facts. It doesn't happen all at once, but in the knot and purl of things, a tug here and a tweak there, such as might go unnoticed from close quarters and soon blend into the accepted weave of history and fact.

The turnout in the Maastricht referendum was 57 per cent, with 69.1 per cent voting Yes – which means that just one in six of those entitled to vote opposed the treaty. Since the outcome of the referendum was linked to the drawing down of the equivalent of about €10 billion in structural funds, the debate was over before it began. Of the main parties, only Democratic Left advocated a No vote. All the newspapers adopted a pro-Maastricht stance. A handful of columnists, myself included, urged a No vote, and were declared insane on that account.

Years later, after the money had been drawn down and spent, a new-found scepticism welled up in the soul of the electorate. During the Nice and Lisbon debates, arguments rejected in 1992 were advanced by born-again radicals who back in 1992 had kept their scepticism to themselves. By then we had made our bed, and our best chance, given the choices we had made, was to hang together with what we sometimes called our European 'partners', if only in the hope of avoiding the prospect of being hanged on our own. By conflating the narratives of the Maastricht, Nice and Lisbon referendums, we have persuaded ourselves that, all the way along, we, the far seeing people, sought to withstand the bullying and blandishments of the political establishment by resisting something that we knew would end in tears. But I have this niggling memory of standing on platforms in 1992 beside the late, great radical economist Raymond Crotty, trying to persuade people that voting Yes to Maastricht would be the most disastrous decision we would ever make. Not only do I not recall those platforms being as crowded as one might gather listening to the born-again radicals who have emerged following recent disasters, but I have this almost certain recollection that most of those now claiming they saw all this coming were the ones calling us mad.

I come from a background in which opposition to Ireland's membership of what is called 'the European project' was passionate and pronounced. My father was one of 211,891 people (17 per cent) who in 1972 voted against joining the 'Common Market'. He believed membership would lead to the destruction of our farming and fishing industries, and make us the paupers of Europe. He insisted that the required trade-offs – especially the exchange of sovereignty and natural resources for infrastructure – would erode our long-term capacity for self-sufficiency. Despite our modern motorways and transnational industries, it would be hard at this moment to dismiss his analysis. This perspective was in my blood, and I articulated it for years, encountering little but abuse and ridicule for my troubles.

I began to rethink my position after our ratification of the Maastricht Treaty, and crossed over into what seemed an acceptance of a different relationship with the rest of Europe and a new idea of Ireland. With that treaty, the EU ceased to be merely a cooperative community, acquiring many of the characteristics of a single political entity. I had assumed that, in voting Yes to Maastricht, we were all pretty much aware of the choice we were making. It seemed obvious that the argument for an independent Ireland was lost. As time passed, I began to feel that our pursuit of a particular approach to economic development had taken us down a particular road, with its own logic, and that it was somewhat irrational to continue fighting what a majority of the electorate had signed us up to. Ireland had become so dependent on the relationship with the Community that, henceforth, almost everything that concerned our future would have to be pursued from an acceptance of this dependence.

In my heart of hearts, I still regarded this as a tragedy. In 1972 and even in the years immediately after we joined, we had hopes of developing an indigenous self-sufficiency, while using our membership of the Common Market, and later the European Community, in ways that might have supported this. But nobody in Irish politics at the time was offering a coherent vision concerning how this might be pursued. Whenever Irish objectives were at odds with the drift of the Community, we chose to accept monetary compensation rather than insisting on retaining certain essential capacities and resources within our control.

In 1972, even in 1992, we had choices; by 2001, when the time came to tick the box for the Treaty of Nice, we had none. Our indigenous economy was virtually non-existent. We depended mainly on outsiders coming in and creating activity from which we gained temporary benefits. Almost nobody among our political class now offered us a vision by which we might proceed outside the EU or in a reduced role within it. There seemed zero prospect of the model of economy we had chosen to follow continuing to be attractive to the external investment it depended on, unless we remained spread-eagled and willing in the middle of the European bed.

In 2008, during the first Lisbon referendum, when I revealed that I would be voting Yes, I got two kinds of response. One, predictably, was the vitriolic bloggerspeak of some on the latter-day No side (none of whom I could remember being around when it might have mattered), who said I had 'taken the soup'. The other was from people on the Yes side who congratulated me on my conversion to good sense. From both sides I detected an insinuation that my changed position had to do with growing older and relinquishing former 'radical' opinions. But I was offered no soup and remained, frankly, unenthused about being welcomed aboard the battleship Yes. This had nothing to do with either conservatism or radicalism. It had to do with national survival. To untangle ourselves from our newly formed relationship, and all that went with it, would be an undertaking of enormous proportions, which in the absence of leaders of the calibre of our founding fathers, it was hard to envisage being undertaken within the scope of my potential lifetime.

Yet the public mood seemed to run directly counter to the evolution of this reality. In the beginning, where Ireland was poor and sovereign, we were 'pro-European'. The more prosperous we became, apparently as a consequence of increasing integration into Europe, the more the doubts seemed to harden. By June 2001, when the Irish electorate expressed its first-thought rejection of the Nice Treaty, it was already too late to prevent the calamity that would unfurl some years later: the euro was at the starting post and we had signed up for it. Indeed, there seemed at the time to be an almost total imaginative disconnection between the currency and the treaty, and indeed between the actually existing economic circumstances pertaining in Ireland and the general attitude to the European project here. When the time came for the Lisbon Treaty to be deliberated upon in 2008, the opposition had hardened considerably, in spite of the fact that the economic catastrophe was as yet just an ominous gathering of clouds on the horizon that those of us who noticed still hoped might blow over.

The slow, odd way we slipped into crisis from about September 2008 led us to adopt certain analyses on the hoof, without more than a glance at the bigger picture. We blamed the banks, individual banking personalities, domestic politicians, accusing them, not implausibly, of recklessness, waste and incompetence. We essayed comparisons with the most recent serious recession, that of the 1980s, in which the causative circumstances were quite different. We focused on the use or misuse of domestic instruments, when the only one that might have saved us – domestic control over interest rates – had long since been surrendered.

What has collapsed in Ireland is not some absolute manifestation of Irish economic or social possibility but the materialist, short-termist option promoted by politicians since the 1960s and acceded to by the people because the prospect of prosperity was dangled in front of them. The stark truth of Irish economic affairs is in fact much worse than anything being considered by our new masters, now universally referred to as 'the troika': it is that, if Ireland were to rely on what it is capable of generating within itself, by its own efforts and initiative, its people would be starving again. Right now, it seems that, even in the passive-aggressive embrace of the troika, we face risks and deprivations potentially as momentous as if we decided to cut loose and start over, but our dependency habit is too engrained for us to weigh the different fear elements and opt for the risks that would involve going forward under our own steam.

Ireland, the conventional wisdom asserts without pause, has for half a century been a society 'in transition' – between what is disparagingly called a 'traditional' society and the kind of society that the elites of Official Ireland seek to put in place. This destination-condition is often unclear, but it is summoned up by certain mantras and neo-values: 'change', 'tolerance', 'liberal', 'pluralist', etc. What is interesting about these concepts when you get right up close to them is that, while having a powerful resonance in culture, they have no precise meanings. They are, at best, vague and vaguely virtuous aspirations, which in the main derive their power from what they imply themselves to repudiate. They are reactive, denunciatory and negative, rather than free-standing, annunciatory and affirmative.

For the moment we are in some kind of interim Ireland, a place we merely pass through on the way to the promised land. When, back in 2005, the Economist Intelligence Unit ranked Ireland the best place in the world to live, the fine print offered a most interesting picture of this place. Dan O'Brien, an Irish economist and then senior editor with the EIU, was quoted in the newspapers as attributing Ireland's position to our having retained 'the good parts' of Eamon de Valera's vision of a strong community and family-based society, in tandem with the prosperity that descended, apparently from nowhere, about a decade before. The EIU found that Ireland, unlike other wealthy countries, had retained strong 'traditional values' rooted in community and family, and that, while Ireland was by no means immune to Western lifestyle-problems like family breakdown and addiction, it remained less affected than other societies.

It was interesting, when you peered closely at the small print, to note that the survey appeared to have awarded points across a range of indices without necessarily applying any particular ideological (or even commonsensical) template to the exercise. Therefore, for example, although Ireland did well for 'family life' and badly in 'gender equality', there was a sense that it must have attracted positive points in both categories, despite the fact that, seen in a certain light, the two concepts appeared to be in conflict. 'Gender equality', clearly, was code for luring mothers from the home to take their place on the assembly lines, and therefore might be deemed a countervailing force to the pull of the hearth or the kitchen range. But the EIC survey aggregated these and other points on what appeared to be a value-free basis.

In passing, one might note the usefulness of the survey in identifying one of the 'tricks' modern Ireland has contrived to disguise its internal conflicts and potential incoherence with statistical conjuring. But even more interesting was that the survey appeared to be suggesting that, right then in 2005, Ireland was more or less at the optimal point of balance between its old culture and some new dispensation, gaining high points for the moment from its 'traditional' values while chalking up increasing scores from its modernizing achievements. The surveyors had managed to quantify something of both the residue of tradition and the spoils of revolution in a single graph.

Quietly, unnoticed, this proposed an entirely different version of reality, in which the cohesion of the passing moment was not exclusively to do with the success of the proposals of the modernizers, but owed something also to the lingering benefits of things they were intent upon destroying. Somehow this seemed to resonate with a recurring sense I had, listening to various proponents of change and liberalism: that, having argued all day for the dismantling of de Valera's Ireland, the self-appointed and determined modernizers of Ireland always went home and had their dinners put in front of them. Their very capacity to demolish what had sustained them continued to depend on what remained as yet intact.

# 2

# *The Faceless Man*

THE PRESIDENTIAL ELECTION OF 2011 WAS TO PROVE NOTABLY LESS momentous than the one that resulted in the election of Ireland's first female president, Mary Robinson, in 1990, and indeed even less so than the bitterly fought contest that delivered another Mary to the Park seven years later. But it was, at another level, far more interesting than either of those two contests. More than any electoral contest of my lifetime so far, it seemed to draw a statement up out of the very psyche of the Irish people, betraying a hankering after something that did not seem to exist.

The presidential election is best seen as a sequel to the general election of the previous February, which resulted in the apparently overwhelming endorsement of a Fine Gael/Labour coalition government. On closer examination, that outcome reveals itself as a default decision, made in the absence of any other viable options. The electorate had more than a mind to punish Fianna Fáil for its unhappy stewardship of the national fortunes between 1997 and 2007, and duly did so with an extreme vengeance.

The election of the Enda Kenny-led coalition had about it perhaps an element of excessive expectation, not unlike the surge of optimism that a few years earlier had put a shoulder to the Celtic Tiger: a kind of irrational faith that, regardless of the lacklustre pedigrees of those associated with the incoming administration, seemed to arise out of the relief of getting rid of Fianna Fáil. In February, Kenny had cut a persuasive figure of a reforming leader, who would restore public faith in politics and rescue Ireland from the peril of Armageddon. As autumn followed summer, the sense had undoubtedly grown – out there in Europe at least – that his government had turned things around, restoring confidence in Ireland as – in Kenny's election mantra – 'the best small country in the world to do business in'.

But back at the ranch, a different mood music was building: a growing sense that Kenny's government was fundamentally motivated by ingratiating itself with the big beasts of the EU, simpering unctuously when they patted its head and promising the further enslavement of the Irish population should this be demanded. It had not escaped public notice either that, apart from embarking on U-turns in relation to many of its pre-election commitments, the new administration had almost immediately begun to manifest symptoms of cronyism and arrogance for which both coalition parties had previously excoriated their predecessors in office. As another winter beckoned – the fourth of the dark, post-Tiger era – the presidential election seemed to offer another chance, if not to change anything, at least to say something.

In spite of everything, Irish people continue to invest great hope in politics, if not exactly to the same degree in actual politicians. This instinct derives from a history which insistently suggests that periodic intervention by passionate and charismatic individuals has the capacity to alter the course of that history – and generally in ways that will make things better. In school, every Irish person has absorbed two fundamental things about Ireland Past: one, that it has been characterized by a process of abuse and radical interference from outside; and two, that, from time to time, some figure, a Robert Emmet or a Padraig Pearse, has emerged to, as Pearse put it, redeem his fellow countrymen from infamy by the splendour of his protest. Perhaps, in spite of much recent effort to erase it, this sense of a themed historical narrative remains strong in the Irish psyche, which – sometimes in spite of what pass for 'the facts' – causes us to investigate every moment of possibility in the hope of finding another redeemer. What is odd is that this sense of latent expectancy should attach itself to the possibilities offered by something as politically tepid and peripheral as the presidency of the Republic.

For all kinds of reasons, the campaign for the presidency seemed, like a heat-seeking missile, to go after several of the key contexts of Irish public life in the previous years and decades. Each of the eventual seven candidates seemed to represent and act out some wider and deeper story. In a long-running controversy involving David Norris and attitudes towards paedophilia, the campaign provided an unexpected opportunity to view the soft underbelly of Irish liberal piety in the matter of child welfare. In spite of becoming embroiled in controversy involving bizarre historical remarks about paedophilia, and a subsequent scandal when it emerged that he had written to an Israeli court seeking clemency for a convicted rapist who had once been his lover, Norris was enabled to re-enter the presidential race. Having started out as the frontrunner, however, he eventually ended up near the bottom of the table.

In the candidacy of Martin McGuinness, the entire history of the previous four decades of war and peace-making in the North of Ireland came under scrutiny.

Seán Gallagher, previously unknown as a political entity, brought something else to the surface: the true nature of Irish attitudes to Fianna Fáil, suddenly revealing a deep ambivalence that nobody had previously detected in the fulminations of the previous three years.

To understand what can sometimes seem like the capriciousness of the Irish electorate under various conditions, it is necessary to have some understanding of the undertows. Unfortunately most of those who think out loud about Irish politics tend to do so in moralistic terms, emphasizing the superficial and fleeting while remaining oblivious of the undercurrents – or, worse, reading them on the basis of what people actually say. If the presidential election of 2011 can be said to be 'about' anything, it was about bringing this tendency into the light.

At all times in a dynamic society, there is always an unconscious awareness of an ideological backbeat, driving things forward. Sometimes – as back in 1990 – this becomes overwhelming: a deep, shared, repeated riff of expectation and certainty. At other times, it dies down to the faintest bass arpeggio, as though inviting a handclap to keep it going. Still, it remains, an underlying idea of what might make things 'better'. It is this rhythm that politicians vie with one another to tap out on the national drum kit.

Back in 1990, it had all seemed straightforward. We were emerging from the primordial mists of tribalism, traditionalism, clientelism and a dozen other isms. These ideologies had been repudiated widely enough and sufficiently to create a clear sense of an agenda of what was deemed to be progress. Having a woman president was an idea that spoke to these notions. The promise was of 'change', a golden age of Irish life, probably heading in a leftward, liberal, more egalitarian and secular direction. Everything would be different, we promised ourselves, once we shook off the binds of our tribal and traditional past.

Padraig Pearse famously rejected the idea that progress and knowledge can be matters of linear growth, insisting that history and human understandings travel in circles rather than straight lines. Thus, things that seem new are nearly always old things that have been forgotten, and the future is always a remixed version of the past. Harking back to that previous moment of acute self-awareness twenty-two years before, it was possible to perceive the truth in this observation. We had not progressed along a straight line, but mostly wended our way around in a circle. In some ways, things were demonstrably better, though not in the ways we tended to emphasize; in other matters it was clear we had slipped backwards. But one thing we were still missing was the deeper self-awareness that might arise from stepping away from the 'progress' viewfinder to look closely at other elements of the fabric of our society: how we might know and describe ourselves now; what words like 'progress' and 'modernization' might actually mean; where human welfare might truly be located.

But by any of the relevant criteria, it is clear that, in the twenty-one years that spanned the 1990 and 2011 elections, our paths had not followed the course we might have predicted back then. We had since seen war and peace, prosperity and bankruptcy, and experienced some jarring changes in the driving rhythms of Irish society. But perhaps the only characteristic that lent coherence to the political life of the Republic over those two decades was the fact that since 1990 we had had a female head of State.

Gazing squarely at the political scene, you would have to say that, by and large, we avoided creating what was back then prophesied as a paradigm-shift in Irish politics, from right-of-centre to left-of-centre. Another pertinent reflection might focus on the fact that it took us until the spring of 2011 to undertake something that was loudly announced after Robinson's election: the renunciation of Fianna Fáil – and indeed even this remains ambiguous.

When you consider how much rhetoric about 'change' in Irish society had emanated from the political context, it was remarkable how little our political establishment has turned over since Mary Robinson's election, with the main political parties still dominated by figures who were in or about the front line back then. For all the hyperbole we indulged ourselves in about the idea of a female presidency, the impact on Irish society had been minimal.

Robinson ticked the boxes of understandings imported from elsewhere, mainly concerning the nature of social enlightenment, and, once we elected her, we banished from our thoughts any serious consideration of how to manage the forward-propulsion of our society. The symbol was sufficient. In the main, we turned the implementation of the social-democratic agenda of equality and fairness over to ideologues with selective ideas about the meanings of such words, and got on with enjoying the party we suddenly found ourselves stumbling into. In due course, a revolution in credit ensured a redistribution not of means but of debt, creating a time bomb that ticked ominously under our noses. But few noticed the ticking. Robinson's presidency functioned as a talisman of pseudo-liberal ambitions but otherwise just came and went.

The presidential election of 1997, which followed almost immediately on the realization that Irish economic fortunes had begun to pick up, announced a retrenchment of the old guard. Fianna Fáil, having had its eye wiped in 1990, now conspired to steal everyone's clothes, reclaiming the presidency with what it fancied to be its very own Robinson-clone and re-entering government just as the sunshine of prosperity began to break through. As an unapologetic nationalist and Catholic, Mary McAleese came much closer than her predecessor to representing the complex, mix-and-match nature of Irish society, and therefore offered us an opportunity to make an otherwise inexpressible statement about the Ireland we desired to bring into existence. But this too came to very little, giving rise to further self-congratulation rather than enhanced understandings or a grounded mobilization of collective energies.

And yet, by the time the next presidential campaign was called for, fourteen years later, a series of revolutions appeared to have occurred across the visible territory of Irish life. Fianna Fáil lay in ruins, as did the Irish Catholic Church. But these apparent revolutions, the standard interpretations notwithstanding, were not of themselves evidence of an awakening Ireland. Rather, they were the default outcomes of serious wrongs, errors and disasters. Looking around with a clear eye, you were forced to conclude that the prevailing state-of-affairs was largely the outcome of a series of reactions to things going wrong, rather than the realization of Irish hopes, dreams and visions.

These circumstances prevailed in spite of the best efforts of various forces who had sought to impose themselves on Irish society, briefly seducing the electorate at various points. Prosperity, or the illusion of it, had naturally had its own influence, persuading us that we had been exceedingly clever in our various past choices, even though we had not been entirely sure what it was we were trying to achieve. Ideologically speaking, we had seemed to move briefly to the left, then back to the centre, consolidated, and then, when everything came unstuck, began to show signs of lurching leftwards again. Now, uncertain of where we had ended up, we vacillated once again, sometimes seeming to be on the brink of fireside anarchism but rarely getting out of our chairs.

The liberal/secular agenda, which provided the score for the 1980s, had seemed to get implemented all of a rush, to the point where everyone was not just 'liberal' but as simplistically and intolerantly so as to bear a passing resemblance to the conservative dinosaurs that seemed finally to have been banished in 1990. In respect of more intimate questions of personal morality and sexuality, there was a widespread sense of self-congratulation at the scale of the enlightenment that had dawned, but little reflection on the contradictions these changes had thrown up.

In the realm of the 'national question', the peace had held, against all the odds, enabling Sinn Féin in 2011 to run one of its leading figures, Martin McGuinness, for the presidency of the Republic it had not long before excoriated as illegitimate.

Because the people of the Republic were, for the most part, not directly affected by the Troubles, the story of that conflict always had a different meaning 'down here', mainly being regarded as an inconvenience and an embarrassment. Twenty years before, most people in the Republic had been hostile to Sinn Féin, but in a rather lazy and ambivalent way. The Provo terror campaign had forced us to jettison a simplistic nationalism under the lashes of revulsion and revisionism. But now, with the inconvenience and embarrassment removed by the peace process, all such sentiments had begun to fade into insignificance compared to the growing impression that greater and more unforgivable sins had been committed by politicians of other hues. Martin McGuinness could point to the prize of allegedly perpetual peace, whereas his opponents stood in front of empty trophy cupboards. The whiff of cordite, far from being a problem, acted as something analogous to an aphrodisiac.

As recently as twenty years before, Sinn Féin's policy portfolio had been a strange mixture of militarism, social conservatism and economic naivety. It wasn't until after the 1990s ceasefires that Sinn Féin had started to review its policy outlooks to the extent of becoming a radical left-wing party under all headings, with policies that were mainly off-the-peg imports from other cultures. This pattern tracked also something of the journey of a majority of Irish people, who now found themselves having far more in common with Sinn Féin than they might have dreamed possible even a few years before.

Running Martin McGuinness seemed a clever tactic on Sinn Féin's part. Once it became clear that Fianna Fáil would not be contesting the election, the opportunity was too good to miss. Here was a windfall chance of a major shortcut in breaking through to the political mainstream of the Republic. It was also an opportunity to defuse many of the reservations that many people 'down here' retained about the Provos, enabling a controlled explosion of the major questions and ensuring that – win or lose – the next outing would be a much easier ride.

But the 'national question' was especially prone to the congenital ambivalence of the Irish people. If McGuinness was expecting to be welcomed with open arms in the Republic by a populace overflowing with gratitude for his efforts to liberate them, he was riding for a rude awakening. As the campaign slipped into gear, he seemed genuinely shocked to be confronted by recurring questions about his history as an IRA member and leader. In one episode, following a television debate between the candidates, McGuinness was reported to have gone to the dressing room of RTÉ presenter Miriam O'Callaghan and upbraided her for her trenchant interrogation of his past career.

That same week, a public confrontation had occurred in Athlone between Martin McGuinness and the son of Private Patrick Kelly, killed by the IRA at the culmination of the Don Tidey kidnap in Leitrim twenty-eight years before. Kelly had demanded that McGuinness reveal what he knew about the killing of his father, and McGuinness had denied any knowledge. More than anything, the encounter revealed the folly of Sinn Féin's seeking to present itself as a party with an unquestionable legitimacy in representing the interests of Irish 'republicanism'. What – that encounter demanded – was the nature of the 'republic' Sinn Féin purported to be working towards? Did it bear any relationship to the one we already had? To put it starkly: was the 'republic' that Martin McGuinness aspired to being president of the one Private Kelly died to uphold? Sinn Féin might feel entitled to dismiss such questions and claim that, in doing so, it was seeking to 'move on' in building the peace process, but it was also discovering that 'down here' the fudges would have to be made to a different recipe. The Provos might have called themselves 'republicans', but the Republic was where we lived, and they never seemed to be thinking or talking about a place we recognized. If you listened carefully to them, you began to suspect that they wanted to abolish the actually existing Republic and establish a new one, but they never came right out and said so. They saw themselves as having inherited our history, but secretly we remembered a rather different version.

This in part accounted for the short-fused menace they now evinced: how dare we question their records and actions when we have not made the sacrifices for Ireland that they had? Caught up in their own rhetoric of peace-making, the Provos had repackaged their fudges as vindications and presented themselves as having achieved significant victories on behalf of the historic tradition of Irish nationalism. This had worked 'up North', but it had rather less purchase in the Republic. The way most people 'down here' saw things, the Provos had been engaged in a local faction fight, with minimal implications for the southern entity. They were pests who saw themselves as heroes. Their insistence on a comparison between themselves and the leaders of 1916 was always deeply nauseating for many people in the Republic, but our public discussion of such matters was insufficiently discriminating to allow for expression of exactly why we felt this.

Perhaps it came down to a simple question of time: Easter Week 1916 had lasted almost precisely one week, whereas the Provos' campaign persisted for nearly thirty years, twisting into criminality and gross inhumanity. Moreover, we looked at the Provos' 'achievement' and couldn't help noticing that, after three decades of fighting for freedom, they had signed up to pretty much the same deal as had been on the table in the beginning. Into the bargain, we had to relinquish our unrealistic but deeply felt desire to 'reintegrate' the national territory. For a quiet life, we had agreed to jettison our claim to national unity, but secretly resented the Provos for putting us in the position of having to do so. In the interests of peace, we suppressed the questions and contradictions, and might have let things lie had Sinn Féin not tried to elbow its way into our politics also.

By 2011, most Irish people, glancing backwards, saw prosperity and its antithesis standing side by side as the totems of the previous two decades, their shadows becoming deeper and merging into one. Both conditions had, in differing ways, rendered us more unthinking: in prosperity because we didn't have to think much; and during its aftermath since 2008 because we became incoherent with rage.

When I was a teenager, back in the 1970s, almost everyone in Ireland was 'conservative'. People voted, as a matter of course, for parties with 'right-wing' policies. Some young people flirted with socialist and other radical ideas, but these were regarded as eccentric and dangerous. The failures of recent years, however, have effected a sudden and massive change in the electorate. Now, most people are, if not outrightly left-wing, certainly increasingly disposed to radical, even anarchistic ideas. In some respects this reflects a backlash against the hubris and grandiosity now seen as having led us towards the abyss. But it might be truer and simpler to observe that many Irish people have lately become politically reckless, perhaps even a little mad. In order to cancel out any impression the world may have of Irish 'conservatism', many voters now seek to make statements that convey the contrary impression. For a moment or two after the announcement of his candidacy, it seemed that Martin McGuinness might well avail of this new disposition, but as the undertows had their way, the moment passed as quickly as it had arrived. As the campaign unfolded through October, it became obvious that McGuinness, after an early spurt, was destined to be an also-ran.

Michael D. Higgins, somewhat bizarrely, became the candidate who would function as a refuge from any form of radical or experimental excursion by the electorate. This would have seemed incomprehensible twenty years previously, but time has a way of making complication seem like the natural order. Michael D. had been around the block a few times, having drifted from slightly militant leftist to liberal darling, and now veering back towards the mainstream from which he had emanated, in an attempt, as he reached the twilight years of his political career, to become father of the Irish nation – but without necessarily understanding just how deep the craving for such a figure had become.

I still have the typewritten note I received from Michael D. in the early days of 1983, when I wrote to him requesting an interview for *Hot Press*. It ends: 'And of course it doesn't matter that you are unable to offer a fee', a response to my naive apology for the impecuniousness of both my employers and myself. That sentence, it struck me reading it almost twenty-nine years later as the presidential campaign got under way, offered an indicator of the sensitivity and instinctual kindness of Michael D. Higgins: in brushing my apology aside, he did not want to draw attention to the gaucheness behind it. It was some time later that I learned that politicians never received payment for press interviews.

In January 1983, when I met Michael D. for the first time, Ireland was a deeply conservative place, its public life character-ized by greyness, stupidity and a repugnance towards youth and spirit. A savage recession was under way. A moralistic Catholicism still held the nation in the vice of its clinch. To be sensible or moral, then, you had no choice but to be left-wing and liberal of outlook, and Michael D. and I ticked both boxes.

If you'd asked me what kept me sane in that monochrome Ireland, I would have said simply: rock 'n' roll. I had recently started working for *Hot Press* and decided to undertake a series of interviews with Irish politicians who struck me as being in tune with the spirit of the music that preoccupied us, and who exhibited signs of carrying that spirit into the public life of the nation.

That January Sunday afternoon, I drove to Galway in my Hiace van, with my sister's two-ton cassette recorder, believing that I was embarking on a voyage into the future. I spent several hours talking to Michael D. in his living room and came away certain that I had met someone who would soon play a central role in changing Ireland for the better. The headline on that piece – the first ever *Hot Press* political interview – was 'Something Better Change', the title of a Stranglers song.

Just short of three decades later, you would need to have been utterly detached from reality not to understand that, whatever it was we now needed or desired, the aspiration to progress could hardly be described in the same 'right-to-left' terms that might have seemed inviting in 1983. Much had transpired that we could not have dreamed that January day. The Berlin Wall had come down and the capitalist system stood tottering. Ireland had been revolutionized by – in no particular order – secularism, feminism, divorce, prosperity, television, cheap air fares, music radio, the global embrace of U2, female presidencies, coalition government, gay rights, immigration and so-called European integration. All these developments, in one way or another, might have seemed in tune with the dreaming and desiring that welled up that early 1980s afternoon between Michael D. and me.

One of the things that irritate me about our political conversation today is that so much of it continues as if nothing at all has changed. Generational gridlock ensures that progress and idealism are still defined in terms that would have made absolute sense in 1983 but have no objective coherence today. Over the uneven course of those twenty-nine years, we had moved through a changing world, in which what Michael D. used to call 'the forces of conservatism' had to a large extent been routed.

Michael D. had long been deeply loved by many and remained a source of bafflement or condescension to many others. There lingered about him a sense that he had some time ago caught sight of a certain cuddly idea of himself and fallen a little in love with it. Thus, he became 'Michael D.', a slightly cartoonish figure, a cult, a 'character', and started to play up to what might otherwise have marginalized him. In some respects, his collusion in his caricature arose from a desire to undermine a more toxic depiction of him by his ideological enemies, of whom there were at one time quite a few.

Things had moved on. From being relatively poor, we had become rich, then poor again. The sovereignty we dreamed of for over eight hundred years had been surrendered to a new power. Marriage was well on its way to being regarded as a lesser commitment than buying a car, and to be Catholic was to be a second-class citizen.

One of the most noticeable things about that presidential election of 2011 was that it illustrated how, in certain respects at least, we appeared to have moved beyond our long-time seeking after tokens to portray our virtuous characteristics in relation to progressiveness and the like. There was a worrying moment for a while when it looked like we might cling to the idea of a Gay President (as opposed, for example, to 'a president who happens to be gay') as a way of again distracting ourselves from reality, but as the campaign entered its final stages that madness seemed to have passed. It was interesting that the two female candidates – and one of them called Mary, too – were languishing near the bottom of the polls.

Back in 1991, I wrote *Jiving at the Crossroads* in an attempt to describe the fundamental nature of the conflict I was experiencing. I had voted for Mary Robinson, something that, observing the chauvinistic way in which her presidency unfolded, I came to regret. In retrospect, it seemed she had employed a bogus rhetoric of inclusion to imply that she would represent all the people of Ireland, when really she, like most of her supporters, was more interested in displaying the head of 'conservative' Ireland on a spike.

I am always fascinated that the word 'conservative' is still used pejoratively as a synonym for 'right-winger' or 'reactionary'. But a 'conservative', surely, is someone who wants to keep things as they are, and this means that the characteristics of conservatism must necessarily change with the ebb and flow of reality. To be a 'conservative' in Ireland nowadays is not to be Catholic, 'right-wing', traditionalist or conventional, but rather the opposite. It is to glory in the vanquishing of the core sensibilities of the Ireland we grew up in, and to demand the retention of all the victories of the revolutions of the past thirty years, regardless of the consequences of these in real life. To be a 'conservative' now is surely to oppose any rebalancing of the scales in the aftermath of the successful revolutions that, since the 1980s, swept Ireland from the liberal-left. Those most at risk from discrimination or injustice today are not, as in 1983, women or gays, but straight, white, middle-class males – this being the only category unprotected by the new dispensation of political correctness under which issues of justice and fairness are nowadays decided.

Listening to Michael D.'s speeches during the presidential election, it seemed to me that, while the old rhetorical flourishes were still present, there was something missing. I was looking for some quality of contemporaneousness that would translate the fundamental desires for justice and truth which had defined Michael D.'s public life from the beginning into a language that spoke to the present moment in terms that I recognized. I did not believe that such speeches could come couched in the terms of 1983: left-wing, liberal, secular and self-consciously 'progressive'. We needed a new language to describe the ailments of Irish society, and it seemed obvious that a radicalism that failed this test was unworthy of the name. As he was a hero of my youth, I wish I could say that Michael D. and I had always walked in step, but that would not be true. Regrettably, I had sometimes found him to be, like many Irish progressives, selective and evasive with regard to matters which did not drop neatly into the liberal in-basket. Watching him during the campaign, it was difficult not to be over-come by the sense that, although he has been on the winning side of many of Ireland's recent ideological and moral battles, he had not adapted his public thoughts to the changing landscape of fact.

As in the general election of February, I volunteered to go back on the beat to report on the election for *The Irish Times*. One morning assignment brought me to a Dublin hotel, to see Michael D. being feted by a bunch of feminists at a press conference under the banner 'Women for Michael D. Higgins'. The assembled women included many who had been at the forefront of the women's rights movement, a recognition that Michael D. had played his own part in various feminist and liberal struggles. Michael D. was in his element that morning, and gave a perky, upbeat speech, which largely focused on the battles fought on this front over the years. These women, he said, had made the case for a real republic.

Then, spotting me in the back row and remembering himself, he looked straight into my eyes and said that the battle of rights also included the rights of fathers in relation to their children. 'It wasn't just women's issues – it was citizens' issues.' But I admit to wondering if he would have been saying this had I not been stand-ing a few feet away.

Still, I had to admit that Michael D. Higgins remained a formidable and deeply serious man, whose politics had been forged in the white heat of a personal experience of acute poverty and heartbreak. A vital clue to understanding the original nature of the force that propels Michael D. is conveyed by the observation that, for someone so renowned for his intellect, so much about Michael D.'s personality and its output is pure emotion. This quality does not fully emerge except when he is making a speech in public. In interviews, he tends to be relatively low-key, in argument verging on disjointed. But when he speaks off-the-cuff to a theme that is fluid in his mind, he creates something akin to music.

He reminds me of The Irish Man, in Tom Murphy's play *The Gigli Concert*: he wants to sing like Gigli but cannot, and yet, unbeknownst to himself, speaks as Gigli might have wished to speak had he by chance happened to hear such speaking. Michael D. begins his speeches quietly, restrainedly, in a kind of deceptive, almost whispered falsetto. There is a kind of exaggerated politeness about him at this point, which makes what follows even more spectacular. Gradually, as he builds his case, his voice develops weight and timbre, his tone, pitch and modulation shifting from bar to bar, from tenor to baritone to bass to baritone, up and down his considerable range of passion. As the aria builds, he moves his hands and arms, as though conducting himself. The remarkable thing is that this occurs even when he is delivering a speech he has delivered a hundred times already. Each time is different. It's all in his head and comes out in multiple forms, replete with new images and colours.

And it is vital to an understanding of this man to remember that, from the age of five until he was eighteen, Michael D. and his year-younger brother lived with an aunt and uncle, because their father, who had fought in the Cork Number 2 Brigade in the War of Independence, was too ill to care for his four children. Michael and his four-year-old brother were farmed out, while their two sisters remained behind. Thus, there conspired to burn in Michael D. a profound moral and intellectual force, which seemed to gain an infinite quantum of energy from the rage still discernible in his public persona – a rage directed at the causes of what he recognized as injustice, and this profoundly linked to the twisted trajectory of post-Independence Ireland.

At face value, then, the outcome of the presidential election, which eventually dispatched Michael D. to Áras an Úachtaráin with more than a million votes in his pocket, might be seen to read as a considered statement of some new understanding by the Irish people. Alas, things were not so, for Michael D. Higgins would become president-by-default, just as Enda Kenny had been elected Taoiseach-by-default after the February general election. The people had had several months to warm to Michael D. and provide him with a ringing endorsement, but had declined to do so. Up to four days before polling, he was running a poor second to a total newcomer, a reality TV star with some clever media advisers.

On 24 October 2011, the seven candidates appeared on RTÉ's *The Frontline*. It was to prove a bloodbath for Seán Gallagher, who at that critical moment, against all odds and predictions, was streaking ahead in the polls. Indeed, his commanding lead was presenting problems for the commentariat, who had not anticipated anything other than also-ran status for him. Now, he was confounding all predictions by climbing to more than 40 per cent in the opinion polls, with less than a week to go.

I am not a great believer in conspiracy – mainly because culture is far more effective at dispensing with uncomfortable prospects than any orchestrated plot could ever manage. Up to that point, just a few days away from polling day, it seemed that something deep in the psyche of Irish society had broken loose and was about to make a statement that would have seemed utterly at variance with conventional wisdom. Now, the undertows started to move again. As on many such occasions, it was afterwards possible to supply a simple 'explanation', but really the surface developments were merely the acted-out alibis of a deeply cunning and self-deluding culture, seeking to post-rationalize its behaviours in a way that pre-empted inconvenient discussion or unwanted analysis.

Like Mary McAleese in 1997, Seán Gallagher exhibited many of those odd, indefinable characteristics that seem to adapt up-to-the-minute sensibilities to elements of the Irish personality.

On the face of things, it is a puzzle why Gallagher wanted to run at all. He was a successful businessman and television personality, whose association with politics had been largely behind-the-scenes. If you'd asked me a year previously, I wouldn't have included him in a list of one million eligible candidates. But once you get over this initial 'Why?', his candidacy begins to make sense.

As the presidential campaign got into gear, Gallagher distinguished himself from most of the other candidates by insisting that the presidency could be stretched beyond its current constitutional and symbolic functions in a way that nobody had proposed before. He suggested that, as president, he would adopt a highly practical leadership role in the battle to restore Ireland's economic stability, and that he believed his business experience equipped him well for such a challenge. Whether this manifesto was plausible or not, his message showed signs of connecting with the public as, having started out at the back of the field, he had become, within a week or so of polling day, the unexpected front-runner and runaway favourite to win.

It was clear, too, that Gallagher was fulfilling a widely unanticipated function with regard to traditional Fianna Fáil supporters. At grassroots level, adherence to FF is not a casual thing but an ingrained condition, which nurtures and affirms a particular view of Ireland and Irish life. All the same, in the previous February's general election, many lifelong Soldiers of Destiny deserted their tribe and some even crossed over to vote for the ancient enemy. For most, such acts of apparent treachery were justified by the exceptional economic situation and the widely felt rage against the outgoing Cowen government. For the moment, 'being Fianna Fáil' was a condition that could not respectably speak its name. But the story of Seán Gallagher's adventure in the presidential election suggests that those who imagined this situation to be permanent might well be deluding themselves.

From the outset of the campaign, Gallagher sought to present his association with Fianna Fáil as a fleeting affair, consigned to the past. He explained his previous membership of the National Executive of the party by saying that he had pursued this role in order to lobby for the rights of building subcontractors who became exposed when building firms went into liquidation. There was also some discussion of his involvement in fundraising on behalf of Fianna Fáil, and in particular some rumblings about a certain fundraising dinner in Dundalk, to which he had allegedly invited some leading businessmen.

No matter that he played down the connection, Seán Gallagher's personality spoke of the qualities which most grass-roots Fianna Fáilers tended to valorize in themselves and in their fellows. From a rural background, he had acquired a reputation for street-smarts. He spoke well and had a good line in drawing folksy but apt connections between the traditional and the post-modern. I had heard him speak at a Fianna Fáil election rally in Monaghan in the course of the February general election campaign, and been struck by the way he spoke about the resilience of the Irish psyche in times of travail. I had also heard him speak in Trim the previous summer and been taken by the witty way he dealt with some of the core contradictions and absurdities of modern Ireland, like how we went from a nation of overcrowded cosy homesteads to a nation of ghost estates. I had had a long conversation with Gallagher that night and, although I didn't for a moment give him a chance of being president, was impressed by his insight and astuteness. He had a sense about him of being authentically of the Irish mainstream, genuinely inter-ested in making things happen – as opposed to feeling entitled to carry out a role on the basis of personal ambition. The more I thought about him, the more I came to feel that, if you could shake off the implausibility of his candidacy, he suggested himself as a possibility of saying something that nobody had yet put into words.

As the campaign gathered pace and the opinion polls began to feed back into the public consciousness, the perception of Gallagher altered noticeably. Initially just another independent candidate, he becomes not just *the* independent candidate but also the surrogate Fianna Fáil baton-carrier in the race, and suddenly a real contender. He was the closet Fianna Fáiler who invited the love that dare not speak its name to tick his name on the ballot paper, the mufti-wearing Soldier of Destiny who *sotto voce* offered to enable his tribesmen, who could not for the moment show their faces, to vote for one of their own, even as he softly denied them. Gallagher's candidacy provided a kind of X-ray of a certain duplicity in the Irish mentality: outwardly there is this almost unanimous joining-in with the baying and repudiating of Fianna Fáil; inwardly there is, in large numbers of Irish people, the DNA-embedded attachment to Fianna Fáil that they were born with. It was as though the country had lapsed into a Janus-faced disposition, denouncing the past actions of those it blamed for the mess it was in, and yet seeking to return to some previous freedom based in a comfortable understanding of itself. Or, if you preferred the prejudicial media version, Ireland was prepared to taunt its own self-righteousness by electing somebody who, at the very least, seemed to have been associated with the culture now widely excoriated for having brought the country to its knees. The truth is that Irish voters remain duplicitous, self-serving and wedded to a 'traditional' loyalty paradigm that continues to endure in spite of everything. However it might be interpreted, what was happening with Gallagher's campaign ran completely against the grain of conventional commentary, which mainly directed a venomous hostility at Gallagher that became more poisonous the more he moved ahead in the polls.

Gallagher adopted, from the outset, a strategy of refusing to engage in negative exchanges or confrontations. He presented himself as the ordinary man with a paradoxically extraordinary life. Quietly, seemingly without cunning, he underlined aspects of his personality that trumped aspects of other candidates': he was younger, more energetic; he had business experience. He created a great drama around himself that fleshed out the cardboard cut-out figure who had been seen for a couple of seasons on the reality programme *Dragons' Den*. He spoke about his sight impairment, about the teachers who wrote him off. 'Last week,' he told an audience in the Mansion House one morning, 'that little guy handed in his nomination papers to run to become president of this great country.' It should have sounded cheesy, but it actually packed quite a punch. There was something about Gallagher's personality that allowed for an exceptional range of expression, from pathos to irony, without going out of tune.

It is difficult to identify exactly what Gallagher's 'secret' was – if indeed he had one. An election is more like a drama than a contest of ideas: we, the jury, make up our minds more on the basis of stories than facts, although we subsequently may seek out facts with which to back up our intuitions/decisions. Gallagher had an advantage because of his restricted back story. As the new-comer, he had a relatively uncluttered frame to present himself in. He also had that capacity first identified with Mary Robinson, of being able to appeal to different factions in different carriages of the same train. He was an ordinary Joe and also a kind of low-key Master of the Universe, both an independent and a recognizable party animal. Even though everyone seemed to know who was travelling in the other carriages, nobody seemed to mind.

One morning during the campaign, when I was trailing Gallagher on Baggot Street in Dublin, the canvass ran into P.J. Mara, the former press attaché of Charles Haughey and a long-time backroom Fianna Fáil strategist. I had had this half-formed question in my mind for several weeks: did Mara dream Gallagher up as a way of saving Fianna Fáil, a Trojan Horse out of which to unpack a reinvented Soldiers of Destiny for a new generation? I got my answer from the mutual wariness visible between the two men. Gallagher made an awkward joke about hoping there were no cameras. The men briefly greeted one another. There was an awkwardness between them that seemed to bespeak some cultural dissonance rather than any sense of an unplanned meeting of allies.

In truth, I had never really believed that Mara could have been behind it. He didn't have to be. Irish politics doesn't work like that, which is why it continues to frustrate those who think in terms of ideologies and conspiracies. Fianna Fáil always had this uncanny ability to develop alter egos, usually arising from internal dissents and counter-revolutionary movements that grew internally to become new versions of Fianna Fáil. Charles Haughey came to power in 1979 as a result of just such a movement.

On the canvass, Gallagher seemed rarely if ever caught short for an answer and managed to hit a true note with almost everyone he met. There was something chameleonic about him, a quasi-instinctual instinct for the personality of the other. On Baggot Street that morning he met a couple of men in working clothes. 'Are ye gettin' a bit of work, lads?' he enquired and immediately they gathered around him to tell him how bad things were. 'Tryin' to get paid?' he rejoined with appropriate melancholy. A young woman called Siobhan approached him and said she would vote for a president 'who smiles'. Seán told her he was the man for the smiling. 'Irish people are renowned all over the world for the warmth of their personality. I would like to reflect that.' He placed an avuncular hand on her shoulder. 'You go and let that percolate down into your psyche,' he said. Gallagher was about the only one of the seven candidates who could get away with using a word like 'psyche' out on the street. From any of the others – for differing reasons – it would either sound ridiculous or stand as a barrier to further communication. But Gallagher's personality seemed to enable him to say such things and trust that they would acquire just the right amount of irony on departing his lips.

In going around with Gallagher, and trying to put a finger on the nature of his appeal, what I hit upon was the idea that he belonged to an Ireland barely visible now at the surface level of our culture. You meet it out in the towns and villages, in the countryside, but rarely encounter it nowadays on TV or the radio. It is the Ireland of the Ploughing Championships, County Finals, Fleadh Cheoils. It mostly votes Fianna Fáil or Fine Gael and, in spite of everything, remains Catholic. It is open-minded but non-PC. It's the Ireland Mary McAleese was first recognized and adopted by as a way of saying in indigenous terms what Mary Robinson had said in terms imported from outside. It likes Garth Brooks and Willie Nelson, but also Westlife and Coldplay. It's an Ireland in which people communicate at a level of humour and constructed familiarity that makes you feel good to be around it. You might call it 'Middle Ireland', except that suggests a place between extremes, and I cannot conceive of any such polarities from which to identify a centre point.

Seán Gallagher emerged from this place. He sounded like 'one of us', an ordinary man who had struggled with a fairly ordinary life, who knew what it felt like to work in the real world, to do a day's work for a day's pay, to scramble to make a tax bill and wonder where the next week's rent was going to come from. When you met him in the street, he managed to sound like he cared about your life, perhaps because he intuited that your life was a bit like his own. Fianna Fáil was written all over him, but in a way that for a time seemed benign, relating to the grassroots of the party rather than its failed leadership and dismal recent record of public stewardship. What he summoned up was a version of Fianna Fáil unburdened by guilt and blame and self-loathing, an opportunity to go back a little and pick things up at a point somewhere before everything started to go off the rails.

We can look at how all this turned out as a matter of happenstance, or we can focus on the roles of particular individuals; as in so many such instances, we tend to account only for the surface events which appear to change the course of history. On the other hand, with one eye on these elements, we can direct our attention below, to the shifting and rumbling that happens beneath the consciousness of a society, of which the surface events may be merely remote agents, seeking to achieve outcomes, corrections, victories, defeats – and in ways that seem implausibly but nevertheless ineluctably bound up with amending the final edition of the historical record, with the reconciliation of dangerous contradictions, with sobering up from whatever dream might be under way. Perhaps, underneath the logic that seems to govern their thought process, societies have ways of avoiding that which might make them look too closely at themselves, and the tumult underneath the agreed façade that afterwards gets turned into words, which become a substitute for true memory.

The trajectory of Gallagher's fortunes, as tracked by the opinion polls between 1 October, when he stood in the polls in the low teens, and the last Sunday of the campaign, 23 October, when he appeared to have entered the low forties, appeared to reveal an appetite for something rather more than a politician. And yet, in the final four days before polling, his vote suffered enough of a shock to result in him losing the presidency to Michael D. Higgins.

In my view it would indeed have been strange had we awoken to a Gallagher presidency, though we came very close to this outcome. Gallagher came second with nearly 30 per cent of the vote, which remains an astounding result for a previous unknown. He was stopped only by a most dubious episode on the RTÉ programme, *The Frontline*, on Monday 24 October. Conventional wisdom has it that what happened was that Gallagher was 'outed' as a Fianna Fáiler, but this is scarcely plausible since we already knew that he was a Fianna Fáiler. Everything that was to become – supposedly damningly – known about Gallagher by voting day was known a full week before that, and yet he continued to lead in the polls – right up to the day before that final, fateful *Frontline* debate.

What happened was not an exposition of anything factual, but a dramatization of something that had sought to remain unspoken, making it a far more interesting episode than the conventional *post facto* analysis suggests.

Martin McGuinness, no longer himself a serious contender, was to become the unlikely agent of whatever deep-set process was occurring in the Irish psyche. About midway through the *Frontline* programme that Monday evening, McGuinness began to question Seán Gallagher about his relationship with Fianna Fáil, the subtext of almost all of the commentary surrounding Gallagher for several weeks. Gallagher had thus far managed to handle the question with no little skill, distancing himself from any formal connection with FF and yet persistently reiterating his refusal to 'demonize' people who became involved in any political party.

On the face of it, Gallagher's involvement with Fianna Fáil had been considerable: he admitted to his past membership of the party's National Executive and also to some involvement in fundraising functions. He had, he insisted, resigned from the party earlier that year, although he was observed on more than one party platform during the February general election, at least once in the company of the party leader, Micheál Martin.

On the *Frontline* programme that evening, Martin McGuinness rendered all this visible and unavoidable, demolishing the doublethink which both Gallagher and his would-be supporters sought to exploit. The issue arose from a question from the audience asking what it said about the country that a former member of Fianna Fáil was now leading the polls. McGuinness piously interjected there was 'absolute nothing' wrong with grass-roots FF members 'but there was something very rotten at the heart of the last administration', and as far as he was concerned, Seán was 'at the heart of that'.

McGuinness then raised the spectre of an as-yet-unnamed 'gentleman' who, he said, had called him that very evening and told that, two years beforehand, Seán Gallagher had been involved in arranging a function which involved the opportunity for subscribers to meet with Brian Cowen during a dinner at the Crowne Plaza Hotel in Dundalk. Seán Gallagher, he said, had arranged it, arranged for the photos to be taken, and afterwards brought the photographs to the businessman's house, where he collected a cheque for €5,000. 'That is indisputable,' McGuinness declared, 'and is an absolute disgrace and clearly shows that the rottenness of the system that went before, in terms of the cronyism, the developers, the speculators and those who effectively destroyed the economy of this country – and Seán was up to his neck in all that and he can't deny it.'

Gallagher did not deny the episode but simply said that he could not recall it. McGuinness warned him to think carefully about his answers. McGuinness expectantly observed Gallagher as he denied the charges, and then he declared: 'Well, he says it's not true, he's begging, he's begging for something to come forward and say that it was true. And I would caution you, Seán, at this stage that you're in very murky waters. Because one thing is for absolutely certain, if I am elected president of Ireland I will stand against cronyism, I will stand against greed and selfishness, and I will stand against the brown envelope culture that has effectively destroyed our economy.'

This speech was calculated to invoke the standard mindset that had been evident in public discussions for the previous three years: a searching for ready scapegoats for a disaster which in truth had deep and diverse roots in the many mistaken choices of both people and politicians for many decades.

Gallagher seemed flummoxed and surprised by the ambush. Like a rabbit caught in the headlights, he stumbled and sought to revert to his tried and tested policy of remaining above controversy and dirty tricks. But it was too late for that.

He had available to him a simple way of dealing with McGuinness's challenge: simply turning to him and saying, 'I wasn't wearing a balaclava, Martin.' Perhaps his guiding strategy of speaking no evil of anyone, which had served him so well until now, caused him to miss this obvious opportunity to checkmate McGuinness by invoking a different moral dimension. In the context of McGuinness's own history, this or some similar retort might have shifted the context of the discussion, but Gallagher seemed to be too uptight to think on his feet, and instead stuttered and prevaricated as though trying to remember what his advisers had told him to say. McGuinness twisted the knife: 'I have to say I think that you're in deep, deep trouble.'

The debate moved on to other matters and for a while it seemed that the matter had lost its fizz. But later in the programme, immediately after an ad break, Pat Kenny suddenly announced: 'Now a development which I want to put to Seán Gallagher: on the "Martin McGuinness for president" Twitter account, Sinn Féin are now saying that they are going to produce the man who gave you a cheque for five grand. Now do you want to change what you said? Or are you simply saying that it didn't happen? Or are they up to dirty tricks or what?'

The tweet subsequently proved to be a hoax perpetrated by a mischievous agent, with no connection to Sinn Féin – although Martin McGuinness, who might have been expected to know whether or not his party was planning a press conference – or some such public intervention – on the issue he had raised, remained silent on these aspects for the duration of the programme.

Gallagher seemed to misjudge the gravity of the situation, seeking to play his 'the presidency should be above all this' theme tune, but it was the wrong tactic for a situation requiring either a forensic rebuttal or some clever rhetorical device to change the moral context of the debate.

Somewhat belatedly, he seemed to realize that piety was useless and he was going to have to fight this one out. He then launched a half-hearted attack on the integrity of McGuinness's 'gentleman', whom he now appeared to recall rather better than he had previously intimated. 'I don't want to get involved in this,' he said, before launching into a counter-attack that suddenly belied his previously angelic disposition. Although he had 'always tried to stay above any negative campaigning', he now felt moved to say that the businessman in question was a convicted criminal, a fuel smuggler, had been investigated by the Criminal Assets Bureau and had rented the office out to Gerry Adams, McGuinness's colleague, in the February general election.

This, inevitably, provoked presenter Pat Kenny to ask him why he had invited a convicted fuel smuggler to a Fianna Fáil 'do'. Gallagher lamely replied that he hadn't known about the pedigree of the individual at that stage. The hole was getting deeper but he was still digging. He provoked hissing when he said that he had 'no recollection' of getting a cheque from the businessman, whom he referred to as 'the said character'. He repeated that he didn't 'want to get involved in this'.

He then embarked upon uttering the three-score of words which would undo his chances of becoming president of Ireland: 'What Martin has said is that I drove to the man's house to deliver a photograph of the event and that he gave me a cheque. What I've done – I may well have delivered the photograph – If he gave me an envelope. If—'

At this point, an instant before laughter erupted in the studio audience, stuffed with acolytes of the various candidates, Gallagher's face became a slow-motion movie. Almost as soon as he had uttered the word 'envelope', he appeared to understand what had happened. His face went into spasm and the laughter served merely to confirm his worst fears. He rushed to correct himself: 'No . . .' [the 'no' here seemed to be directed at the laughing members of the audience rather than intended as part of a correction – like an accused responding to the reading out of a charge against him] 'If he gave me the cheque it was made out to Fianna Fáil headquarters and it had nothing to do with me.'

At a rational level, his defence was entirely plausible. What he described is precisely what happens in the operation of political parties all over the free world. To suggest that the agents of such transactions are guilty of wrongdoing would be to say that almost every politician can be similarly accused. The following day, Fianna Fáil would reveal that the businessman's cheque had been banked several days before the dinner in question, suggesting that at least the letter of McGuinness's allegations was questionable.

But none of this was anywhere close to the point. The point was not even that Gallagher had been caught out in prevarication and evasion, but that he had aided and abetted his accuser in rendering it impossible for many of the watching public to any longer collude in achieving the outcome they had up until that moment seemed intent upon achieving. The word 'envelope', uttered from Gallagher's own lips, was what did it. It was the return of the repressed, the eruption into full view of something that the unspoken contract between Gallagher and his would-be followers had depended on remaining out of sight.

Pushed to 'explain' this, I would do so as follows: There is a deep historical ambivalence in the Irish personality towards excessive moralism in matters monetary or fiscal. This goes way back into Ireland's history of suffered radical interference from outside, which ensured that a repugnance of the State was instilled in the Irish DNA. The financial crisis of 2008 onwards, however, having seemed to implicate this culture in the collapse of the economy, caused a retrospective public Puritanism to manifest itself. This prohibited any acknowledgement of the 'old' culture, even as that culture continued to exist in manifold forms, most of them relatively harmless. The dilemma that sections of the electorate faced with Gallagher was that they recognized him but could not give voice to the complexity of that recognition. It was necessary for him to remain unblemished, to avoid implicating his supporters in the forbidden culture that, publicly, everyone agreed had been banished, and rightly banished, for good.

But actually, it may well be that what did for Gallagher was not some issue of ethics, or some emerging, previously unrecognized truth about him. Perhaps what did for him was his reaction and the response of the audience to it. From one side of the cultural divide, this looked like he had confessed to some complicity in the prohibited culture. But from the other side the damage may have been even more fatal: he looked like he wasn't cute enough to handle himself under fire from the enemy.

When Gallagher blurted out that word 'envelope', the audience laughed and jeered, and Gallagher could be seen dying in the water. Up until this moment, he had survived the questions, the charges, even the facts. But he could not survive the ridicule, which became a political force far more deadly than facts or accusations.

Suddenly, by just one word out of his own mouth, and the hilarity it engendered among those present, Gallagher was proclaimed guilty of the offence of which he stood accused. That charge was not so much factual as cultural. For weeks he had succeeded in staying ahead of the accusation, gathering votes as he went. Now, he had blurted it out, apparently of his own volition:

'envelope'. Perhaps no other word had such a capacity for reverberation in the still-smarting sensitivities of a country that had, in its own mind at least, dropped out of the air just a few years before because a bunch of cute hoors with envelopitis had blown a hole in the fuselage. Seán Gallagher, by his own announcement, was part of a 'culture' of envelope-passing that had, by common consensus, destroyed his country. It was not the literal charge that did it, but the dissolution of gravity that accompanied his involuntary admission. After that, even he himself would have had to admit that the prospect of him becoming president of Ireland was, frankly, laughable.

Watching him that night, it was obvious that he already knew this was the end. He floundered and stumbled as though trying to remember what advice he had been given for this or that situation. It was like he was undergoing a kind of political out-of-body experience in which he could only look on at his own undoing and his own part in it.

Had Martin McGuinness not intervened with what was actually a very dubious allegation, had *Frontline* not breached some of the most basic principles of good journalism by reading out a fake tweet (and then failed to alert the audience when the truth became known), and had most of the Dublin media not been against Gallagher from early on – indeed in the absence of any one or more of these factors – Seán Gallagher would probably be president today.

He could have avoided the meltdown by getting his story a little straighter from the start. Had he said that he had been in Fianna Fáil until the February general election, but had finally come to despair of the party and decided then that a new dispensation was required, he might have survived McGuinness's challenge. The idea of a man whose idealism had finally been exhausted would have appealed to people in the state of mind then possessing the electorate. Had he been thinking straight, he might have come up with a little anecdote about the moment he resolved that enough was enough, when he decided that his sense of the extent of the failure of Cowen & Co had left him with no honest choice but to put himself before the people. 'Yes,' he might even have added, 'I even went around the place collecting money for those guys!' We would have been putty in his hands.

I was one of six members of the Compliance Committee of the Broadcasting Authority of Ireland who upheld a complaint by Seán Gallagher about his treatment on *The Frontline* that night and the next day on *The Pat Kenny Show* on RTÉ Radio One. It was a straightforward enough decision: Gallagher had been confronted, and arguably badly thrown, by unverified information of dubious provenance. The media's obsession with, and reverence for, the new-fangled 'social media' had caused the *Frontline* team to bestow upon a tweet a degree of trust that would never be extended to information gleaned by word-of-mouth or some other random 'offline' means.

The committee did not consider the political implications of the episode, this being outside our remit, and far beyond our competence. Indeed, whether or not the bogus tweet was the critical element in the scuppering of Seán Gallagher's hopes of the presidency is a question we will never be able to answer. We can't rule it out, but neither can we construct an explicit equation to prove the case. Although there is little doubt that the *Frontline* episode was what did for Gallagher, it's not possible credibly to quantify the various elements and scientifically decide that the fake tweet was absolutely the decisive factor.

The *Frontline* debate didn't really bring any new information into the public arena, but rather seems to have crystallized something in the public mood, to Gallagher's disadvantage. Martin McGuinness's intervention and the bogus tweet, together with Gallagher's responses to both, appear to have flushed out the nod-and-wink compact with assorted elements of the electorate that, all things being equal, they would give Gallagher the stroke. Perhaps what did for him in the end wasn't so much McGuinness's attempts to present him as a Fianna Fáil bagman as his own inability to handle himself in a scrap. If he had said all the things he was to say subsequently, Gallagher might well have disposed of the whole thing there and then, but by dropping the ball he allowed the accusations to stay current for another 48 hours. The car-crash nature of his performance seems to have scared off enough potential voters to allow Michael D. to overtake him on the left flank.

So, Michael D. was to prove the victor, but it was Seán Gallagher's election, and its meaning for the future of Irish life ultimately relates to what happened with his candidacy. Coming from nowhere, he edged to the front in the final furlong, revealing an unexpected and previously unrecognized rump of dissent and desire in the electorate.

In the aftermath of the election, there was a strange sense of confusion and denial as people tried to make themselves believe that nothing exceptional or odd had happened at all. The agreed version was that Gallagher had seemed to offer 'hope' but had been exposed just in time as a fraud, or at least a thinly disguised version of something people felt they knew only too well. By this telling, the electorate rejected Seán Gallagher because he repre-sented a form of political and business life that had become repugnant to them, which is to say that he was the epitome of the Fianna Fáil insider, a man steeped in the very attributes and culture that had led to the unfolding of Ireland's economic ruin three years before. To have elected him, one reader wrote to me afterwards, 'would have proven Irish peoples' worst fears about themselves, namely that they are superhumanly naive, perhaps doomed because of their own gullibility to never be able to look after themselves'. By this analysis, rejecting Gallagher represented a sort of change; it showed that Irish people were not as naive as they once had been, had grown a little tougher, had grown up a little.

In many ways, our public discussions are remarkably restricted where it comes to pursuing comprehension of political events. One difficulty is that political analysis tends to restrict itself to classifying under narrowly focused political/ideological headings: the parties, 'Independents', left–right designations, and so forth. Another is that subterranean but strictly policed rules-of-engagement place less orthodox modes of exploration out of bounds. Political correctness and other unwritten strictures debar the possibility of deeper understandings concerning the state of the collective psyche and the archetypal yearnings that impinge on collective representation of individual democratic choices.

But democratic leadership, in addition to its political dimensions, tracks a deeper archetype: that of parenthood. The qualities we seek in our leaders derive from an unfathomable, inherited need to be parented at the level of nation. If you apply this idea to the 2011 presidential election, you notice patterns that have been overlooked. After twenty-one years of 'mothering', we appeared keen – although this remained unsayable – to put a man back in the Áras. Perhaps this was down to our undergoing a crisis unprecedented within living memory, suggesting that, in moments of uncertainty, we glance anxiously around for Dad.

Early in the campaign, this desire remained obscured, but as things progressed, the frontrunners emerged as representations of different types of male strength, climaxing in an epic struggle between the athlete-cum-manager and the teacher-father: Seán Gallagher as latter-day hunter-gatherer versus Michael D.'s embodiment of the elder-guru – Keith Wood wrestling John Scotus Eriugena.

We desire that our fathers be wise yet genial, dependable and restrained, strongly empathetic but frank, prudent but unafraid, stoical but unfanatical, tough yet patient, thoughtful but not incontinent of speech. Our grumbles notwithstanding, we feel safer with leaders who quietly require that we postpone gratification and commit ourselves to sacrifice for our own long-term good. These are the father values erased from our surface culture by forty years of aggressive feminist agitation.

That the two female candidates for the presidency ended up bottom of the table has been noted but in a timid, unfocused way that elided its significance. Anyone who ever thought another woman candidate would ipso facto be a shoo-in had not looked closely at either Mary Robinson or Mary McAleese, both of whom were not so much exceptional women as exceptional at being women in a public world ordered to male responses. Both exhibited that quality of emotional restraint that is among the male qualities feminism has most energetically sought to disparage – as well as rich baritones with which to advertise their possession of it. You had to listen to just ten seconds of Mary Davis and Dana to divine that neither of them enjoyed similar capacities.

In terms of public achievements, David Norris and Martin McGuinness ticked several of the father boxes. However, each in turn broke the spell by virtue of poor responses in the face of criticism, resorting to most unfatherly modes of riposte – a plaintive boastfulness in the case of Norris and, on McGuinness's part, a baffled and – once, infamously – unchivalrous rage in reacting to the insubordination he encountered. Both men came across as adhering too closely to all too recognizable 'Irish father' stereotypes. Gay Mitchell, the Fine Gael candidate, was too shrill and ornery to be a reassuring father-figure, and besides was too closely identified with the main ruling party to convince us that he could be a truly independent parent to the nation.

Seán Gallagher was largely a projected image, but an effective one: the strong, silent type who looked like he might be good in a scrum. His body language was uncompromisingly masculine, but in a way that seemed unaffected, even unconscious. Lined up behind a table with the other candidates, he would reach across his opponents for the water jug with a certainty that said more than a thousand speeches urging a renewal of national self-confidence. Until the final few days, he remained matter-of-fact, calm under pressure, uncomplaining, quietly disdainful of bitching and recrimination. But when the Dragon's father-mask slipped, Michael D. became our default choice, the thoughtful, teaching father, the kind whom his offspring respect and adore but also tease on account of half the time not having a clue what he's going on about.

Seán Gallagher spoke to those who wanted to restore that which had been taken away, all that had gone wrong. He was like a fantasy character in a dream in which none of the bad things had happened. His message of positivity combined with a wholly fantastical idea of the presidency as a means of generating economic activity managed at once to distance himself from the game of politics while suggesting that as president he could shoulder-charge politics into a different direction.

He was the Lone Ranger. He refused to shoot to kill, but still sought to disable his opponents and make them amenable to the justice of the people. He did not accuse anybody, and yet still stood as a benign accusation against those who had officiated over the mess we found ourselves in. He didn't engage in deconstructions or analyses, but, by his repeated insistence that an economy could be run in a way that would provide hope and support to people who were prepared to get out of bed in the morning, he implied something that came close to what most of us believed. His candidacy spoke of the end of nonsense, of the need for a politics based on industriousness and energy, on recognizing that the chief resource of this nation was still the work of those who want to work, that there is no silver bullet which will enable us to become self-sustaining by simply pretending to be 'modern', that we had to roll our sleeves up as well.

It was clear in retrospect that Seán Gallagher saw things nobody else did. He was a complete unknown, politically speaking, and yet went from the back of the field to the front in a matter of days, indicating a yearning for something not otherwise to be detected. He himself had a strong sense of what he wanted to tap into and what he wanted to communicate, but he also had behind him people who knew how to press the right buttons by looking a certain way, speaking a certain way, seeming to come from a certain place. And it was the disintegration of this carefully constructed image, far more than any sense of actual wrongdoing, that did for him in the end. None of the charges against him were fully proven, but together they created enough misgivings to destroy the image.

Seán Gallagher had announced early on in his campaign that he planned on pursuing a deliberate strategy of not having election posters. It seemed risky. Nobody is quite sure how election posters work, but most political strategists regard it as imperative that their candidate's mug be up there with the others, if only to offset the 'reminder factor' which posters offer the other candidates. Just as conventional brand advertising works on the principle that only the most visible can remain in contention, political posters seem to work more out of a fear of absence than any particular bonus that arises from maintaining a presence.

Not having posters was a crucial element, enabling Gallagher to become the 'absent presence' on the highways and, by doing so, he seemed to manufacture a new brand of poster, a kind of blank space on the roadside pole that enabled him to smile out invisibly from the line of candidates representing the main parties. Some other candidates, for resource reasons, ended up with either a paucity of posters or none, but Gallagher was the only candidate who made a virtue of not having any. By opting not to litter the countryside with his image, Gallagher did more than exploit a latent 'Green' vote with no place to go – he also tapped into the subliminal public feeling that the real cause of Ireland's difficulties had to do with those guys grinning down from the roadside poles. Thus, every image of another candidate became a reminder of Seán Gallagher.

The idea of the faceless man is a powerful one in human culture. It exists in science fiction, as an archetype of ghost and horror stories and in many traditional folk literatures. The *Noppera-bō*, or faceless ghost, is a legendary creature of Japanese folklore, a kind of hobgoblin known primarily for frightening humans. The *Noppera-bō* appears at first as an ordinary human being, sometimes impersonating someone familiar to the victim of the scare, before causing his features to disappear, leaving a blank, smooth sheet of skin where the face ought to be. The archetype of the faceless man relates at once to hope and terror. He is both myth and symbol. In his book *Apollinaire and the Faceless Man*, Willard Eugene Bohn describes the faceless man as symbolizing the human condition, having come to be adopted by writers and artists as an early, perhaps prophetic symbol of twentieth-century existence. 'By turns a domestic, a pirate, or the last representative of the human race, he reassures us and menaces us simultaneously.'

Seán Gallagher was the faceless man, the blank space on to which were painted the features of a someone we suddenly realized was missing from our lives, a shiny-pated mannequin on whom all kinds of enticing garments could be draped. He was the candidate with the featureless face, on whom the voter was invited to place his own impression.

Martin McGuinness restored Gallagher's features, making him real again, returning us from the dream of desiring that nothing bad had happened at all. McGuinness broke the spell that Gallagher had managed to weave, with the complicity of an electorate longing to be seduced.

Something deep happened here. Something that none of the

conventional explanations seem to come near accounting for. This story went close to the heart of longing in a society that nowadays talks too much and too long for anyone to really get to the bottom of anything.

The real message of the election, then, was not really about the winner, but 'something behind', something that is not clearly visible in the results and would not be reflected by international headlines declaring that Ireland had elected a veteran socialist and poet as its president. Waking up under President Gallagher would have been a strange experience, but almost certainly truer to prevailing Irish realities than the belated election of our slightly retro philosopher king.

Certainly, it would have afforded us a superior opportunity for self-scrutiny, although I'm not so sure we would at this remove be able to explain it even to our own satisfaction. All the same, it would have forced us to look more carefully at one another, and take rather less seriously the things we say when someone with a roving microphone or a pollster's clipboard asks us what we think.

But the 2011 presidential election was certainly an educational interlude, all round. Perhaps even now other unknown hopefuls are out there studying the Gallagher trajectory and planning how to avail of the same mechanisms and electoral doublethinks, while avoiding the soft margins that ultimately did for the bald dragon.

Meanwhile, we have to go on with the president we have chosen, even if only by default. As time moves on, we will become emboldened in the pretence that we intended all along to put Michael D. Higgins in the Áras – while still, from time to time, looking back and wondering: what if?

# 3

# *Diehards*

WHEN I WAS A CHILD IN THE CASTLEREA OF THE 1960S, I SPENT AN inordinate amount of time at home in bed, suffering from various ailments arising from what my father spoke of as my 'delicate constitution'. I had bronchitis, or perhaps asthma, and at the slightest sniffle or sneeze, my mother and/or father would insist that I stayed home from school, which suited me fine. Most of the time I spent reading books I borrowed from 'the back room', where my father had stored the treasure trove of literature he had acquired at auctions in some of the local 'big houses', when their owners sold up or died out.

When I was tired of reading, I would listen to the traffic and the sounds of the street: the shouts of people going and coming to the pubs or shops; the click-clacking of high-heel shoes; the hum of motor cars, as they were still called, to distinguish them from the horse-drawn variety; a lorry engine starting deep in the heart of the town and moving in slow changes, gathering speed and pitch then gaining volume as it laboured against the hill from the fair green up the main drag towards our house. Day and night I listened to this symphony and perhaps unconsciously started to interpret it as a soundtrack to the town, with its hierarchy of importance and self-importance. At nighttime I would listen and put faces to all the vehicles and their drivers and watch their passing lights make shadows on my ceiling, and then close my eyes and sink into the idea that this town was not Castlerea at all, but some other town, or even a city, close by but undiscovered, a town no one talked about, which hummed and breathed and sighed and groaned within earshot of the real world but could not be visited except in the imagination.

During daytime, whenever I heard an unfamiliar car, I would jump out of bed and run to the window, and in this way had acquired the ability to tell one car noise from another and put a face on its driver as it approached and passed underneath my bedroom window. It wasn't as amazing a feat as it sounds now: there weren't that many cars around at the time, and most of them made more – and more idiosyncratic – noises than the modern variety.

The two cars I had the greatest trouble distinguishing from one another were the squad car, a black Ford Prefect, and the blue Ford Prefect owned by Dan O'Rourke, a former TD, retired teacher, one-time president of the GAA and – his most elevated qualification in a locality in which he was venerated – ex freedom-fighter. The two Prefects had the same rattle, and I never quite achieved certainty in telling them apart.

Dan O'Rourke was a familiar figure around town, a tall man crouched over the steering wheel of his incongruously small car. He wore dark suits, a grey moustache and seemed a little too tall for the dark blue Prefect. Occasionally you might see him stop and clamber out to conduct some piece of business. Sometimes, when I was out with my father, we would meet Dan on the road, and the two men would exchange salutes. I never saw them go further, and assumed this was because of differing political views, or perhaps some arcane sense of the niceties of the town's complex hierarchy, in which Dan had a special, elevated place, though – unusually – not for reasons of wealth or property.

Dan, though he started out in Sinn Féin, had long been a Fianna Fáiler, and had served as the local TD until the early 1950s, and for a brief time thereafter as a member of Seanad Éireann. In those days, a man was in large part defined by the attitude he had taken to the Treaty of 1921, which established both partition and the Irish Free State. My father, having been pro-Treaty, was a Fine Gael supporter. Many times I heard my father excoriate de Valera and his 'bowsie' followers, whom he blamed for starting the civil war and 'setting brother against brother'. I always assumed that Dan must have belonged also to this abominable company, even though I never heard my father say a bad word about him. When I was fifteen my father sent me to Dan's funeral with a Mass card. It was my first time to see in real life a coffin draped in a tricolour, and it stoned me with awe and reverence.

It was only relatively recently that I was able to figure it all out, after a friend from home handed me a sheet of paper with the text of a short speech delivered in the Treaty debate in the Second Dáil, in the Mansion House, Dublin, on 7 January 1922, by Dan O'Rourke, then a Sinn Féin TD for Mayo South/Roscommon South.

Something about this speech enthralled me with its sense of something familiar yet no longer detectable in our culture. I read it repeatedly, seeking to name some of the qualities it exhibited. It was of another time and yet, it seemed, urgently relevant to the present. I had noted similar thoughts and sentiments before in, for example, the essays of Padraig Pearse, in the way words seemed to step out of history and imply a timeless view of what Ireland was, is and might become.

Dan O'Rourke's Wikipedia entry says that he 'supported the Anglo-Irish Treaty and voted in favour of it'. But the story is far more interesting than this arid citation suggests. The thing about O'Rourke is that he was actually opposed to the Treaty but still voted for it.

In this speech, O'Rourke was explaining why, although he remained a Republican, he had come to decide to vote in favour of the Treaty. Before getting to this, he explained that the first he had known about being elected to Dáil Éireann (he was an unopposed Sinn Féin nominee to the Second Dáil at the 1921 general election in Mayo South/Roscommon South) was when he read about it in the newspapers. Had he known his name was to be put forward, he said, he would have objected.

He then moved on to the point of his speech, firstly explaining that he was unhappy with the manner in which the Treaty had been signed.

'Until I came here I didn't know how the matter stood. When I found out how things happened I must say I did not like, and I do not like, the idea of the plenipotentiaries having signed without having brought back the Treaty for consideration.' He was referring here to the Irish negotiators, including Michael Collins and Arthur Griffith, who signed the Treaty without reference to their leaders in Dublin.

'When I came here first,' he said, 'I was opposed to the Treaty, and on principle I am opposed to it still.'

But he had changed his position, if not his mind. His 'great ambition and prayer' was for unity. 'I am prepared to do anything for unity because I realise that the great curse of this country has been disunity.'

If a division had been taken before Christmas, he said, he would have voted against the Treaty. Now, he explained, he was going to vote the other way.

'I returned to my constituency at Christmas and I went there to the people. Not the resolution passers – to the people who had been with me in the fight, the people whose opinion I valued, the people who are, I believe, diehards. And I consulted with them about this question and I must say that, unanimously, they said to me that there was no alternative but to accept the Treaty.'

In these words, or somewhere about the back of them, Dan O'Rourke was expressing something about the entrenched but qualified quality of nationalism that I breathed in as a child. In the West, the Fianna Fáil/Fine Gael division had little or no 'class' dimension, as it seemed to have in other places. The Fine Gael of my childhood allegiance was never the party of the merchant classes or the big farmers, but as much a populist movement as Fianna Fáil. It was not possible to tell a Fianna Fáiler from a Fine Gaeler merely by considering questions of background and occupation. The main outward difference was one of character: Fianna Fáilers were usually somewhat wild and unpredictable, whereas Fine Gaelers were more restrained, pious and, for these reasons, often a little more forbidding. Fianna Fáilers laughed more, but often pointlessly, as though as a kind of camouflage. It is not that Fine Gaelers were joyless, emotionless creatures, but that their humour or expression was noticeably more subtle and restrained. When a man spoke, and a particular kind of seriousness became obvious, you identified him, on the balance of probabilities, as a Fine Gaeler. The attentive ear could detect a quality of refinement in the tone of voice, in the pitch of the laughter, and an added dimension of uprightness, of moralistic literalism in what he said. It was subtle but concrete, a nuance that I doubt an outsider could detect at all.

I have a strong memory from growing up also of the aura of moral purpose that was attached to the Fine Gael view of the world. It was a political outlook associated with compromise and accommodation, a strange mixture of fanaticism and adaptability. In the years since the civil war, this had seeped into the culture like a bloodstain into a bandage, a kind of reminder of the limits of ideals and the danger of rhetoric that failed to take this into account. This view had about it an element of weariness with conflict, but was mindful, too, of the historical experience of subjugation, and of the foolhardiness of taking on an impossibly powerful foe. It did not seek to deny or revise anything, but merely owned up to the difficulties and costs associated with grand gestures. It saw the pursuit of pure principle as representing an extravagant luxury, which placed idealism of outlook against the immediate welfare of real people. While honouring those who had led the various bursts for Irish freedom, it was also conscious of the hurts arising from that experience and wished to avoid their repetition. It elevated not so much high ambition, intention and speechifying, as wisdom, coolness and a preparedness for the long road.

This was my father's kind of patriotism, a kind that embraced both the ideal and the consequences of pursuing it, and took both into account. It did not attach itself to vain or hopeless gesturing, but blended ideal with a pragmatic sense of other choices. It represented no less a burning desire for freedom, independence, justice or egalitarianism, but it was not prepared to engage in the pretence that these came without price, or that the value of a flamboyant act was enough to outweigh that price. My father would frequently voice in righteous terms a rejection of recklessness, which he associated with the other side. It was, when you came right down to it, the key distinction between Fine Gael and Fianna Fáil.

In all the talk we've had about the 'civil war divide', it is forgotten that originally, in the main, this factor related to respective dispositions, as opposed to ideological positions. The true knot of difference related to the question of warfare. The tribe that would become Fine Gael had lost its stomach for war and would come to despise the other shower for unleashing a vicious conflict. The bellicosity of Dev's tribe nowadays manifests itself mainly in yahooing and back-slapping, but the contrasting sensibilities remain intact, and may account for something of the relative fortunes of the parties in the past eight decades or so. The warmongers lost the war but, by stealth and cunning, won the battle for the Irish heart, if not the Irish mind.

Dan O'Rourke was a Fianna Fáiler, but not a warmonger. His disposition, now that I come to think of it, was not unlike my father's, even though he belonged to the other side of the argument, the other tribe. My father, a non-participant political animal, about whom I wrote at some length in *Jiving at the Crossroads*, was a pro-Treaty republican, who believed that the interim settlement achieved in 1921 would have led in a short time to a United Ireland. Thus, his gripe with the irredentism of Fianna Fáil did not include a concession of the final nationalist ideal, but actually the contrary: he believed they had scuppered the prospect of a United Ireland by affecting to be passionate about it. This was the view of many Fine Gaelers in the West in my childhood years, rather than any formal view of the Fine Gael party, then or since.

'Everything that is personal to me,' Dan O'Rourke went on, 'is against this Treaty. I yield to no man in my hatred of British oppression, and in my opposition to any symbol of British rule in Ireland. But I say I would be acting an impertinent part by putting my own views and opinions against the views of my best friends, the men who are the best fighters with me.'

For himself, he would be 'just as well pleased' if the Treaty were rejected. But he would not take responsibility for throwing the young men of his country into war, 'for I know what war has meant'. His desire was that 'the members of the Dáil will come together and come to some common understanding to work our country in the interests of the people'. If the Treaty were rejected, he concluded, and war the result, he would do everything possible to unite the people against the common enemy. 'And I promise to fight to victory or death to secure the Republic.'

The Treaty was passed by the Dáil by a majority of just seven votes, with three deputies abstaining. O'Rourke's contribution was by many accounts decisive.

*

Reading this speech today is strange and moving in a way that leads to deep sorrow. For it is instantly clear that we have lost almost everything of the values and qualities that underpin these words of Dan O'Rourke. To read such words in the current climate is almost like looking into a strange culture as a tourist, a culture in which different things are important and these shifted priorities are visible, consistent but also strangely opaque.

It is hard to articulate what it is that strikes me, and immediately, on writing this, I know that 'strikes' is the wrong word. I should say, rather, that something unsettles me on reading what Dan O'Rourke said. Something moves me. Something stirs in me a sense of loss that is almost unable to glimpse the nature of itself, never mind to express itself. I am not 'struck' by anything: I am affected in a profound way that is beyond words and yet appears to have at its core the very problem of words and their limits as a means of calling people to the same cause or idea.

O'Rourke was outlining a hard choice, between an ideal and an honourable form of expediency, but his motivation was clearly rooted in a feeling for the common good of his country and its people. He was eschewing the option of high-flown speechifying in favour of a salutary warning, but the power of his words was by no means dulled on that account.

In this speech, O'Rourke was articulating a monumental personal decision and also expressing a strain of thinking that was to define the Ireland that was to achieve his dream of 'the Republic' within his lifetime. This existence would be founded on the compromise that O'Rourke described himself making. He was, in nationalistic terms, resiling from a menu of agreed and well-established principles: ourselves alone, a nation once again, the reintegration of the national territory – all those ideals which have since so often been dismissed as shibboleths, perhaps because they ceased to seem attainable or became contaminated by gratuitous and cynical violence.

But O'Rourke did not dismiss them. He spoke of them with respect and affection, before walking away from them with a regretful determination. What he was expressing was a principle, too: the principle of accommodation to a compromise that could not be bettered at the time. His changed position, however, was not being expressed as a dogma or an ultimatum. He was saying, 'We have no choice', but he was not saying this in a manner designed to silence or intimidate those who might not agree, who had not – or not yet – reached his state of clarity. He was outlining something of his own tortuous journey, hoping perhaps to inspire others to see things in the same complex way, but he was also bowing to the other side of the argument, and acknowledging, by virtue of the struggle he described concerning his own crossing over, that it too had merit and honour.

The speech acknowledges, too, a higher authority than Dan O'Rourke, an authority captured succinctly in the word 'diehards'. In this word there is so much that the meaning seems to burst out from it, a word that in modern usage usually has a pejorative connotation. Here, it has about it an almost overwhelming sense of affection.

He takes us back to Castlerea at Christmas: 'I went there to the people.' This phrase summons up an image of O'Rourke as the willing mouthpiece of his people, going first to ask them what they wish him to say. A leader, yes, but of a particular kind. Is it possible to imagine a modern-day politician uttering such a sentence? I do not mean to suggest that modern politicians do not see themselves as representing their people; but can we imagine any of the present-day generation having such a sense of humility in the face of the grandeur of his own people as to speak of them in this way?

And then, the reference to 'my best friends', the beautiful sense it evokes of a nation in the building by people who know each other intimately on account of the common purpose of Ireland.

O'Rourke evokes an Ireland in which bureaucracy has not yet taken hold, in which 'The State' is not the dominant concept of the public life of the nation. It is as though he is speaking about the endeavours of a football team, a common enterprise in which belonging and participation, even a form of ownership, are taken for granted.

Perhaps O'Rourke had expected that his people would agree with his stance against the Treaty. We get the feeling he has been surprised, awakened, before being convinced. They had not agreed with him. We see a picture of him listening, nodding, arguing, nodding again. We get a sense of his surprise in the phrase '. . . I must say that, unanimously, they said to me . . .' We can see him coming away, his mind unchanged but a new resolve rising to the surface of his soul. He would support the Treaty. The diehards had spoken.

He had come back not chastened but changed.

And then that remarkable phrase, 'I would be acting an impertinent part', tendered in explanation for why he has decided to disregard his own opinions on the Treaty. How, in the age in which we now live, are we to understand the moral basis of which Dan O'Rourke was speaking? There is here an echo of something that seems almost to predate the idea of democracy: a sense that the individual view offers merely a partial insight into the duty of that individual, whose relationship with the public realm is not defined by interests or opinions, but by something deeper and more enduring.

Underlying this speech are several quantities which no longer exist in our culture: the belief in war, obviously, as a last-resort remedy, and the willingness to fight, and, if necessary, to die for Ireland. But there also is a belief in 'the people' as the final arbiter on things, and the ringing endorsement of the value of unity. There is a sense of the public representative as the voice of the people, rather than as conduit for the orders of powers and agencies which have already decided everything. There is a sense of the struggle that needed to occur in the heart of Dan O'Rourke before he could have brought himself to make this momentous speech. There is a sense of the hurt of that struggle, the sleepless nights, the sorrow and the clarity giving way, perhaps, to relief.

But behind all this there is something else, something clear and tangible and yet no longer accessible in our culture, and therefore likely to be overlooked: a love of Ireland that is neither self-interested nor sentimental, a love of country that is commonly held, self-evident, unapologetic and necessitating no elaboration – no, not just unapologetic but utterly uncomprehending of any alternative way of seeing things. O'Rourke does not need to engage in high-flown rhetoric to communicate his love for Ireland: he simply describes an everyday series of exchanges and thought processes saturated by this love.

The speech has in it a considerable measure of O'Rourke's soul and personality. He declares and explains his decision and its motivation, unexpected in the context of his history and known outlook. He deals with big ideas: the conflict between a deeply held personal principle and the necessity to avoid war, which he does not seek to elevate into a competing principle but simply records as a necessary and decent objective. He is 'opposed' to the Treaty, a personal position that he holds dearly, and yet is pre-pared to go against his own deepest-held desire so as to avoid a conflict that will involve others, perhaps the sons of his friends. He will himself fight, if necessary, but will not be the one who insists that others do so because of his need to hold to principles which others whom he trusts have come to see as redundant. It is all clear and reasonable, rather than moralistic and preachy. He is not trying to curry favour or present a gracing aspect to popular piety. Neither does he seek to attack anyone else, to make those who hold other views appear less moral or good. He is speaking against a certain backdrop of urgency and touches implicitly on an agreed code of priorities, which he presumes to be widely shared. He speaks fluently and yet economically, saying a great deal in a few words. He seems oblivious to the possibility of encountering any resistance or objection, certainly to his authority, in stating his position as he has. He is confident, despite the fact that what he is saying has the potential to end his life in a bloody fashion.

In this short speech, it is possible to see deeply into the character of this man, to perceive his principles and his struggling with them, to note his efforts to reconcile conflicting emotions with a greater necessity and do the right thing for his own people and his country. But it is also possible, using the speech as a prism, to look differently into the culture of our own very different time, to measure what has changed and what has remained. There is a naked humility about the speech that is impossible now, as well as a sense of purpose, close to absolute, equally impossible to imagine. Although the name of Ireland is never mentioned, the speech is all about her. It is the speech of a man who thinks of little else but the ultimate destiny of his country, and who assumes that his listeners are similarly preoccupied.

In those days, when 'Ireland' was spoken of, what was summoned up was not an economy or a society or a state, but a place in which people lived, loved and died, a place that, as Padraig Pearse had explained so beautifully, was a spiritual reality much more than a political or geographical one. From this idea there flows an ineluctable moral reality, on which Dan O'Rourke was touching in this speech.

Although there is no allusion to a deity or a divinity, implicit in every word is the idea of an authority greater than Dan O'Rourke, a sense of events that are ordered from elsewhere, an ethic that is defined by absolute values that find their expression in the concept of country. There is the sense in O'Rourke's words of the call of Ireland as something greater than anything else that might concern him in the normal run of events, but also an acknowledgement that this demand is not a matter to be discharged with beautiful words or even beautiful thoughts. There is a deep patriotism in the very thread of the speech, but not of theconventional rhetorical kind. This brand of patriotism is matter-of-fact. It sees no requirement to name itself. It is obvious that, as a politician, Dan O'Rourke saw himself involved in something much bigger than himself or his own will, something that could be accessed only through the heart of the community, the people.

O'Rourke's suggested destination must surely move us to tears now with the irony and pathos of it all. The Republic: an entity that men like O'Rourke at first but dreamed of, fought for, lived to see and died before it could be taken for granted. 'The Republic' was something that mattered more to men like Dan O'Rourke than their own lives. It was, in some sense, a human objective, but it also transcended individual human needs of a more everyday kind, even the need to live, if such a sacrifice was to be called for. In the casual, matter-of-fact manner of its delivery, this pronouncement offers us a challenge that we cannot dismiss, as we might when listening to the rhetoric of other Irish patriots, as mere bellicosity or sentimentality.

It goes without saying that Dan O'Rourke's speech could not be imagined arising from our own times. Leaving aside the questions of its content and focusing on its tone and subtexts, it is impossible to imagine a politician today being able to speak like this about anything, to invoke his deepest personal desires in this way and then go on to explain why he is disregarding them, to summon up an idea of Ireland that is so self-evident that he scarcely needs to refer to it. It is impossible to imagine a politician speaking about Ireland in this way without inviting sardonic grins or causing people to burst out laughing.

O'Rourke was speaking in a language I understand, a language I recognize as English, the same language we speak in Ireland today. But the mode of his expression, the awarenesses and sentiments he was calling up, the sense of proprietorship of his own citizenship, as well as his sense of his role as leader of his fellows – all these are alien now. Alien too is the implicit air of entitlement to speak of the destiny and welfare of his country, in a way that was neither economistic nor sociological, neither moralistic nor sentimental.

There is something elusive here, something that seems, when read in the context of our culture today, to jump ahead before it settles, to dart away as soon as focused upon. The difference is not so much in the way people think nowadays as in the incapacities of the language we nowadays rely upon. This language seems incapable of conveying great thoughts like Dan O'Rourke's.

The problem seems to lie in the range of possibilities open to anyone who would address himself to the idea of Ireland and its public realm – the capacity of the culture into which such thoughts might be spoken to understand them more or less in the way they were intended. We cannot imagine someone speaking like this, any more than we can imagine someone speaking in the manner of Padraig Pearse at the graveside of O'Donovan Rossa: 'Our foes are strong and wise and wary, but strong and wise and wary as they are, they cannot undo the miracles of God who ripens in the hearts of young men the seeds sown by the young men of a former generation.'

Whatever we may nowadays decide about such sentiments, we can hardly deny that they seem to suggest an entirely different kind of relationship between speaker and listener than anything we can remotely imagine.

Arthur Miller, in his essay 'The Family in Modern Drama', wrote about the dramatic incompatibility of public and private language. Poetry, he argued, was the language of the public arena; prose that of the domestic space. Private life lends itself to realism; public life does not. These dichotomies spring from different aspects of human experience, and appeal to different receptivities in the audience: 'When one is speaking to one's family, for example, one uses a certain level of speech, a certain plain diction perhaps, a tone of voice, an inflection suited to the intimacy of the occasion. But when one faces an audience of strangers, as a politician does, for instance – and he is the most social of men – it seems right and proper for him to reach for the well-turned phrase, even the poetic word, the aphorism, the metaphor. And his gestures, his stance, his tone of voice, all become larger than life; moreover, his character is not what gives him these prerogatives, but his role. In other words, a confrontation with society permits us, or even enforces upon us, a certain reliance upon ritual.'

There is, obviously, something in this. One does not imagine Dan O'Rourke speaking to his family in the same way as he addressed the Second Dáil. But it is not the full story. Miller's analysis makes something clearer, but it also skates over something about the nature of political speech in the present time. Dan O'Rourke's speech in the Treaty debate did not contain any aphorisms or metaphors, or even a great wealth of well-turned phrases. We can but speculate on the manner of its delivery, but its content was such as to suggest that it was a low-key speech, spoken at the pitch of a street conversation. And yet it carried within it great burdens of feeling and thought.

Perhaps the point to be made about Dan O'Rourke's speech is that such a fusion of intensity and deliberation, affection and reason, passion and clarity, is possible only in times of conflict and war. Perhaps, the further we move from risk or danger, the more blasé our public pronouncements are destined to become. Or perhaps the problem today is that, because political rhetoric has become almost exclusively bound up with economistic concerns and technocratic solutions, there is no longer room for genuine inspiration, or breadth of vision, and therefore no language in which the deeper strands of collective meanings and attachments can be expressed. It is rare to hear a political speech now that does not sound like the address of a chief executive of a factory producing some indeterminate articles for some unspecified purpose. The only values capable of being summoned to such an occasion are those of self-interest and what is called 'progress' or its economic equivalent: growth. The idea of 'Ireland' is, apart from sporting occasions, something of a joke. If you pluck at random a sentence or two from a speech by a political leader from the age of butter boxes outside chapel gates, and compare it with a passage from almost any modern-day speech in Leinster House, you perceive that there has occurred a debasement not just of the intensity of the message but of the language itself. What has been lost is not poetry, but something else: heart. We no longer feel that our leaders truly love us, and this causes us to withdraw affection from them.

The result appears to be a kind of withdrawal from the public realm except for the purposes of recrimination. You might call it cynicism, except that such a term tends to create a short-circuit of meaning that ensures we become caught up in tautological concepts of the problem.

Nowadays, we do not look to the public square in search of the towering figure of the political demigod or demagogue, but snort our disdain to our nearest fellows, infecting them as they have infected us. We look balefully now not just at our present-day leaders but at all those who came before: at Pearse and de Valera as much as at Haughey and Ahern. We convince ourselves that the bitter complaints we direct at their departed backs represent a judgement by us on them that somehow implies an improved awareness and moral growth. Others – Garret FitzGerald, Mary Robinson – our culture contrives to remember in a more benign way. When we look closely at this 'morality', we can perceive that it is overwhelmingly connected to agendas of what is called 'progress'. Perhaps as a way of justifying to ourselves the deeper, unacknowledged costs of progress, we remember well those who allegedly 'dragged us kicking and screaming' out of the past. This, more than anything, is the moral criterion to be applied to the record of Irish leadership in the near-century since Independence. Mostly, the memories are false for in truth there was very little objective difference between the public lives and contributions of these leaders and the ones we excoriate. Almost invariably the denunciations and benign remembrances are retrospective and based on circumstantial evidence of limited reliability.

The basis is always moralistic. We target certain individuals with an irony steeped in condescension and contempt, ostensibly because we disapprove of them on some moral basis or other. But it is moralistic according to a specific pattern: either that of self-interest or of ideology: these people have damaged us, or betrayed us, or stolen from us. Or, 'This guy had some ridiculous ideas'. Those who led us in the past become either secular saints or the butts of our rage and, simultaneously, of our jokes.

There are few exceptions, but the most interesting is Seán Lemass. He, virtually alone of twentieth-century Irish leaders, has managed to retain a degree of respect through the decades, but this is mainly because his technocratic pragmatism is contrasted with the alleged Catholic mysticism of de Valera, to the detriment of the latter.

By and large, the ones who survive our wrath, like Garret FitzGerald, are those who did not challenge us overmuch in terms relating to our deepest natures – who told us what we wanted to hear, what suited us and suited our sense of what personal freedom amounted to. Most of those who called us to anything higher, or harder, are dismissed and disparaged. A new morality has entered in: one governed not by objective, external consider-ations, but exclusively by consideration of how public events and public decisions will affect the interests of the individual or the group. Patriotism is simply a concept to be employed as a weapon against those you accuse of lacking it. Ideals are still expressed, but they are always coded expressions of the idea that greatness resides in giving people what they demand. For as long as a leader continues to do this, he remains a hero. When he has outlived his usefulness, he becomes a villain, the object of ridicule, or both.

There is a strange contradiction here; on the one hand, such hostility is frequently expressed in irony and a dark humour, but on the other it is invariably characterized by a withdrawal of openness to the complexity of the character being disparaged. We make jokes about Pearse's myopia, while denying the power and range of his observations about the Irish condition. We sneer at de Valera while distorting his vision, the better to mock it into oblivion. We scorn Haughey while overlooking the extent of his imaginative grip on his country for nearly half a century, not to mention the way his life and lifestyle seemed to prefigure something in the national romance. The shocking thing about this persistent attempt to ridicule is the literalism of it, the way it purports to discover elevated notions in banal concepts of grievance and recrimination. Dripping scorn and derision, our responses are utterly lacking in the irony bestowed by self-awareness, wit, empathy or comprehension, but seem to gain vigour and venom precisely by virtue of this deficiency.

We laugh and laugh at those who built our nation on their ridiculous pretensions and sentences, but still we cannot imagine ourselves belonging to a country that loved itself so much it could not wait to be whole. Above all, we cannot imagine a way of building a country if we had to start again from the beginning.

4

# The Dead Great Father

ON 11 APRIL 2008, NEARLY A MONTH BEFORE BRIAN COWEN BECAME Taoiseach, I wrote an article for the *Irish Mail on Sunday* expressing bemusement about how his alleged qualities of leadership were being prematurely touted in media assessments and warning that the impending coronation was as wrong for Cowen as it was for the country. Reviewing what I wrote then, my only mistake was accusing Cowen of exhibiting 'competence rather than flamboyance'. I observed that, in contrast to Bertie Ahern, he was an ordinary kind of politician, more likely to get into trouble because of a budget deficit than, for example, a marital breakdown. I worried about our capacity to love him in the way we had loved Bertie.

With Bertie lining his luggage up in the exit lounge, I wondered aloud if Brian Cowen might not perhaps lack the magic ingredient to make a great leader. Whatever kind of intelligence he possessed, I felt, it was not of the visionary kind, nor of a kind that in any way transcended the capacity for, at best, proficient management of 'Ireland Inc'. I voiced my suspicion that Cowen's aura of strength had been almost entirely to do with his complementariness to Bertie Ahern in a time of unprecedented prosperity and assurance, and that, now the tide had turned, he was in for a rough ride. I overlooked at the time the since increasingly plausible hypothesis that Bertie's period of leadership might not have amounted to much had he been presented with the situation inherited by Cowen in May 2008.

The decision to crown Cowen without a contest got things off to a bad start. A good, honest leadership contest might have shaken the cobwebs off both Cowen and his party, and given everyone a sense of a new direction. In its normal besieged state, FF tends to see its leadership elections as family romance, when they are actually societal affairs. A paranoia about divisiveness – born of its long besiegement by external enemies – has led to an excessive belief in unity and consensus. Anyway, Fianna Fáil long ago let go of the idea that it should elect leaders with ideas: the chief priority was to elect leaders who could win votes. The general belief within the party was that Cowen was quint-essentially FF, the best-on-board at that particular time, that he was well adapted to that party's needs at a moment when a period of wound-licking and recuperation was anticipated. There was a sense of both FF and its enemies preparing for the next bout of cultural siege rather than for the next phase of national progress.

The national mood at the time was of increasingly fragile denial. Within months, media commentators would come to describe the new Taoiseach as a disaster, the worst ever. But, for now, the talk was all about his unparalleled intelligence, his toughness on the football field, the fact that he could hold a pint or ten and sing a song in the snug of any public house in which the gauntlet was thrown down. Deeper down, the implication of such commentary was that we were still on the pig's back. What we needed was another affable actor to maintain the mood of the previous decade. To suggest otherwise might have been to acknowledge what was already known in the bones of the culture: that we were in deep trouble. There was a general sense, which later seemed almost surreal, of things continuing as normal, of the heir-apparent stepping into his rightful role.

Almost immediately upon Cowen's coronation as Fianna Fáil leader and Taoiseach, the chill winds began to blow. For weeks and weeks, bad news was followed by worse. For reasons nobody could adequately explain, the Irish economy appeared to be back in the basket from which it had been retrieved in 1987 by Charles Haughey and his finance minister Ray MacSharry.

Listening to government ministers talk about the state of the economy was reminiscent of the fairly familiar experience of watching an Irish soccer team trying to get its head together after going a goal or two down in the opening minutes. The chief sensation was of a battery of headless chickens rushing about in search of rhythm and direction. The Taoiseach and his ministers tried to break the bad news – at first gently and then rather more forcefully. But their words were unable to penetrate the public mindset.

When, eventually, the reality began to sink in, there was a growing mood of dismay at the unfairness and unexpectedness of it all, and this seemed to harness itself to a doleful view of Irish fortunes rising up from deep in the historical memory. The national mood began to resemble that extended instant just after you've had a prang at the traffic lights, when, as you get out of the car in slow motion to survey the damage, you think, 'I don't need this, therefore it can't be happening.' At such moments, there is a sensation of being lost in time, of feeling, against the apparent facts, that the past is still recoverable, though the future is already making itself clear. The rhetoric of the previous decade had so convinced people that we had finally emerged from the mists of history and penury that this could only be a terrible misunderstanding. The utter unfairness of it all seemed to render the circumstances momentarily implausible, and therefore appealable. But then reality reasserted itself. Time found its feet. The facts began to sink in.

Cowen's coronation as Fianna Fáil leader had been attended by an ecstatic commentary which alluded to his long experience, towering intellect and amiable personality. But from the outset of his time as Taoiseach, even these qualities seemed to desert him. Within weeks, the worm had turned, and Cowen's political obituaries were being anticipated in doleful analyses. At first, the commentators began to note how unfortunate he had been to inherit the earth at a time when it was starting to fall apart. At the beginning of that summer of 2008, nobody could have predicted that the Lisbon Treaty would be defeated, that oil prices would skyrocket, that an international credit crunch would bite hard at the property market and construction industry, or that the national kitty would be three billion quid shy. Above all, nobody could have suspected that the entire Irish banking system was already crumbling from the inside.

Some less kind commentators were heard to observe that, having for several years been minister for finance, Cowen might have been reasonably well placed to know about most of this. But, at the time, this seemed unfair, since there was by then no definitive evidence in the government's handling of the economic crisis to indicate that Brian Cowen was directly responsible for anything that was happening or indeed that he was performing especially badly as Taoiseach. Things were bad and getting worse, but the extent to which this has to do with government policy, present or past, was unclear. In fact, the most fateful decision made by Cowen, in relation to the bank bail-out of September 2008, was not recognized in all its gravity until long after Cowen's popularity had plummeted beyond redemption. At the time, indeed, it was hailed as a masterstroke by many commentators, who later appeared to overlook their initial enthusiasm for it.

The problem with Brian Cowen seemed to centre on confidence, and this worked both ways. As the gravity of the situation became clearer, Cowen and his ministers seemed utterly at sea and unable to find any way of communicating with the public to allay the growing feeling of disquiet. We, the people, did not feel safe in his hands because we sensed that he would not be able to hold together if things got even a little rougher. For his part, even when he had not yet done anything outrightly disastrous, his general demeanour and body language suggested that he was just about handling himself in a job he had probably dreamed about for most of his life and now had inherited as a nightmare.

In September 2008, he appeared on the first edition of *The Late Late Show* presented by its new host, Ryan Tubridy, and already seemed a bag of nerves. Actually, to begin, it was difficult to say which of the two men was the more nervous. Tubridy introduced the show like a rabbit in the headlights, and Brian Cowen came on as though picking up the vibes and adding them to his own tendency to be uneasy in unpredictable situations.

It was, on the surface, an uncompromising interview. Tubridy asked several are-you-still-beating-your-wife style questions. Was he sorry for anything? Would he apologize for his mistakes?

Cowen replied: 'If people want me to apologize, I apologize in the event that people think I did something purposely wrong.'

Was that an apology, asked Ryan Tubridy, or not?

Often it seemed Tubridy was asking questions for the sake of asking them, rather than for the answers – as though he wanted above all to avoid the accusation that he had dodged putting his man on the spot.

Then, taking his cue from recent newspaper references, he asked Cowen about his drinking, which – having first been the topic of intense and explicit internet commentary – had latterly been taken up by the mainstream press. Tubridy, having mentioned the unmentionable, all but apologized for asking. Was he, he wondered aloud, annoying Cowen? Maybe, he mused just as Cowen started to answer, it was too personal a question? This, interestingly, was when Brian Cowen seemed to begin relishing the encounter, receiving a round of applause for telling Tubridy he could ask what he liked: 'It's your show.'

It was a fascinating exchange, but not because of the surface content. It told more about the interior lives of the two participants than about what they strove to say about themselves, each trying to prove himself in his own position. But, at a deeper level, it showed that Cowen was not happy or comfortable in his new role, even though in response to a direct question he said he was. The most telling moment was at the end, when Tubridy started to wrap up the interview. The relief on Cowen's face when he realized that his ordeal was over was a picture to behold.

The pattern continued into 2009, with Cowen seeming to hide away from the public, to confine his public statements to economistic pronouncements littered with jargon and clichés. And, then, one morning, the Irish people awoke to the news that he had made a speech that had 'electrified' his audience at a Dublin Chamber of Commerce function at Dublin's Four Seasons Hotel.

Cowen had spoken off-the-cuff, delivering a rousing oration such as in the past he had been famous for giving at Fianna Fáil ard fheiseanna at the RDS arena. There was the time, still mentioned, when, two decades before, with his party entering into an uneasy coalition with its long-time nemeses, the Progressive Democrats, he had aimed a famous sideswipe at the junior partners, declaring, to the delight of the party faithful, 'If in doubt, leave them out!'

As it happens, I had been in the vicinity at the RDS some hours beforehand when the script of that speech was being finalized. Cowen was working on the text in the press area, and was being informally assisted by a well-known political journalist, in whose company I happened to be that afternoon. Cowen was sitting at a table musing over what he might say under various headings and had came to the knotty problem of the PDs, between whom and Cowen little love was lost.

Looking up from his draft script, Cowen growled, 'The PDs?', grimacing by way of asking whether or not he should mention them. His journalist consultant was doubtful. 'If in doubt, leave them out,' he advised. 'Brilliant!' said Cowen and wrote it down.

The Four Seasons speech was, by comparison, pedestrian, but the fuss it engendered says a lot about the sad state of inspiration in the Ireland of the immediate post-Tiger period. In this speech, Cowen had set forth fairly starkly the dreadful state of the country's finances. He predicted that living standards would drop by 10 to 12 per cent over the next few years. He called on his audience of business leaders to 'work together' and 'believe in our capacity to confront the challenges that lie ahead'. He said that Ireland had gone from a position of unknown prosperity to, all of a sudden, 'the survival stakes'.

'If we decide to wallow in the sea of doubt,' he said, in the only line that jumped out of the transcript of his speech, 'do not be surprised if we remain in the turbulent waters that we are in today.' It was enough to cause the media to go into raptures, suggesting that, nine months into the job, the new Taoiseach had found his mojo.

I wrote at the time that the speech seemed to me to have the potential to be a turning-point, but not for the reasons being widely cited. Most commentaries, including the favourable ones, treated the speech like an act in a talent competition, giving marks for 'passion' and 'conviction', praising its 'spontaneity' and so forth. But when you studied it line-by-line, the speech was not especially brilliant in any of the ways being suggested. Mr Cowen's delivery was not particularly passionate. About 95 per cent was standard, pedestrian stuff: some flannel about the entrepreneurial spirit, a lot of guff about social partnership, a couple of sideswipes at those who voted against the Lisbon Treaty. There was no good news and very little in the way of obvious hopefulness. The keynote themes had to do with sacrifice and effort. Essentially, he was saying that we had to come to terms with the fact that the good times were over. If we could work together, he proposed, the tide could be turned again.

It occurred to me that the strength of the speech lay in its understanding of an archetypal need in both the human psyche and in the soul of society, one of the most fundamental human needs of all. Brian Cowen's deeper themes that night were postponement and reassurance, the great themes of fatherhood. What he was doing, very simply, was announcing himself as father of the public realm.

In my adult lifetime, which embraces the period of what we now colloquially think of as Irish modernity, Fianna Fáil has had three ordinary leaders sandwiching two extraordinary ones. The extraordinary leaders have been Haughey and Ahern; the ordinary, Lynch, Reynolds and Cowen. I have in mind not ability or competence, or even political skill, but mythic status. It is as if, from time to time, Fianna Fáil needs to take a rest from myth-creation. Having thrown up a leader who in his personality seems to summon up the kind of society he will leave behind, the party retreats for a while into a self-protective conservatism.

The myth-creation and the conservatism are equally vital elements of Fianna Fáil's spiritual dynamic, and together form the unassailable moral resource so envied by outsiders. It may nowadays sound a little satirical, but Fianna Fáil might be called the living political conscience of the Irish nation, for it is in the soul of that party that the great moral questions are ultimately resolved in a manner best adapted to the emerging culture.

And this is why the party unconsciously adopted this two-steps-forward-one-step-backwards approach to choosing its leader in the years since de Valera's isolationist mysticism was unsettled by the pragmatism of Seán Lemass. Had Haughey come next, recent history might have been different, but the party lost its nerve, causing Haughey to become ingrown and stunted. His turn, when it came, unleashed a series of frustrations born of the original cowardice and resulted in a fraught time for all. Albert Reynolds followed but was too obviously a creature of his predecessor, and of his party's need for a break, to survive for very long. Then came Bertie, who had clambered to the top because of his profound functionality as a praetorian guardsman to his inspiration and mentor, Charles J. Haughey, whom John Healy famously named The Great National Bastard. Everyone hated Charlie Haughey except the people. Yes, but his enemies hated him to begin with precisely because of his empathy with the people, whom they hated far more.

Sick societies normalize at the top, pretending wellness where there is nothing but disease. When a society is debilitated following radical interference by outsiders, much of the pretence takes the form of aping the occupier. Reducing itself to the largest entity capable of passing itself off in this way, the elite creates a version of reality as deluded as it is exclusive: 'This is civilization. We are the civilized. We don't understand this talk about colonization. And as for those reprobates threatening to overthrow the so-called occupation with guns . . . we are horrified and ashamed.'

This is the context in which the story of Charles Haughey must be seen. But precisely because of the tenacity of the delusions, the truth eludes. Because we depend on the former occupier for words, and on the elite of settled natives for logic and an ethical framework, all discussion drives us deeper into delusion.

Haughey was a subversive – his enemies were right about that. He sought to subvert the delusions of post-colonial Ireland, to manipulate the iconography of wealth and power so as to deliver himself and us to our potential. He spoke in the language of the national spirit (a volume of his speeches was once published with the title *The Spirit of the Nation*) but addressed himself to reality as if it were exclusively a material phenomenon. There was here, it is true, a certain corruption to begin with, but his proposals represented, approximately, a blueprint for the beginnings of self-realization and seemed at the time to gain favour with his people.

His enemies were right, too, when they called him a thief. He stole Ireland back from the elite who had stolen it for themselves – by aping their pretences and self-importance and exposing the inadequacy of their charades; by creating a new drama of elitism: spectacular, attainable and potentially democratic in offering his people the opportunity to reinvent themselves in their own ways.

He preached of the deep tradition of a peasant Catholicism and yet lived the life of a Renaissance prince. He turned our heads with his Georgian mansion, his sharp suits and crisp shirt collars, his air of masterly charm and certainty. His life was manifesto and lived-installation, a representation of the possible. Think loaves and fishes. Everything about him – his history, house, fortune, adultery, disgrace – became codes by which we discovered ourselves. He supplied the narrative for an otherwise inscrutable journey. Perhaps no other Irish leader since Independence has represented so well the inner life and aspirations of his people, who, having asceticism forced upon them, had pretended to be more virtuous and self-denying than they actually wanted to be.

We can argue that Haughey was the one who led us into a cul de sac of materialism, but we cannot gainsay the fact that, of all those who led us or aspired to do so, his life and likes and lifestyle came closest to dramatizing what we would become when he was no longer there to blame for it. In his life and lifestyle, Haughey was a prophet of the Ireland he would leave behind him. When he walked into Government Buildings following the 1987 general election, 'Ireland Inc.' was on the verge of bankruptcy. Shortly after he left office five years later, the foundations had been laid for an economy that within five years or so would become 'the envy of Europe'.

It is not just that the circumstantial evidence points towards some gift for alchemy on Haughey's part. This, in a way, is obvious. Much more interesting is that this turnaround in the national fortunes came to offer a reflection of the manner of

Charles Haughey's own enrichment. Perhaps unable to achieve release from the cocoon of post-colonial literalism, the sceptic will point out that Haughey was himself the prime beneficiary of his own dramatization. For Haughey, in the circumstances in which he found himself, there was no other way of being. But there was also a considerable measure of good intentions resting alongside the self-interest and egotism. We, his subjects, were caught between the manifest impracticality of the old values of frugality and asceticism, and our continuing emotional attachment to them. This unleashed in us a neurosis that was later to cause us to lurch, almost in a single moment, from one extreme to the other.

Conventional ideologies presented us with a stark choice: reject the old values outright so as to move forward, or sink back into the bog. Haughey, and Haughey alone, seemed to understand that the price we were being asked to pay for prosperity was too high. For him it did not have to be a stark choice between poverty and jettisoning everything we had been. He offered us a third way: to tiptoe into the modern world, while still wearing our old values as a cloak.

In a society where limited imagination and ignorance of its own colonized mentality had prevented an organic development from tradition to modernity, Charles Haughey was the inevitable product of his times. He lived and ruled through an era when old values were being dissolved and turned into money. Bereft of a personal vision, he tried to simulate the impression of a visionary based on parodying ancient values and their adherents, even while he was up to his oxters in the green slime of the material world. He used the money he got from merchant princes to create the illusion of magic.

Male nature – and most great leaders have been males – tends towards extremes. The average female is smarter than the average male, but there are far more men than women of brilliance and genius, and also a lot more male idiots. The greatest leaders appear to be people in whom these extremes are balanced: dark and light, vision and myopia, great intelligence and crass vanity. And this balance of extremes appears, ultimately, to make for the most seductive incarnations of humanity. It was out of such characters that Shakespeare rendered his greatest works – figures of whom, when they occur in real life, we continue to speak long after they are gone. Our public discussions about contemporary politics tend towards sanctimony, but history, like a red-blooded woman, tends to valorize not the leader with the pure heart, but the one who was a bit of a bollox.

To speak in public these days about the nuances of political culture – to lament, for example, that something was lost in the recent push towards a more transparent and accountable politics – is as risky as making a speech about ethics at the average Fianna Fáil cumann meeting. Both forums belong to the same society but recognize utterly different sets of meanings. We are talking about the murky depths of a culture, the fruition of generations of organic growth, impossible to plumb or parse. The truth of this culture nowadays betrays its existence only in moments of crisis, and these are likely to become fewer as the assault from the new literal, rational culture drives the subterranean model into extinction.

Understanding this culture and why it exists is at least as important as bringing it under control, if only to ensure that we do not lose anything vital in embracing the new. Sketched simply, this culture is an expression of the residual subversion of a once subjugated society which saw authority and regulation as the prerogatives of the enemy outsider, because usually they were. This culture survived into Independence and became a way of circumnavigating the system on behalf of those left outside the loop. Fianna Fáil built its power base on this brand of perpetual revolution, looking after its friends and steering its enemies to the hind tit. Ethically speaking, this became problematic only as the cake grew bigger, and hoodwinking the system came to involve far bigger stakes. Since there was no clear-cut point at which this moral transition was made, many on the inside failed or refused to acknowledge that anything had changed at all.

In the story Haughey dramatized for us, the iconography of materialist pretension lay side by side with an acknowledgement of hard facts: radical interference, famine, cultural asphyxiation, enforced ignorance, squalor and the bloody hangovers of history. Haughey did not turn away from the facts, but neither did he confront them in a way that would have permitted him to be patronized as an honourable failure. He wanted to succeed, on terms he felt capable of attaining, not to create a new iconography of glorious failure. He sought to lead us from the swamp of history not with a rhetoric of egalitarianism but a programme of action and a drama of attainment. To the people of flawed pedigree, Charles Haughey said: 'Anything is possible, poverty is not natural, and, no, you do not have to accept your place.'

This exercise in subversion was successful, except that, by virtue of its methodology, it left many of the governing delusions intact, allowing the deluded not simply to forget what it had been like before but to deny the meaning of what was happening now and what we were becoming. It was as though the prosperity that came afterwards was an immaculate conception, a reward perhaps for some virtuous behaviour, rather than the inevitable consequence of certain choices and decisions.

Doing the State some service was the least of Charles Haughey's contributions. His fingerprints are all over the transformation of Ireland in the 1990s. The explanations are too complex and amazing for easy acceptance, and so, without a dramatic transformation of current thinking and sentiment, unlikely ever to become more than seemingly mischievous and ironic propositions. History, oddly enough, belongs to the living.

If you wish to take materialism as the measure, the circumstantial evidence in Haughey's favour is overwhelming. Before he came, there were hovels; after, a housing boom. Before he came there were dirt tracks, then, motorways and flyovers. Before he came we were afraid to speak in whispers; afterwards, we proclaimed our worth to the world.

Charles Haughey, as my father would often say, was the Fat Chieftain who promised to make his people as plump as himself. This is why it was important that he be seen to be wealthy, extravagant, omnipotent. Haughey, you might legitimately say, attained power by playing to the deep insecurities of a post-colonial people, suggesting that what he could do on his own behalf he could do on theirs. We looked at his ample belly and felt reassured.

What we cannot say is that it did not happen, that he did not deliver on this implicit promise. The thought occurs that, left to get on with things, he might have delivered twenty years earlier, and that the differing circumstances then might have enabled us to handle the experience better than we eventually did. But this is our tragedy, not Haughey's.

A decade ago, seeking to divine the secret history of the Celtic Tiger, I wrote:

> I suspect that, in due course, we will observe in the entrails of that excavated feline skeleton a similar pattern of dodges, strokes, funny money and hard neck as we now observe in the fiscal history of Mr Haughey. In other words, if our previous financial embarrassment bore a passing resemblance to Mr de Valera's notions of frugal comfort, our present shut-your-face-and-take-a-look-at-my-wad style of prosperity is undoubtedly modelled on Charles Haughey's brass-necked approach to the management of money.

I tried to say these things without moralizing. Haughey did not make us poor in making himself rich, still less did he make himself rich by taking from those who had less. On the contrary, to the extent that we became rich, it was because Charles Haughey was the kind of man he was with the kind of faults he had. The main reason we grew mad at him in the end is because we discovered that there was no magic, that he accumulated his own riches not by wizardry but by supplicancy. The truth, of course, rendered us disappointed about him, but more fundamentally about the illusion he had helped us nurture concerning the possibility of material acquisition in general. In due course, we would come to read the tale of the Tiger in the same way.

To deal with such a legacy by counting 'good' and 'bad' and weighing the difference is simple-minded and pointless. At full throttle, politics steers closer to magic than logic. To calculate the impact of Charles Haughey, we must add positives to negatives, hate to love, to know the sum of what he inspired and what he overcame to make the impossible banal.

If I wished to be perverse in some ultimate defence of Charles Haughey, I would present the following, admittedly rather risky closing argument. I would say that in a society which had no clear values of its own, having rejected all existing values on the basis of their lack of material potential, the difference between what has emerged about Charles Haughey and what has emerged about other politicians and about the party system in general is simply one of degree, a mere matter of the number of noughts on a cheque. For if it is legitimate for a political party to ask businessmen for money, how is it possible to draw a line between this and the solicitation of money to maintain a Fat Chieftain in the manner to which he has become accustomed in order to maintain the belief of his followers? For is this not also the purpose to which political parties put the proceeds of their own begging? In other words, is it possible to say with absolute certainty that, in a society on the cusp of modernity in the precise circumstances in which we found ourselves, the payments by businessmen to

Mr Haughey were not, in some convoluted way, just as 'legiti-mate' as the payments to the election campaigns of Fine Gael, the Labour Party or virtually any candidate running for election under any banner in any democratic contest in the free world?

I ask the question only half in earnest. In the full glare of the logic of the new ethics-preoccupied Ireland, it is a ludicrous question. Since light is always created by the victors it is right and fitting that the question be withdrawn. Those of us who counted on Charles Haughey in any way, who thought him not entirely a bad thing, who loved him even a little, had better button our lips and slink back to our filthy hovels in the countryside – there, perchance, to wait for a new champion, with a more subtle grasp of the essentials of magic.

In the fable of the Fat Chieftain, the people, once they have decided that their corpulent chief has outlived his usefulness, lose little time in cooking and eating him for lunch.

For all the mixed fortunes of the first seventy-five years of Independence, there had been a certain consistency to our political leadership, which was, generally speaking, geared to find-ing ways of proactively generating wealth from within. The Ahern/Celtic Tiger years spawned a new style: that of manage-ment of good fortune arising from forces beyond the control of government. Ahern's lack of ideology, love of consensus and much-vaunted affable disposition made him the ideal manager while the supposed economic miracle lasted. But the management of crisis is an entirely different matter.

It is interesting that this shift in the culture of leadership follows the pattern first outlined by the American poet Robert Bly and the German psychoanalyst Alexander Mitscherlich. Bly had actually borrowed his concept of the 'sibling society' from Mitscherlich, who warned of the approach of a Peter Pan world where nobody would ever grow up, where adults regressed towards adolescence, and adolescents stayed where they were. This, argued Bly in his seminal foreword to Mitscherlich's book *Society Without the Father*, and later developed in his own book *The Sibling Society*, is characterized by a turning away from the vertical plane, comprising tradition, service and devotion, in favour of the horizontal plane, with its self-referential culture of the young and the wannabe young.

At the heart of this process is a vacuum left behind by the departed figure of what Bly called 'The Great Father'. In the consciousness of humanity there are three layers of fatherhood: God the Father, the State Father and the Great Father. All three are now deceased. They have been killed off by Elvis Presley and the Rolling Stones, Gay Byrne, Mary Robinson and Nell McCafferty and all the sundry other voices of post-1960s rebellion and protest. The trouble is that none of these has had even the most modest proposal about what to put in place of that which they had destroyed. As Alexander Mitscherlich has written, the father as a force for good in society has been exiled, leaving behind 'a gigantic army of rival, envious siblings'. Sibling society has no time for glory, or effort or justice, or greatness, or duty, or patriotism, but is content with consumer durables, celebrity and shallow forms of freedom. Is this beginning to sound germane?

In a scintillating analysis, Bly outlined how the Industrial Revolution had destroyed the four-million-year-old Great Father, by removing him from the home and making his powers invisible, and then removing his political equivalent from the public square. It was not, Bly observed in a passage that summons up the ghost of the Western world's dead fathers, a premeditated killing: 'Industrial circumstances took the father to a place where his sons and daughters could no longer watch him minute by minute, or hour by hour, as he fumbled incompetently with hoes, bolts, saws, shed doors, plows, wagons. His incompetence left holes or gaps where the sons and daughters could do better.'

For Bly, this absence of the domestic sphere was just the first in a series of bereavements. But, here, prefiguring what would follow in the public sphere, there were three absences: the physical absence of the father from the vicinity of his children, the psychic absence of the father from the human heart, and the spiritual absence of the very *idea* of 'father', once represented by a Loving Father called 'God', from the human being's sense of his own soul. These absences were soon to be replicated at the level of political leadership.

If we are to take Bly's prognosis seriously, what he described may be a self-accelerating condition, from which the means of salvation is cut off by virtue of the principal symptoms. The banishment of the father creates in the children a sense of rebelliousness which has no means of reconciling itself.

In the normal cycle, the revolt of the child is managed within a relationship rendered safe by the father's firm guidance and resolve. Within this relationship, the child imagines himself to have a genuine problem with the father, perhaps even, for a time, to hate him. The child says 'I want', 'I want to', and the father says 'No'. The child says, 'I hate you, I didn't ask to be born.' But the steadfastness of the loving father allows this natural process to work itself out. In time, like Mark Twain, the child comes to wonder at how much his father's thinking has advanced over the course of a few short years.

All true, human-centred societal growth, which is to say reliable change, demands a process of renunciation, which in turn requires a strong, safe, generous agent to act as buffer and punchbag. In other words, a person of benign authority. A good working definition of the word 'authority' might be: the capacity to endure unpopularity in the interests of good.

But when the father is absent, this does not happen. Instead, the child's emotions, deprived of a legitimate target, lack the safe provocation that nature intended. It was an essential element of the make-up of the Great Father that he was prepared to be hated in the interests of doing what he had to do, a burden mothers did not have to carry, relying on the father to impose discipline, sometimes at the expense of his own parental popularity. The role of stoical authoritarian receptor for society's anger and outrage has been decried and displaced, and with it many of the positive values of father-organized society, like security, order and fair play.

In the post-father society, there is nothing at which to target our anger, which turns inward against ourselves. Moreover, since there is no longer a father there to withstand our anger, to stand rock solid while we pummel his coat, to calm us with a pat on the head and a stern admonition to go away and be better, our anger destroys everything regardless of virtue. Without the Great Father, we cannot tell right from wrong, good from bad, or truth from mere information. There are certain criteria which, if exhibited by a phenomenon, action or concept, will inevitably attract the destructive tendencies of the siblings; these include, in particular, that it be the creation of the father and have proved its merits through time.

The effect on males is worse than on females. With increasing industry and zeal, we build a society where fathers have no words to speak to their sons. Masculinity is demonized and our education system impresses upon adolescent males that their fathers are inappropriate role-models. The result, by Bly's analysis, is the creation of generations of young men who are numb in the region of the heart. The umbilical cord has been severed, but no more than that. The father can find no way of protecting or guiding his son, who remains tied to his mother's apron. Still, deeply aware of his maleness, he shies away from adopting the emotional life of the female, and chooses to have no emotions at all. Thus, the male becomes incapable of taking on the father role himself, and the cycle gathers speed.

The paradox of this situation is that men now stand where they would if they had retained the stature of the Great Father, but without any of the strength or resilience that allowed him to withstand the onslaughts of the past. Today's man stands accused, pummelled, denigrated, not on account of his greatness but because he is weak and refuses to carry the burden of society's grievance. His position is understandable: you have taken my power away, and so cannot expect me to absorb your resentments. This double-bind is visible in the domestic arena of the home, where the father carries the dilemma in his very gut: as a child of the 1960s, his instinct is to spurn, to forfeit, the authority which his own children still expect him to wield. It is also visible in the public arena, where the only successful leader is one who panders to the most immediate desires of the electorate, promising reduced taxes, increased public spending and solutions to everyone's problems.

Bly and Mitscherlich argued that the enforced fatherlessness of both the private and public realms led to chaos, regression, and a narrowing of collective horizons to selfish group and individualistic interests, as the siblings set to squabbling about the division of the spoils.

There is every evidence that these changes in the public sphere are being played out in Irish society. When the father is absent, the siblings remain contented for as long as they get their way. When the good times stop rolling, when the money runs out, the emotions which have lain serene and unengaged kick in with a vengeance. My generation, born in the 1950s or 1960s, was perhaps the last in Irish society to experience the healthy form of engagement with a public realm dominated by strong father-figures. Indeed, when we look again at the turmoil of the 1970s and 1980s, it is possible to see, emerging from the mists of those turbulent decades, a new, previously secret history of what was going on. For what is suggested by the lengthy sagas involving the attempted overthrowing of tradition and authority, the bursting out of freedom battles of various kinds, and, at a more concrete level, the beginnings of deficit budgeting as a respectable approach to the running of an economy, is a pattern uncannily close to that which Mitscherlich and Bly sought to identify and describe.

For four decades, we have had leaders who played at being fathers, McDonald's Dads who, married to what Robert Bly called the 'multi-breasted State', begged us to like them and let us do what we liked. Seán Lemass was the last Taoiseach who offered the old kind of fatherhood, the sober, teaching kind who said 'No' as often as he said 'Yes' and never spoke until he had arrived at a clear understanding somewhere in the depths of himself.

It was then, rather than with Haughey especially, that it started to go downhill. Jack Lynch, with his hurling past and mellifluous accent, was more of a visiting uncle who patted your head and dipped into his pocket for a half-crown. Liam Cosgrave was more in the way of a grandfather, who takes over as head of the household because the father has died or gone to work in England. Cosgrave had the air of authority, but never really earned more than a grudging respect, and certainly not much affection. Charles Haughey made the right noises but his rakish air undermined everything. We didn't know where he got to at night and spent long evenings waiting for the rattle of his key in the latch.

With Garret FitzGerald it was back to uncles, and of the kind you'd like to swap your father for – until the first moment of crisis. We loved his absent-mindedness and the way his hair seemed to burst out of his head much as the words burst out of his mouth, but we didn't take him all that seriously. He tried to persuade us to do lots of things to improve ourselves, but more by way of suggestions than demands, and they emerged from his mouth with such fluidity and speed that we became more fascinated with the intensity of his speech patterns than with what he was actually saying. He was a nice man who doubled the deficit in his efforts to stay in our affections.

As though understanding his own implausibility as father-figure, Haughey, on returning to the Taoiseach's office in 1987, gave us someone who remained in our psyche as the most recent imprint of the sober, guiding father. Ray MacSharry stepped into the shoes that Haughey could not fill to lead us out of the most serious domestically generated crisis since Independence. When he took on the stewardship of the national finances in 1987, qualities of thrift, frugality and familiarity with life's harsh realities, which had attached themselves to him in the tough years of his child-hood in 1940s Sligo, were forged into a strategy for saving the country. But MacSharry never developed the itch to assume the king's crown, stepping aside into the role of European Commissioner, from which he drifted into retirement.

This left the field open for a different style of personality, Albert Reynolds, the kind of uncle who smiled and talked too much. And yet, underlying his rather sleek exterior was a shrewdness forged in his many years as a businessman. But his reign was too short for him to do any more than leave behind a regretful question-mark concerning what he might have done had he been allowed to stay for longer.

John Bruton, suddenly and dramatically becoming Taoiseach against the run of play, was a kind of stepfather figure who never really got his feet under the table. We didn't take him seriously and in the end he disappeared.

Bertie was the kind of older-brother father-figure you some-times get if your father bails out or dies young, but who himself has never quite grown up. He treated us as equals, pandered to our whims and only occasionally lost the rag. His indulgence dovetailed with the times. For ten years he presided over a society that was convinced that the wind of history had changed. We grew up feckless and selfish, but it felt good. Having staked his claim to political seniority as a facilitator of consensus, Bertie marked a departure from the old-style ex-cathedra leadership represented by a line of Taoisigh from de Valera to Reynolds.

Seen in this light, the lengthy moral tussles of the 1980s,

between Charlie the Bad and Garret the Good, reveal themselves not as literal battles for differing perspectives on the moral universe, but as two different approaches to carving out a niche. When you stand right back from that period, what you see is not some clear moral distinction between the two men, so much as two men trying to discover a means by which they might pander to demands of their sibling people and stay in the game. In both instances, we observe a pattern in which indulgence is followed by panic, followed, once the scare abates, by more indulgence. Both men vacillated in a time of great economic crisis, here arguing for austerity and restraint, there letting the deficit grow. Both men laboured under the delusion that they could cheat reality. The only true differences between them were of style. In truth, both men led us into perdition, from which we had to be rescued in the end by Ray MacSharry, perhaps the last Great Father of Irish politics.

Nowadays, such a figure could hardly expect to survive in the prosperity-induced complacency of post-Tiger Ireland – as Brian Cowen and Brian Lenihan discovered from 2008. Accustomed to the good times, the Irish people have lost all sense of perspective, not just on the realities of self-sustenance, but on the capacities of leadership. In the new dispensation, our leaders are no longer figureheads and anchormen who summon us to effort, sacrifice and realism, but merely punchbags for us to batter gratuitously when we do not get what we want. They are unknowing creatures of the culture who imagine themselves in a line that flows from the past, and, although they understand that things have changed in certain ways owing to 'progress' and so forth, seem still to imagine that the conditions are broadly the same.

But something fundamental has shifted in the contract between the leaders and the led: the roles have switched, and now we lead them, with our populist outrage, hyper-democratic opinionating and self-interested agenda-setting. For as long as everything is going well, this reality remains invisible, but at the first signs of trouble we emerge, as though teenage tyrants, to harangue our leaders and beat them up. They only appear to be our leaders, when really they are our vassals – affable vassals but vassals nonetheless. Our so-called leaders have become the rag-doll impersonators of our fathers, and of the father-figure leaders who preceded them.

We have a sense, conveyed best by the word 'patriarchy', that there was a time, not too long ago, when the State created itself in the image of the father. The State was tough, straight, straight-talking and demanding of its citizens. The State did not waste energy in communication, but made clear, in a minimalist way, what its expectations were. The State, as it used to be, did not care whether people liked it or not, and so could ask people to postpone gratification and reward, to give unselfishly. But over the past forty years, we have witnessed what might plausibly be characterized as the feminization of the State, which now resembles mother more than father. Now the State is tolerant, indulgent, talkative, given to explaining itself in great detail. The modern State longs to be liked, although it retains an inscrutable capacity for viciousness when pushed beyond certain limits. Men still try to lead this entity but cannot do so. It does not come naturally to them. That is why, fundamentally, none of our leaders now seem in any way to resemble either our fathers or the men our fathers spoke of with awe.

A further twist is provided by the fact that, in a society headed up and administered by these affable vassals, the natural and necessary antagonism towards authority, authoritative or otherwise, is no longer possible. The result is a constant venting of unfocused rage, directed at the most obvious and immediate targets, who by definition are powerless to answer or defuse it.

'In the old father-organized society,' wrote Robert Bly, 'the citizens simply looked up at the men at the top of the high stairs and opposed them with an outrage that was partly fuelled by anger at one's own father and his power. But when the father is absent . . . then how does the citizen fuel his political anger? How can the anger be accurately focused? It's possible that our whole Western tradition of fiery outrage will fade.'

Here we may need to refine Bly's point. What he meant by 'fiery outrage' was the natural and legitimate reactions of a people who demand that their leaders serve them competently and trustworthily and are legitimately indignant when this does not occur. One could not look at Irish society at the moment and diagnose an absence of outrage, fiery or otherwise. But what we see is an outrage that has no coherent target, that seems to enter into a vacuum of powerlessness, that transfixes our so-called leaders in its headlights and makes them afraid. It achieves nothing but its own expression. It has no target but the rag dolls who crumple before it. We assume that this is the same process as always existed, the one Bly refers to, but it is not. Without a process of engagement, even the rage and outrage will begin to burn out. In the absence of someone worthy to battle with, or someone who will stand and allow us to exhaust ourselves, we will exhaust ourselves anyway out of sheer frustration.

Bertie was a different kind of myth-maker to Haughey. He entered the highly ritualized and formulaic world of politics and began to subvert it with a personality both ordinary and anarchic. In the beginning he seemed ill suited to running a country. He was hard to take seriously and seemed only to be there because of a cheeky manner that was good for pulling votes and offered a refreshing counterpoint to CJH's Napoleon complex. But then he began to use precisely these incongruous aspects of his personality to organize the country in a new way, simultaneously refracting the changes that resulted from this new approach. His broken marriage, his celebrity family, his high-visibility engagement with ordinary pursuits – all these contributed to the creation of a new myth of leadership, a sibling mythology which subtly redefined the role of Taoiseach in accordance with the changing nature of Irish culture.

It is obvious, when you think it through, that politicians always carry their fatal flaws from the beginning, but also that we simply don't notice until near the end. From the moment the curtain goes up, the ending is already implicit in the character of the subject. When disaster begins to unfold, as it must, we think of this as natural attrition, whereby the growing complacency of the powerful comes under pressure from events, leading to the stories which become the undoing of the dream. But really there is another process, a kind of initial blindness deriving from the idealism of the observers, a refusal to see anything but the shining newness in relief against the rejected dullness of the old, gradually succeeded by a seeing born of disillusionment and the recurring and inevitable boredom.

So it had been with Bertie. His departure in the early summer of 2008 was marked by a level of ambiguity unparalleled among the ranks of Irish leadership. From the moment he announced his departure a month earlier, commentary had been almost uniformly positive. Before that, it was unrelentingly negative, and in the immediate future, it was to become negative again.

It is doubtful if Bertie would have emerged from the pack had it not been for his suitability as a foil for Charles Haughey. In the turbulent Haughey years, his easy, emollient personality became useful by virtue of the Boss's need for someone plausible to sweep up in his kingly wake. In those years, Bertie was like a child with a difficult parent: hypersensitive to the next crisis, a low-key counterpoint to the ego of his master, a fixer, a gofer, a diplomat, a cleaner-upper. He always seemed to be running around putting an acceptable face on things. He learned young how to gloss things over, how to keep the neighbours sweet, how to create diversions at the slightest change in the atmosphere, how to placate the affronted and comfort the crushed, how to coax people back from the brink of finality. Bertie emerged in the Haughey era as something of a cartoon character, a figure of necessary light relief, a reassuring caricature, a shambolic Dub you couldn't help liking. Something about him made you laugh instinctively, though without malice. In the mingled menace and macho of the Haughey years, he contributed a different tone. But he also attracted a degree of condescension, which he pretended not to notice, but which he stored up as both motivation and ammunition. He was a man who enjoyed being underestimated because it allowed him to shuffle in where others could not go.

We tend to forget now that, even as late as the early 1990s, Bertie was an unlikely Taoiseach. He was attractive politically but not particularly impressive as leadership material. His skills, developed in the Haughey bunker, seemed inappropriate to the top job. The inevitability of his becoming Taoiseach seemed to be more to do with Fianna Fáil's family dynamics than the national interest. But nobody minded very much because it was Bertie.

In retrospect we can see that he came to chiefdom in a time when the talents he honed as Haughey's ambassador to reality became opportune to an extent that, even in the deep unconscious of the nation, could not have been foreseen or planned.

One of the reasons the Dan O'Rourke prototype is no longer tenable as a political template is that the magnification of politics by modern media has reduced the politician to the role of acting out a careful version of himself. Mass media have not simply changed the nature of politics – they have altered the very molecular structure of politicians, or at least of the kind who end up as leaders. Once, the primary talents required of a leader were megaphone skills, flamboyance and charisma. On television, however, such qualities overwhelm everything, bursting out through the technology. TV, because it magnifies and amplifies, requires subtlety, understatement and a kind of natural plausibility that can only be faked. This suited Bertie, who merged with his new role in a way that changed him as much as it changed the role. The old expectations of flamboyance and menace lingered for a while, and in this period Bertie seemed an oddity, a misfit, the cartoon figure he had always appeared. But slowly he redefined both himself and the position. He had already begun to change his appearance, dress and hairstyle, though never in a way that undermined his underlying Bertieness. Now he acquired an air of authority, though without losing his affability.

Politics is no longer much about standing at the head of your people and leading forward, but of going around whispering in ears, persuading the maximum number to see things differently. Bertie was a master of the intimate, conspiratorial whisper, capable of persuading almost anyone that he was on their side and somehow bringing everyone with him despite the permutational impossibilities this implied. He had that knack of getting people on the front of the wagon without losing some off the back. He was fortunate to hit the top job at a time when negotiating and diplomatic skills were the assets most in demand: domestically in coalition, in the EU, in the Northern talks.

Bertie grew into the times and the times grew into Bertie. Leadership is about more than innate qualities: it is also about alchemy. But unlike his wizard mentor, Bertie was a leader who found his greatness in the crucible of power, rather than coming to power because he was great. He had become confident enough under Haughey to realize what he was capable of. Gradually he brought to bear on his role and office precisely these aspects of his personality that had made him such an unlikely Taoiseach to start with. His public persona was a mass of contradictions. Separated and in a new relationship, he never failed to appear on Ash Wednesday with a dark blob of ash on his forehead. Ostensibly inarticulate, his personality did a lot of the talking, but there was, too, a talent for the kind of symbolism that makes words superfluous. This enigmatic everyman seemed to embody the contradictions we all found ourselves living, and in doing so gave us all a little more sure-footedness in fast-changing times. Gradually we began to understand that, although Bertie was very much one of us, he possessed an extraordinary capability to make things happen. We began to relax and congratulate ourselves on our prescience in choosing him.

The image he had so carefully constructed in the beginning to create a force field through which Haughey could stride back to power – of a humble political journeyman, uninterested in the trappings of power or wealth – was badly compromised by revelations suggesting his private finances were as flush as they were chaotic. The idea that Bertie might be interested in money and houses was as damaging to him within his own culture as the taint of corruption was to him outside it, because it summoned up the ghost of his mentor and caused a new meaning to seep into the leadership persona he had forged for himself. It was the return of the repressed and occasioned a chilling revisitation of the thought that Haughey might not have been joking when he called Bertie 'the most skilful, the most devious and the most cunning of them all'.

In the end, Bertie stepped off the ship just as it was about to go under. As he had always been able to do, he sensed that the wind was changing. He had come from an era when things were done in unorthodox ways, but this culture was being replaced by a new literalness with which he was less comfortable, in which his contradictory elements did not translate cleanly. His own public had begun to see through him, not necessarily in some fiercely ethical sense, but in the sense of being reminded that Bertie had sold them a version of himself that was, even if necessarily, only partly real. It had worked for a while and was no longer working. Bertie had tried to be the reassuring antidote to Haughey, but gradually the cloak of ordinariness had started to slip and it began to become clear that all was not as it seemed.

*

The long-standing cultural antagonism towards Fianna Fáil, exhibited in so much public discourse over most of my lifetime, and especially the high-octane moralism attaching itself thereto, conceals a vital truth about Irish society: that Fianna Fáil is the organism which has produced most of those whom, looking backwards, we recognize as our significant leaders.

This is why Fianna Fáil drives crazy those who have never been embraced by it and cannot bring themselves to try to understand it: because it was the Labour Party, or Mary Robinson, or some such 'progressive' phenomenon, that was supposed to lead the way into the new Ireland, and always it has been Fianna Fáil doing it. Somehow, Fianna Fáil, which has been synonymous with conservatism, manages to sneak into the driving seat at critical points in the progress project and do the things its enemies imagine themselves predestined to do.

People have been predicting the end of Fianna Fáil since its foundation. I've done it myself, prophesying the emergence of a left–right divide or intermittently declaring Fianna Fáil to have finally and fatally shot itself in the foot. It never happens like we think it should, because 'should' holds no sway in the relationship between a people and the truths that govern that people's inner life. Hence, Seán Gallagher's meteoric trajectory through the electoral firmament in 2011.

Fianna Fáil is the black swan of our political ballet, the exterior phenomenon that dances out the part of our inner psyche which would otherwise manifest only in outward incoherence and contradiction, the entity on to which we project all our selfish, shadow energies and desires – our cynicism and self-interest, and, when things go awry, our rage and self-hatred. From time to time, we tire of all this and seek to go straight, stretching out our arms for a waltz with the white swan. But, after a time we grow even more weary of virtue, and Fianna Fáil emerges as the pied piper of our sneakier hopes of redemption and salvation by some painless intervention. The white swan is, at different times, played by other entities: Fine Gael, Labour, celebrity economists, journalists, charismatic independent candidates. But the white swan doesn't float our boats. She is plaintive and fragile, but also pious, incompetent and uninteresting, and nobody wants to dance with her for long.

Every leader of Fianna Fáil has arrived at that position as the saviour of the party or the nation or both. Sometimes, as with the shift from de Valera to Lemass, the necessary act of salvation has been defined by some dynamic of modernization; or, as with the installation of Jack Lynch, as an attempt to divert the storyline by suppressing the black swan. But it never works out. Each leader in turn has become possessed in one way or another, and in due course has had his human personality obliterated by the projected blackness of a culture in search of someplace to deposit its misunderstood or unacknowledged dark side. After brief periods of apparent rejuvenation, Fianna Fáil repeatedly acts as a conductor for all the things we refuse to look at in ourselves and in our dysfunctional public culture. A trauma follows and, in the end, the party responds to the implicit general behest by changing its leader, and the whole process starts over.

This has been the drama of Irish public life for eighty-five years. We may wish for a different drama or a more effective governing narrative. But we are drawn to this one, again and again. Thus, renewal is followed by a further period of degeneration, followed by another rebirth, followed by what sometimes seems like the black swan's final career towards self-destruction. From time to time we try to kill the black swan, but always it rises again from the wreckage, because, deep down, that's the only drama that really satisfies us. The white swan cannot satisfy the darker appetites of a political culture more attracted to the playing out of its psychic dramas than to creating a functional political reality. We speak fondly, even longingly, of the white swan, but the black swan inhabits our dreams.

# 5

## *The Tyranny of Indulgence*

IN PRESENT-DAY CULTURE IT IS ALMOST IMPOSSIBLE TO OFFER A critique of certain aspects of modern living without it being assumed that you are utterly and comprehensively opposed to the phenomenon under discussion. For example, anyone who criticizes below-cost selling of alcohol is immediately assumed to be a teetotaller, and if it emerges that he enjoys a tipple at the weekends, he is instantly deemed a 'hypocrite'. This is not, in fact, accidental, but is rather a symptom of an ideological view of freedom. What is being talked about in these discussions is not really alcohol per se, but the idea that certain behaviours fall within a particular definition of 'freedom' and are prone to being questioned only by those seeking to reduce or attack this. A choice must be made between freedom and something else.

To understand what the 'something else' might be, we have to step back from our culture and study it in a wider perspective. In fact, we need to step back far enough to take in a period of nearly sixty years, enabling us to see the totality of the development of modern culture in many of its key dimensions.

If not the central element of this narrative, then certainly the source of the accompanying backbeat, was the emergence in Western society in the mid-1950s of rock 'n' roll. It began, really, with Elvis. From the very first notes of his very first songs, Elvis Presley urged the world to awake to freedom, desire, change, revolution, life. Elvis called on the world to 'Awake!' and thus called an end to the post-war period of uncertainty and weariness.

Sam Phillips, the man who recorded those first songs of Presley's in Sun Studios nearly six decades ago, said that, until Elvis walked in the door, he hadn't known what he was looking for. But he did know that it would be something not just good but unique and uniquely new, something that didn't fit, that didn't make any sense of or reflect life in America as it then was. It would be something that made everything a little bit irrelevant, something that created confusion, that didn't allow people to feel totally safe in the way they'd grown used to.

Those early Sun records were, and remain, annunciations of what sounded like the endless possibilities of personal freedom – the manifesto of a new sensibility that declined to conform to the strictures of existing authority, the rejection by the young of the infallibility of the old. When you heard them you could not fail to be alerted to the idea that everything around you was capable of being rendered completely different to the way you had been told it should be. That was, and remains, the rock 'n' roll 'proposal'.

This message dropped into a grey, monochrome reality, defined by caution and conservatism, and was therefore, in its time, an irrefutable witness to something in the human spirit that had been suppressed and subdued. Culturally speaking, it defined a generation in a way no generation had ever been defined: a generation that would take the affirmation of youth as the guiding force of its actions and perspectives. The spirit of those early moments later came to energize a whole decade, the Sixties, and particular moments within it, especially 1968 and its connotations of youth rebellion and repudiation of the political values of the time. Fundamentally, this revolution was existential rather than political: it rejected all forms of authority, from the parental to the divine, and asserted the vindication of human desire in its most immediate form as the defining ethic of the age. But it also seemed to believe that something new had been discovered about human nature: that only the distorted will-to-power of the old and disappointed stood between humanity and perfection.

Because youthful idealism had been placed at the centre of this revolutionary endeavour, it was impossible to dissent from it without immediately being identified as defending the agenda of the old guard. To question any aspect of this freedom project was immediately to reveal oneself as a 'reactionary', a counter-revolutionary who wished to restore the fallen authorities and their prescriptions. Thus, as with all revolutions, this one became blind to its own limits and contradictions; and so, when it lurched forward into excess, or failed to perceive the limits of its own expressed idealism, there was no voice from within capable of suggesting a rethink or a change of direction. In fact, as with other revolutions, one of its key achievements has been the preservation of the idea of the 'old guard' as a salutary reminder in the event of anyone whispering that the revolution had limits or was capable of mistakes.

The influence of this revolution has carried on right up to this very moment, defining the consensual ideology of mainstream Western society, including, and indeed markedly, that of Ireland. It has redefined virtue and progress in ways that have yet to be analysed – because they appear to be neutral and naturalistic elements of reality, and because the commentary is almost exclusively provided by adherents of the revolution. And here resides a remarkable irony: the cultural power of rock 'n' roll and its magpie ragbag of unpolished sentiments has been appropriated by a generation in power that once exalted youth beyond all other values, but which has itself clung to power more tenaciously than any of the generations that preceded it. This is at least as true in Ireland as it is anywhere else.

Throughout the Western world, societies are by now labouring under the ideological weight of these prescriptions that once, half a century ago, seemed the blithest, most seductive and un-exceptionable proposals for human possibility. The core 'idea' of this revolution was that the world could be rendered simple and beautiful by peace, love and understanding. The generations espousing this philosophy were not called upon to put these ideas to the test, because, being raised in the wake of World War II, they were enabled to affect contorted postures during the passive-aggression of the Cold War while being protected from the horror of actual conflict by the policy of mutual deterrence. Meantime, they had the full run of their cultures, in which they were enabled, if not encouraged, to exercise their pre-Oedipal confusion by despising their own political leaderships, their own government, even their own parents. The consequences of this are scarily out-lined in Bly's *The Sibling Society*, in its depiction of the modern generations of half-adults pounding hysterically at the chests of their fathers and calling them fascists. The new ideology is four-legs-good; that which belonged to the past is two-legs-bad.

For a generation now, the liberal ethic, which has gone hand-in-glove with this movement, has been in the ascendant, climbing into the consciousness of Western society, preaching freedom, tolerance, individualism, libertarianism and equality. Until recently, this ethic had been unchallengeable, because it flew in the face of what had been an inflexible and unyielding conservatism, the destruction of which might well be celebrated by anyone with even a few red corpuscles.

Time passed, and in due course these revolutionary ideas moved into the mainstream, where the revolutionaries soon accom-modated themselves to power. This led to freedom, certainly, but only of a certain, limited kind. And it also, just as surely, shut many Western cultures off from more fundamental understandings of what real freedom means.

Essentially, there are four generations currently implicated in the culture bequeathed us by the revolution of the 1960s. The first was what is often called the 'baby-boomer' generation, the children of the immediately post-war – or in Ireland post-Emergency – moment who, adopting the cultural values of the 1960s, gained cultural and political power from the 1970s onwards. This is the generation that initially responded to the 'Awake!' of Elvis and staked its claim in the student rebellions of 1968.

Then came my own generation, born in the 1950s, following in the slipstream of this initiative. We came to the revolution a little after its beginning and bought into most of the ideas of our predecessor generation, while remaining, generally speaking, somewhat detached. We participated but, because we were not, in the main, accorded positions of power and authority (having been too young to participate in the first waves of revolution), we remained on the sidelines, observing and cat-calling, but occasionally reflecting. I've noticed that people of my precise generation – those born between the mid-1950s and mid-1960s – tend to be misfits, people who never quite came to take the modern world at face value but nevertheless immersed themselves in it with the appearance of enthusiasm. Some among us even affected to look a little like hippies, although most of us managed also to retain our mental faculties. It is not possible to anticipate or categorize us, either in terms of attitude or positioning on the political spectrum. We confused people, because we seemed not to be one thing or the other – a little 'left', a touch of 'right', at once neither and yet a little bit of both.

What distinguished us from the older revolutionaries was that we loved the music and lived the freedom, but we also, not being centrally involved in the project, had enough time on our hands to see where it had gone off the rails. We knew about freedom, having enjoyed it as much as anyone. Yes, we loved Elvis, the Beatles, Hendrix, the Kennedys, Martin Luther King, and 'hated'

LBJ and Nixon with the same fervour as our immediate elders. But the absurdities and contradictions were not lost on us either. We noted that, although JFK had started the Vietnam war and Nixon had finished it, it was Nixon who was remembered as the villain and Kennedy the hero, and we wondered, sometimes aloud, if this wasn't because Nixon didn't have a pretty face.

Having no ideological stake in the issue, we became interested in the effects of freedom on ourselves and were less afraid than the founder revolutionaries to admit when the promise remained unfulfilled or the pain gauge had twitched ominously towards the red. We took to the revolution with at least as much zeal as our predecessors, but we did not have the same investment in its outcome. We were able to enjoy it without assuming proprietorship, and thus became observers and commentators rather than protagonists in the arenas of mechanical power.

But whereas my generation insisted on staking its claim to a public voice, the two generations that followed us – born, approximately and respectively, in the 1970s and 1990s – retreated into irony and detachment. By and large those born after the early 1960s did extremely well in the years of peace and prosperity that continued to the end of the twentieth century, but remained mainly invisible from the public sphere. Many of them were good at business and good at enjoying themselves. Occasionally, they entered politics and the media, but were never able to elbow their way to the centre of things, or set out an alternative vision of how things might be seen or done. This was partly because the key positions were already occupied by their elders, and partly because these younger generations lacked any sense of what they wanted to do in a political/cultural domain that seemed to leave little space for radical positive interventions. This created a brand of existential detachment from the social sphere that expressed itself in satire and ironic nostalgia, but which had its roots in a confused sense of genuinely youthful idealism lacking any sense of how it might express itself.

One of the key symptoms of the society created by the Sixties revolution is that attitudes, energies and activities once rightly considered the province of the young are now embraced by the middle-aged and older – sometimes by the very people against whom, in a naturally evolving social context, these attitudes, energies and activities might very properly be directed. After all, if the mainstream culture has attained the optimal expression of idealism, what is there left for the young to say about anything?

Because human idealism is by definition incapable of outright satisfaction, but is at best an energy directed at an approximate sense of good, this distortion has resulted in a culture that does not appreciate the limits of a freedom defined as the pursuit of desire in its most immediate form. This results in a blindness towards the possibility that this understanding of freedom may have its limits.

But here there is an interesting anomaly. Whereas the baby-boomer generation is fanatical in its devotion to its own concepts of freedom, subsequent generations are not. They have enjoyed the experience of this freedom, up to a point, but have been perplexed by (a) its failure to deliver outcomes fully in line with the desires of the human heart; and (b) the failure of the culture to remark on this other than by way of occasionally acknowledging that, for particular reasons, there will inevitably be casualties of any attempt to make life better for everyone. Even the death of Elvis, from a collision of uppers and downers, while sitting on his toilet, failed to alert the culture to the possibility that his 'Awake!' would have been better heard not as an absolute and final injunction but perhaps as the first in what might have become a series of steps towards a better understanding of the human journey.

Rebellion is an integral element of growing up. Young people need to have an outlet for their frustration with the world and their contempt for grown-ups. But if their parents are 'grooving' in the next marquee, how is the adolescent malcontent going to express his or her dissent? Or do we expect the new generations to become hip to the same groove that blew up their parents' skirts?

In truth and in short, the Sixties revolution, lacking a healthy dialectic, has been allowed to proceed to the point of its own logical disintegration, largely unchallenged in cultures that have come quite seriously to believe it possible to defy the very nature of man.

These general conditions have achieved a particular configuration in the Irish context, gaining exceptional traction on account of the manifest failures of the isolationist strategies of the mid-twentieth century, when Ireland sought to redefine itself in accordance with some 'authentic' resurrected notions of itself, in contradistinction to ideas imposed or imported from outside.

This backdrop has made exceptionally easy the pursuance of a revolution that, although necessary in the beginning, has long overstayed its usefulness. The post-Emergency generations, which found their raison d'être in debunking the values of their parents, have crept into power without admitting to being there. The dominant chords of public discussion still relate to opposition to some dark and troubling past that seems to threaten to return unless vigilance is maintained. Liberalism, denying that it is now the absolute ruler of all things, pursues a war against a defeated opponent, issuing from the citadels of power its daily bulletins implying that the battle has not yet been won. A phantom enemy, inspired by forces long banished or dead, is daily placed before the people, lest their anger abate and a different perspective rise up in them.

I have, for much of the past two decades, found myself belonging to this culture and yet being troubled by it. Instinctively, I find most of its ideas appealing. The people I think of as representative of the post-1960s revolution have, for most of my life, seemed to me the most interesting, entertaining, creative and fun-loving of any discrete and recognizable groups I can think of. Confronted with a choice between accepting their entire world-view and inviting a return of the greyness that preceded them, you would need to be crazy not to embrace wholeheartedly the changed world they ushered in. And yet I have been troubled, too, by the inconsistencies of their prescriptions, by their own blindness towards the flaws in their beliefs and their denial of the strengths in some of the values they have devoted themselves to sweeping away. The problem with them is not so much with the values they preach as with their absolute unwillingness to admit that human freedom did not begin in 1968.

What I describe is really a new kind of tyranny, but it is impossible, for all kinds of complex cultural reasons, to speak of things in this way with any hope of penetrating the defences this culture has devised for its self-protection. On the outside, this 'tyranny' has all the appearances of a new and previously unimagined dispensation of freedom, where individual rights and self-interest are at the centre of all consideration of the public good.

This freedom, however, is not real freedom, but a reduction based only on what man seems to desire by the evidence of his most immediate cravings. The new dispensation convinces us that it has raised us and our needs to the highest value. But the freedoms are illusory and the rights are not really rights in the strict sense, which is to say absolute entitlements by virtue of a human existence ordained from above, or below, or wherever we nowadays seek to locate our sense of a source of life and thought and everything. Rather, they are concessions, awarded under specific headings to approved recipients by a power that reserves the right to withdraw them. Thus, we become as children, siblings cast adrift at the mercy of a dispensing power that grants us freedoms not because we exist, were born, have human dignity, but because we conform to the ideological prescriptions of the 'regime'. Our freedom becomes contingent upon our willingness to trade our deeper desires and their meanings in return for the satisfaction of our more immediate ones. Our oppressors are also our benefactors, our protectors, our jailers. They purport to elevate our humanity to the highest value, but really their munificence is qualified by a pact that we must enter into on pain of being excluded from the benefits of both freedoms and rights. These new invisible masters nurture and pamper us, but only for as long as we acquiesce in their omnipotence. It is a new kind of oppression, never before imagined, in which we become the prisoners of our own instincts: our own greed, lust, thirst, hunger and fear.

The new 'regime', then, is 'enforced' by dint of the gratification of instinct and desire, an apparently painless form of dictatorship that never becomes visible for what it is. When things go wrong, as sometimes they do, it is because the natural order that has been challenged by the new dispensation begins to rebel or creak under the pressure of delivering all that is promised and demanded. But this rarely occurs, because the systems created to facilitate the smooth running of the new order have acquired for themselves an almost unlimited capacity to push any problems into the future, to be dealt with by future generations, whose freedoms are not really an issue for us now.

In truth this is, or ought to be, an utterly transparent trick. The reasons it isn't so are complex and difficult to articulate, not least because many of the logics required to deconstruct this culture have stealthily been replaced by new forms of thought which do not lend themselves to disassembling that which sustains them.

The institution of marriage, for example, intended to protect the family as the crucible of the next generation, becomes indefensible in a personal-freedoms-obsessed, rights-based culture, because it appears to 'discriminate' unfairly against certain apparently excluded categories of citizen and thus, by osmosis, appears to be the gratuitous legacy of outmoded and prejudiced thinking. Those who feel confused by this have to content themselves with scratching their heads and wondering how it was that they missed all this 'discrimination' that was practised so callously before. When, they speculate, did it cease to be axiomatic that a marriage occurred between a man and a woman and the chief point of this was the protection and nurturing of the next generation?

Such phenomena are part of the growing senselessness of our cultures, which, having eradicated from their thinking the most fundamental understandings of man's situation, are now at the mercy of arbitrary and capricious forces that seek to mould reality anew behind our backs. This imposed senselessness has been a constant theme of my good friend Desmond Fennell, one of Ireland's greatest essayists and perhaps our only truly modern philosopher, who attributes it to the loss to Irish society of the sense-making framework previously provided by what he terms 'European civilization'.

In an extended email correspondence between us, he outlined the basis of his observations of this destruction of sense:

My working term for a satisfactory framework for human existence is a 'civilization'. Essentially, as history shows, that is a distinctive, hierarchical set of accepted rules, which lasts a long time because it makes sense to its adherents, and therefore motivates them to keep reproducing themselves and it.

European (alias Western) civilization took shape after the year 1000 and lasted almost a thousand years. A chief rule of that civilization, as of all known civilizations, was 'The community must honour, and seek the aid of, the supernatural Power/Powers.' The Western community accepted and did this at least formally –

in Ireland very intensely – until the decades after World War II.

However, that rule implemented on its own would obviously not suffice to give sense to life. It can only *help* to do this in conjunction with, and as chief element of, a *hierarchy of rules covering all of life* – international and interpersonal rules, rules of reproduction, political rules, artistic rules, economic rules, etc. To construct and apply the particular hierarchy of rules that makes sense to a particular historical community is to make a civilization i.e. a sense-providing framework for life.

Western civilization gave sense to life for a long time for Europeans, in Europe and overseas. With the abandonment and capricious replacement of many of its core rules – including the rule about relations with the supernatural – life in the West, Ireland included, has lost sense, and instead of presenting sense presents senselessness – an affront to the rational and sentient human being. This has dire effects on people of all ages, but especially on the most sensitive of the (naturally life-probing and life-assessing) young. Only a new civilization can redeem the situation.

For a post-European rules system to enduringly replace that of European civilization, it would need to make lasting sense to the great majority of westerners, as the European rules system had for many centuries so evidently done. In other words, it would need to offer a new civilization. But the production and presentation of civilization-creating sense is the fruit of creative interaction, employing all the human faculties, between a people's rulers and ruled over a considerable period. The post-European collection of rules – new ones combined with some old – that by the 1990s had come to hold sway in the West did not and could not make sense to the human collective, white westerners in the first place, on whom it was imposed. Thrown together by a late-European ideological sect and its supporting governments, to promote justice, virtue, consumption and power, its sponsors had treated overall sense as superfluous.

In practical political terms, I believe, the senselessness so perceptively described by Desmond Fennell arises as the consequence of a pincer-movement involving the operation of vested interests on two distinct but inter-working kinds of folly. On the one hand is the folly of the managerial political class, which implements the will of assiduously campaigning ideologues behind the backs of the allegedly democratic entities over which they preside. On the other hand is the moronic cacophony emanating from the lower tiers of public opinion, orchestrated by shit-stirring commentariats that contrive to elide the accumulating absurdities in order to provoke a lucrative dissension in which one element of society is pitted against another.

Sometimes it seems that what began as a youthful desire to destabilize intolerance, rigidity and hypocrisy has, by virtue perhaps of its immunity to the interrogation of age, drifted away from any kind of moorings in wisdom or common sense. The liberal ethic, having fulfilled its mission, has failed to self-collapse, and so it runs virulently on, like a genetically modified weed. And since it is refusing to self-collapse, it is inevitable that it will seek to collapse, instead, the norms of societies in which it now lingers like a virus.

It is difficult if not impossible now to combat by argument anything that seems to offer unconditional freedom and easy to dismiss as obsolescent anything that seeks to summon humanity to a higher sense of what fulfils it. People tend to support that which promises them the most, soonest. Thus, 'debate' on such matters is invariably governed by the phenomenon of foregone conclusion. The promise of imminent freedom, however superficial, will always win out over a call to patriotism or long-haul endeavour. While things are going well, the merits and virtues of the programme are self-evident, and even when things begin to slide, the capacity of the regime to control the scope of the discussion ensures that fundamentals never get too closely looked at in a way that might draw attention to any possible line of causation that implicates the dominant version of freedom in the mess that has ensued.

In this process, the younger generations have been reduced to the status of beneficiaries, onlookers and sideline commentators. Their actual involvement in running things is minimal. In the Celtic Tiger years, for example, the younger Irish generations, those born after, say, the Pope's visit of 1979, did not, when they came of age in the new millennium, achieve any visibility in Irish society in the way that, for example, my own generation had begun to do some twenty years before. They went to college, had jobs and social lives, but they did not, culturally speaking, seek to express themselves in any recognizably coherent way until the meltdown of the Irish economy in 2008. And then, the principal tones they emitted were disgruntlement, rage, lamentation and, above all, cynicism.

It is customary, in this context, for the older generations to condemn the young, but I would like to proffer a different analysis. It seems to me that, although cynicism is now the dominant note of youth in Irish society, this does not accurately reflect the sensibilities of these younger generations. Rather, I believe it is the outcome of a process of cultural imposition, whereby young people, having been offered pampering instead of participation, have in effect been constructively excluded from engagement with their society.

Often, when you look really closely at what passes for democratic discourse in Irish society, you begin to suspect that what calls itself a commitment to diversity of opinion can actually be the orchestration of a narrow consensus combined with a reluctant agreement to facilitate what are regarded as cranks and crackpots in the belief that the ostentatious toleration of error will validate the correctness of the consensus and help to let off any problematic steam.

Underneath the surface tensions and antagonisms of media debate concerning social and political issues in Ireland, things are rarely as they seem. For a long time, Irish journalism has seen its primary role not as the unearthing of facts or the facilitation of open discussion, but the instigation and pursuit of a particular model of social change, with the facts providing a kind of scaffolding in the construction of a new Ireland. On the surface, debates about nationalism, abortion, unmarried mothers or whatever appear to be authentic confrontations between opposing opinions, with the media operators as neutral conduits and facilitators. In fact, these discussions are mostly staged debates between those whose views are manifestly 'correct' and those who are obviously 'wrong'. The purpose is not to ventilate whatever issue is under discussion, so as perhaps to enable the public to make up its mind, but rather to dramatize the confrontation between 'truth' and 'error' so that the public will become even more convinced of the 'truth'. To this end, it is vital that those participating in public debate to defend what is manifestly 'incorrect' must enter into a tacit agreement with their media hosts. This agreement incorporates a number of unstated but implicit conditions, viz.: Thou shalt defend the indefensible (for example, clerical child abuse) by dint of dissembling or prevarication; thou shalt wear strange, old-fashioned clothing, whereby to signal an out-of-touchness with modern society; thou shalt become incoherent with rage in the course of the programme; and so forth.

It is not difficult to see why educated, intelligent younger people might not wish to have any truck with such charades, which appear to miss almost everything about everything. So, instead of seeking to become involved, the young have gravitated to the sidelines, where they stand whistling and jeering, which funnily enough is the response that the 'regime' seems to have been hoping to provoke in them.

154

One of the exceptions to the general exclusion of these generations from public debate was a younger colleague with another newspaper who at the height of the Tiger years wrote an intriguing article about the failure of the Irish media to create new forms of debate with which to propel Irish society in a different direction. 'The comment pages', he wrote, 'have become places where the consensus – economically liberal, politically revisionist – is almost entirely unchallenged. Even when it is challenged, as by John Waters, the result is rhetoric less postmodern than antediluvian.'

This contribution was fascinating on a number of counts. One, most immediately, was for its proposition that any new perspectives on Irish society must perforce be 'postmodern' ones. And since no definition of 'postmodern' was offered, the immediate suspicion was that the word was being used precisely because it has no clear meaning. The frustration being expressed was not on account of certain adumbrated perspectives being missing from public discussion but because there seemed to be no way of engaging with public issues without seeming uncool. Indeed, when I wrote about this in a previous book, *Lapsed Agnostic*, and was subsequently interviewed on the *Ryan Tubridy Show* on RTÉ Radio One, he referred to the book's preoccupation with religious questions and asked: 'Do you not worry about being uncool?'

This position is commonplace among younger people now, including many who have achieved positions from which they could speak if they could think of something suitable to say. Many young people are bored and discontented with much public discussion, but are not quite sure what options there might be. Most appear oblivious that they have absorbed as axiomatic, and broadly accepted, the model of modernization with which they have been presented, and are encountering an imaginative blockage as to what should happen next. They do not want to go back, but cannot conceive a space into which to move forward. They search desultorily for some 'postmodern' way of responding to reality, but nobody is really sure what this might mean. The result is that they are immobilized by a studied languor that has often seemed like it could become a lifelong disposition.

This demeanour and outlook depends for its sustainability on the existence of certain conditions. Firstly, of course, it depends on the continuance of peace and prosperity, so that nothing arises to subject the pose to a sudden jolt. Secondly, it assumes that the running of things will all the time be taken care of by others, enabling the languid one to frown amusedly, raise an occasional ironic eyebrow, emit the odd snort of derision, but otherwise not be required to hazard an involvement in events or discussions by saying yes or no, left or right, old or new, black or white.

In a sense it is to be anticipated that young people will not wish to be seen to be on the side of the past. It is among the functions of the young to wish to tear everything down and start again, to proffer a new analysis that rubbishes the prescriptions of their parents and announces a new dispensation for the coming generation. The problem is that this natural cycle has been frustrated in Irish society and elsewhere by virtue of the refusal of the post-1960s generations to yield power and allow the younger generations to take over at the wheel. This refusal is largely invisible, being cleverly concealed behind the incessant pretence of celebrating youth culture, but if you look closely you will see that the indulgence of youth is a trade-off in exchange for a process of cultural set-aside. It is as if the older generations are now saying: 'As the ordained prophets of youth culture, we can be assumed to understand youth so well that we do not need to consult the actually existing young about their wishes or understandings. We already know what they must think.'

The actually existing young, for their part, do not know what to say in response. Something about it does not seem quite right, but they have no way of responding that will not make it seem that they are reactionaries in the guise of youth, or 'young fogeys' as the ideology-shielding phrase would have it. Thus, they rack their brains for some 'postmodern' way of responding, but nothing comes.

And then there is the drink. Going around Irish cities and towns, especially at certain times – like after dark, at weekends, on the occasion of festivals or rock concerts – it is impossible these days to avoid noticing that something that used to be mythological about Irish people has now become true. I have in mind our reputation for drinking alcohol, a worldwide legend which for generations was perhaps undeserved on account of the fact that it was mainly our expats out there in the wider world who were drinking enough to keep both themselves and the folks back home in the world record books. This drinking had its roots in alien-ation, a protection against the forced adoption of a new culture and society. Now we've brought it all back home, and increasingly it becomes impossible to ignore the evidence of the alienation of the younger generations of Irish citizens from Ireland rich or poor.

In September 2010, for example, I was invited to the Electric Picnic festival in Stradbally, County Laois, to read from my books at one of the many sideshows they have there alongside the main diet of music. The Picnic is a different take on the traditional rock festival, combining the usual ingredients of rock 'n' roll, tents and mud with poetry, theatre, polemics and strange interventions of various kinds.

I was involved in two quite different events. One was a straight-forward reading from my books about God and reason between songs sung by a friend of mine, Johnny Duhan, former lead singer with Limerick band Granny's Intentions. We called ourselves The Prodigals and were toying with the idea of going on the road for a couple of months to check out the response to a combination of music and readings from some of my 'religious' writing. Somewhat ironically, I had also been engaged to deliver a ten-minute speech on 'hedonism' as part of an event called 'Chaos Thaoghaire', as in 'Dun Laoghaire'.

The hedonism gig was first and went great. I wasn't so sure what I was supposed to be doing until I ran into the legendary B.P. Fallon, aka 'The Beep', and asked him what *he* was doing.

'Some verbals,' he replied. Ah!

By way of dodging the hedonism issue, I embarked upon what The Beep would have called a 'rap' about missing most of my hedonistic past because I was drunk at the time. It went down a bomb, and then I moved two tents up the line to do some verbals about God.

It was then I began to think that the Electric Picnic was probably a better idea in theory than in practice. I noticed at both of my gigs that people were drifting in, lazily surveying what was happening and drifting out again. One moment the tent would be full, and then you might look down to read a passage, look up again and find it half empty. I might have developed a complex about this had I not observed the same pattern at other performances, even the musical ones. (There is an interesting comparison to be made between this tendency and the way people pursue information via the internet: they browse and graze, skipping from one link to another and reading until their attention is again shorted out by another distraction.)

One factor undoubtedly was that there was so much happening at any moment that everyone was going around thinking they were missing something. But then I began to sit and watch.

For nostalgic reasons, I wandered into the *Hot Press* tent and listened to some live interviews with various artists. There were some interesting-looking acts drifting in and out, but in the interviews they seemed to be talking about everything that didn't matter – touring, recording, drinking, sex. I wondered if it was self-consciousness, but then it struck me: everyone was so intimidated by people drifting in and out that nobody had the bottle to go deeper. A fear of – literally – losing the audience was causing everyone to stay on the surface of things.

Gradually I felt this build-up of distraction and dissatisfaction, and finally it dawned on me that this overall feeling of dissatisfaction was the Electric Picnic's most striking feature. It offered a little of everything, but nothing seemed able – or was permitted – to penetrate beyond a certain limited depth.

And, as the day wore on, I was deeply struck by the hordes of young people – in their twenties and thirties – who seemed to constitute the majority of the audience: beautiful and friendly and gentle and full of a stunted enthusiasm.

But I couldn't help noticing that most of those I met after a certain hour in this field littered with plastic beer-tumblers were completely blasted. I had recently had the opportunity to observe people of a similar age profile attending a broadly not dissimilar event in Italy. There was drink available there also, but nobody I encountered was either drunk or drinking. And, beyond that superficial observation, what distinguished that event from this was that the young Italians seemed to be able to find total satisfaction in delving into the content of what they were experiencing, of remaining in touch with the nature of their own desires and seeking to push them farther. The young Irish at Electric Picnic were in a place where they had been led to believe they might find what they were searching for, but they could not find it. And so they were guzzling soul-poison in the hope of locating it. Or perhaps, wandering into a fog of inebriation, they imagined themselves to be already where they desired to be.

The culmination of Saturday was the appearance, for the first time in two years, of an interesting Irish band of the previous couple of decades, The Frames, preparing to celebrate their twentieth birthday and still looking like they might be The Next

Big Thing. This highlight was also, in another sense, the lowlight of my Electric Picnic. While The Frames played, I was aware of the effects all around me of a reckless if good-humoured drunkenness. As the gig climaxed, a young woman collapsed beside me and her friends bundled her up and carried her away. And Glen Hansard sang: 'I want my life to make more sense/I want my life to make amends/I want my life to make more sense to me.'

I wrote about this in *The Irish Times*; my observations were not intended to be moralistic. They were, rather, a kind of lament for the loss of much of my own youth to a culture in which alcohol is offered as a substitute for experience, and a lament for the new generations being offered the same raw deal. It wasn't the furthest thing from my mind – it never is as I survey the blighted landscape of 'modern' Ireland – that I had a child of my own now, who had just crossed the threshold into her teens.

The audience at Electric Picnic was, by and large, a generation of young people who have on the surface of things received everything, but really have been deprived of the most essential ingredient of all: a comprehensible map of the greater meanings of things. I could see that our 'pop kids', as we would ironically call ourselves back in my own *Hot Press* days, were lost in a sense of pessimism and confusion that was already beginning to destroy them. The music, poetry, politics etc were just convenient alibis to enable the young people to imagine that they were engaging in some form of cultural and/or intellectual activity, when really they were engaging only with the experience of getting pissed. There was plenty of material to engage with, but very few people were getting to it, and most of those who were trying to do so were becoming frustrated because the entire event was constructed around the superficial demands of those drifting from one happening to another with plastic tumblers in their hands. The only penetration being achieved was of the buzz provided by the alcohol. The rest was just an elaborate backdrop.

There is an unwritten rule of Irish culture that you should not query people 'enjoying' themselves, on pain of being labelled a 'killjoy'. In the context of alcohol, this has become a capital crime, because it is taken as self-evident that the function of alcohol is as an enhancement of enjoyment. We see someone with glass in hand and do not think: 'drug'. We observe the outward symptoms of intoxication and take it for happiness. It is an easy mistake to make, especially if you have vested interests in making it. But the joy achieved through chemical assistance is not real, or has already been killed before the first sip. The curiosity, appetite, desire has already been short-circuited into a condition that takes on the characteristics of experience but is actually its antithesis. We construct elaborate pretexts and alibis to conceal this from ourselves, and most of the time manage to fool ourselves. It is only when we go elsewhere and watch how other people live that we have the opportunity to reflect on how different and strange our culture actually is. And this is the culture which our children grow up to inherit, assuming it to be natural and unalterable. And so they blunder along the same blind alleyways we staggered down ourselves. If we half close our eyelids, we can imagine that they are 'enjoying' themselves, but in our hearts we know that they are plunging into a bottomless pit of empty promise and missing everything worth catching.

Because our era seems to value youth above all other character-istics, it has become difficult to insert into public discussion anything that seems to run against the youthful desire for total freedom in all things, or even to issue a challenge to young people to look again at what they have taken for granted. To outline, for example, the possible risks of an imbalance between freedom and responsibility immediately identifies itself as a reactionary response. To speak about the past is to set oneself up for a satirical impersonation. To warn about the self-murder involved in consuming drugs of any kind, is to be dismissed as an old fogey killjoy.

All this is deeply convenient to the 'regime'. The media, which act as the conduit of our discussions, have become dominated by a view that seeks in all things to pander to what is perceived to be the natural position of the young, but which is really an *interpretation* of such a position arrived at by people who are actually close to retirement. It is based on their memory of being young, but in a different time, with different conditions and needs. Meanwhile, the actually existing young have been culturally disabled, by drugs and other distractions, waylaid into forms of self-expression that enable their energies to be subjected to controlled explosions before they can come to represent a threat to the regime.

Those who should be mentoring the young and inducting them into a responsible engagement with their own futures are perfectly happy to see them fritter their idealism and wonder in a vacuous dance with meaninglessness.

The problem with much of the kind of progress that is so loudly and pervasively celebrated in Irish society is that it has occurred without a great deal of thought being applied to the complexities which such change inevitably brings. We have not developed, or been permitted to develop, a language in which to cultivate true ideas about our desires.

Even to question some new proposal with a view to seeing if its sponsors have thought it through has this effect. 'Are you with us or against us?' they demand, and the embarrassed questioner falls silent. The result is that those who speak out on any subject, apart from those advocating what has already been 'agreed', are contributors who, because their perspectives are readily recognizable as 'reactionary' or 'nostalgic', are easily disposed of. It is rarely possible to open a debate up in a new way, and so the regime's intimation of a conflict in which there are only virtuous progressives and reactionary traditionalists is validated and consolidated.

There has been no emergence of a language of critiquing change that is non-ideological: i.e. not instantly recognizable as emanating from the logic of either modernization or traditionalism, but simply representing the commonsensical outlook of people who do what sensible people always do: investigate the implications and likely consequences of every new proposal with a view to judging its efficacy and benefits. This, really, is what is meant by those who seek some 'postmodern' way of looking at things. They want to speak about the future without being condemned as reactionaries before they get halfway into their second sentences. The problem is that there is no 'postmodern' way of creating a dialectic out of which a society might contrive to move forward. The process tends to follow a pattern that has existed since men and women first engaged in community with others of their species: each new proposal is vetted against the old, its merits assessed both on what benefits it is likely to bring and on what it will cause to be lost. The old way is not thrown out until the new way has sufficiently proved itself, and even then its benefits are venerated and remembered in case a change of circumstances might require a return to the former approach.

'Change' has been one of the most over- and misused words in the lexicon of the Ireland of recent decades. For more than half of my lifetime we seem to have been subjected to almost continuing reminders of how much Ireland has changed since that or then – since 1950, since the coming of Seán Lemass, since the first woman president was elected, since Bishop Eamonn Casey packed his bags and headed for the airport. Invariably, the implication is that change can only be for the better. The very idea of it has been attributed a moral quality of and for itself, which makes it impossible to challenge any more any initiative that is not self-evidently a step backwards. But one of the things that can surely be said without controversy is that the present state of Ireland reflects the consequences of at least some changes that were not well advised. What these might be may well be debatable, but surely we should at least be entitled to consider the possibility that some of the prescriptions in which we have placed our faith have let us down.

Many young people, and some who are not so young, nowadays contemplate the drift of Irish society and, although disaffected with what they see, cannot put a finger on what the problem is. Thus they decide that the root of some failure resides in what – or whom – they are told is the issue, or they choose to see it purely in so far as it affects their own lives. The idea of discussing matters in terms of their value or implications for 'Ireland', as our parents and grandparents did as a matter of course, has become alien. 'Ireland' is now simply the entity that enables – to the extent that it does – a material existence to be maintained, and loyalty to this entity is almost invariably of a pragmatic or sentimental essence.

This was less of an issue in the years of apparently endless prosperity, when the most the young seemed to have to worry about was obtaining an income and getting on the property ladder. Now, however, with the Irish economy in ruins, they sense that something fundamental must be wrong but they have no means of formulating an analysis of why things are so.

Many young people have accepted at face value the rhetoric of the present generation in power, which holds that the journey that started out in the 1960s is the One True Journey, the only possible route towards enlightenment and contentment. You would have expected that, in the wake of the economic meltdown of 2008, a radical reassessment of this project would have been put in train, but in the main the discussion has focused on the blaming of individuals caught with the most traces of spoil on their snouts. In the ensuing clamour, the voices of the post-1970s generations have been heard, for the first time, but their contributions have in large part comprised splenetic condemnation delivered in blog, tweet and similar postings, satirical denunciations in comedy routines and pure rage vented on radio phone-ins. Far from questioning the edifice of ideology which has delivered us to this moment, they have joined in with the analysis of the 'regime', pointing fingers at the most immediate scapegoats and avoiding any attempt to probe the deeper nature of the malaise.

In the four years since 2008, the drama of a society divided between those who have allegedly created our economic difficulties and those who allegedly innocently suffer the consequences has been staged daily by a media presenting itself as on the side of the 'victims'. This storyline can be heard most clearly in the listener texts read out ad nauseam by radio presenters. These texts are an important revenue stream for most radio stations, which may partly explain why terse and ill-tempered communications are treated as a profound expression of the will of the people. For 30 cent, 'Tommy from Tullamore' and 'Ciara from Clara' can bask in the tacit approval of a media tribunal represented by a presenter who seems never to reflect on the contentlessness of what he or she is reading.

As predictable as they are banal, these texts simply affirm and consolidate some populist intuition concerning the outrage we are all supposed to feel about 'Them'. If a guest on a programme is one of 'Them' or seeks to make a point that does not join in the generalized excoriation of 'Them', he or she is subjected to a barrage of texted accusations of being 'part of the cosy consensus'. The texter is always 'outraged', 'appalled' or 'gobsmacked', or simply wants to 'throw up'. If, on the other hand, the guest has harmonized with 'public outrage', the texts will be approving. 'Fair play to so 'n' so,' they will applaud, 'for speaking up for us.' The worst crime is to be 'out of touch with the man-in-the-street'. The difficulty is that the 'man-in the-street' is a creation of those who preside over the discussion. Before he picks up his phone to call or text the programme, he has already been told what to think. He has been addressed in the terms of one of his most heartfelt grievances and his response is as predictable as the dawn. He speaks or texts as though to a script, but with a moral authority from his man-in-the-streetness that cannot be questioned and brooks no dissent.

On a number of radio programmes in recent years, I've been intrigued to observe that radio presenters think these communications are a weathervane of public opinion. Of course, they represent merely the regurgitation of a repetitive sense of grievance emanating from people with time on their hands and nothing interesting to say for themselves.

This trend has at least four worrying elements. Firstly, it reduces the public narrative to opposition between the 'guilty' and the 'innocent'. Secondly, it grounds the common discourse in concepts of blame and punishment. Thirdly, it allows the media to hide behind a bogus notion of 'public opinion' to pursue agendas which may be to the long-term detriment of Irish society. Fourthly, it enables the continued avoidance of the idea that the Celtic Tiger was the consequence of a collective psychology, of which the media was the principal driving element.

Back in 1955, the year I was born and Sam Phillips recorded those first tracks with Elvis, if you had been reflecting on the promises offered by the coming age of mass media, you might well have predicted that this development would render us freer to speak of what mattered in our lives. You would certainly not have foreseen what has actually happened: that, instead of opening up our societies to greater possibilities to exchange our innermost thoughts and feelings, what seems to have occurred is that the power of the media operates in the opposite direction. Instead of asking us what we feel, media instruct us on what to think. Instead of inviting us to share our deepest thoughts and hopes, media provide us with a menu of approved options and ask us to tick the box marked, for example, 'progress' or the one marked 'retreat'. Many of the feelings that we think are worth sharing are unwanted or unapproved within this discussion, and so are driven back where they came from by a studied rallying of orthodoxy and neo-moralism.

As we go along, the human heart hears less and less to nurture it, but only things that confirm it in its darker aspects, its tendency itself to nurture, along with hope and love, some darker sentiments, like pessimism, fear, hatred and rage. But more and more, these are the entities which draw us into a conversation that exists for the purposes of keeping us doubtful, fearful, hateful and enraged – contriving, with a daring that smacks of genius, to sell us these implanted emotions of ours as a spontaneous eruption of popular sentiment, recycled again and again as the core discourse of democracy.

## 6

## *The Ear of a Dog*

IN MARCH 2009, AS THE FULL PICTURE OF IRELAND'S HORROR WAS settling in public focus, a terrific public controversy erupted when two paintings of the then Taoiseach Brian Cowen, one a nude, the other depicting Cowen wearing Y-fronts, were surreptitiously hung in two prominent Dublin art galleries, the nude in the National Gallery in Dublin and the not-quite-nude in the Royal Hibernian Academy. The matter might have gone unnoticed had not the national broadcaster, RTÉ, carried a report which was the subject of an immediate complaint from the government, precipitating an apology from the broadcaster for any personal offence caused to Mr Cowen or his family and for any disrespect shown to the office of the Taoiseach.

The episode was variously described as 'guerrilla art', 'satire', 'political art', a 'prank', a 'joke', a 'stunt' and a 'statement' on the state of the economy and the performance of Fianna Fáil-led governments in the previous twelve-year period. Fine Gael, then the main opposition party, issued an enthusiastic statement declaring that the affair was 'more reminiscent of Russia in the 1930s than Ireland in 2009'.

The artist, a teacher in his thirties from County Mayo, said that he wanted to let the paintings 'speak for themselves'.

The public square today is often ignorant or unfair, but sometimes the best thing to do or say is do and say nothing. Let it pass. Rise above it all. Trust the thinking public's capacity to read the subtexts. Behind the newer façade insinuated in the media, there remains another Ireland: unhip, unmanipulated, ignored, but still present and watching everything with the same odd mixture of engagement and ironic detachment I remember from listening nearly half a century ago to my father talking to his friends. I often notice this when I'm caught up in some public controversy and begin to think that, because of expressing some unapproved opinion, I have become a pariah. I walk about the place with my head down, or with my mobile phone glued to my ear. But then, gradually, I realize – yet again – that I am over-reacting to a media misrepresentation of reality. The 'real' Irish people are still as present as they ever were: observing what is happening to their own country but remaining largely wide to it all.

Behind the shell of received opinions adopted from the media-generated conversations, the Irish public remains shrewd and sensible enough. Often, when you tune into the kinds of discussions that occur in bars and trains, you realize that people have taken the public record as their starting point and interpreted events according to a deeper sense of human character and behaviour. They speculate about things, and in doing so often give credit for grace and silence. Life is both trial and drama, but not to be treated in the manner of a budget speech. A tweet is something a bird emits.

Brian Cowen must once have understood this. Perhaps he still did. But perhaps after being pummelled continuously for nearly a year by an orchestrated discourse that presented him in an unrelentingly bad light, he simply decided that enough was enough.

He had not been known as thin-skinned. A few years before, when he was foreign affairs minister, the Reverend Ian Paisley had made some ugly and decidedly unChristian remarks about

Cowen's personal appearance, and Cowen, though he must have been gravely hurt by such an unprecedentedly personalized attack, shrugged it off and carried on with his work as foreign affairs minister, in which he was required to have frequent contact with Paisley and his party. As a result, the public mood came down entirely on Cowen's side, even though, by that time, the historical sense of Paisley as the Devil's brother had all but dissipated and he was well on the way to becoming a cuddly icon of Irish life – south of the border almost as much as in certain pockets of the North.

The Paisley episode was perhaps one of the most important in Cowen's ascent to the Taoiseach's office, conveying to the public imagination some sense of the steel and resilience in his character. Here seemed to be a politician who did not allow personal abuse to get in the way of public duty, and who had it in him to reach out his hand to someone who had subjected him to a cruel and utterly unjustifiable personal attack.

The old Cowen might well have shrugged those paintings off. Regardless of their crudity and general awfulness, and irrespective of the inappropriateness of RTÉ's handling of the matter, there remained the matter of proportionate and prudent response. The attack was indeed personal and poisonous: Cowen had every reason to take legitimate offence. And, contrary to the predictable interventions by mischievous agents who had never been required to exercise major public responsibilities, the issue had little to do with any lack of a sense of humour. The paintings were offensive, vindictive and lacking in any great artistic merit. They would never have been heard of had RTÉ not misplaced its editorial instincts and, faced with choosing between soberly reporting a minor crime and colluding in a thoughtless exercise in humiliating the Taoiseach, chose the latter. There was no joke here, as such, merely an exercise in schoolboy toilet humour given undue credence by poor editorial judgement at the national broadcaster.

The handbook of sage political counsel, which the old Brian

Cowen would hardly have needed to consult, advised, 'Say nothing.' But the old Brian Cowen was by now nowhere to be found. Thus, rather than being seen for the cheap stunt it was, the paintings episode came to colour even further a public discourse which had Cowen down as someone who just couldn't handle himself, and raised further questions about the temperament and emotional equilibrium of his administration, and its shrewdness in dealing with the continuing public narrative, dominated by rage, recrimination and a lust for scapegoats. On show here were both an oversensitivity to personal affront and a worrying lack of political savvy.

It was reasonable that some form of protest be made to those in RTÉ with editorial responsibility for the paintings item. But it was not prudent that the protest was made to the director general, which made the intervention seem high-handed and intimidatory. Government sources later stressed that no apology was sought, but everyone knew that, in certain circumstances, when a complaint is made in emphatic terms by certain forms of authority to certain other forms of authority, an apology will follow willy-nilly. Journalists have long been familiar with this syndrome of managerial mind-reading, which from the outside can be indistinguishable from spinelessness.

All the government had to do was wait and allow the subtext of the RTÉ report to seep into the public consciousness. All Brian Cowen had to do was look plucky and wry, perhaps issue a throwaway remark to reporters about getting to work on his washboard stomach. Reading, as usual, the deeper level of the narrative, the public would have been laughing with him and the prankster would have looked like a plonker with a potty fetish. But Cowen lost both ways: he suffered the brunt of the ridicule and then became the subject of anger and further ridicule because he couldn't take it, couldn't see 'the joke'.

Immediately, there were those who sought to defend the paintings on the basis of their allegedly humorous content. On his morning radio show, Pat Kenny implied that RTÉ should not have apologized for reporting the story as it did. If someone produced a similar portrait of himself, he said, he would buy it and hang it in his toilet, so that visitors there could get 'a bit of a laugh'. The difference between himself and Brian Cowen, he asserted, was that he, Pat Kenny, had 'a sense of humour'.

In fact, there were differences apart from this. One was that Brian Cowen was Taoiseach and Pat Kenny was not. Another was that the paintings had not been hung in the toilet of a private house, but illegally placed in two prestigious galleries in the centre of Dublin.

There were multiple layers of meaning to this episode. On the one hand, an intrinsically harmless prank was elevated into a national controversy by RTÉ's decision to report the matter on the main evening news, magnifying something that might otherwise have remained underground. On the other, the saga showed in striking fashion the inability of modern politicians to deal with the form public responses to politics are increasingly taking. The paintings were fairly typical of a public discourse by then grievously degraded by internet-driven cynicism and an obsession with 'humour'. They sought to dress up a crude and contentless statement as something meaningful and intelligent just because it was 'funny'. It was all very much of a piece with a lot of the commentary emanating from young and youngish contributors to public discussion in the explosion of public rage and grief that followed the sudden departure of the Celtic Tiger, shortly after Brian Cowen's arrival to the office of Taoiseach in 2008. For these reasons, it tells us many things about how the public sees and thinks about politicians, and how the politicians are being affected by these responses.

Pat Kenny's reaction was interesting for the way it gave expression to what is a persistent theme of public discussion in

Ireland nowadays: if something is deemed to be 'funny', it acquires a degree of untouchability suggestive of an elevated form of morality. Public figures now need to convey, above all other messages, that they have a 'sense of humour' – even when something isn't funny.

There is, of course, an honourable tradition of political satire in Ireland as much as in other free societies. Writing about the Cowen paintings, I found that, yet again, I received a few genuinely irate communications from a few disgruntled blueshirts complaining about the treatment of the 1973–77 Cosgrave coalition by *Hall's Pictorial Weekly*, a hugely popular television show of the time. 'Where were you then?' one correspondent demanded to know. I responded that I had been working in a railway goods store in the West.

The difference is to be located in both the content and the intent. Frank Hall, like the great satirists anywhere – from Charlie Chaplin to Rory Bremner – went for the ball, not the man. Their purpose was to lampoon the political deeds and words of those elected to lead, not to assault the humanity of the person occupying a public office. If this sounds today like a platitudinous distinction, it is nonetheless a necessary one. Without political content, mockery is just gratuitous derision. Satire is not the same thing as scorn. A politician is accountable to the public for what he does or says, not for his weight, shape or size. A cartoon or burlesque can, of course, include personal elements, but there remains a difference: the emotions of the public are engaged against the object using some tic or idiosyncrasy of the individual being satirized, but the sting is part of a statement that is of its essence political. Cartoonists like the great Gerald Scarfe, for example, operate in a long tradition of exaggerating physical characteristics of politicians in order to point up some resonance with the deeper character of the public figure. The Cowen paintings were devoid of any such quality or intention, but were intended merely to ridicule Brian Cowen by engaging in a graphic public speculation as to what his naked body might look like.

After oxygen, water and food, laughter may indeed be among the most vital ingredients of a healthy life. A joke is the means by which, in the collective dimension, we conduct or participate in managed releases of our darker individual thoughts. A good joke brings together the incongruous and the culturally subversive, creating a resonance with that secret impulse, offering permission to laugh at something that, deep down, we always felt, knew, wondered about, but didn't feel permitted to articulate. A joke tells us, perhaps more immediately than any other form of communication, that we are not alone in our fearful and irreverent thoughts. And so, even the offence intrinsic to much humour can offer a release from the loneliness of individual impiety, relieving an otherwise total subjugation by the culture of collective insincerity.

On the other hand, laughter can be corrosive and destructive. In his book about the British media, *What the Media Are Doing to Our Politics*, John Lloyd cited David Steel, the former leader of the British Liberal Party, in his belief that his portrayal in the *Spitting Image* sketches of the 1980s destroyed the chances of the then alliance between his party and the Social Democrats replacing the Labour Party as the main party of opposition. *Spitting Image* invariably showed Steel as the fawning lapdog of SDP leader David Owen. Elaborating on the power of such crude stereotypes, Lloyd (a namesake of the producer of *Spitting Image*) wrote:

Once again, choices made by electors were being very substantially altered by media; and because of the nature of the culture which assumed a right to intrude ever more decisively into what had been forbidden territory, not only was nothing being done about it, no

174

serious questions were even being asked about it. Politicians became, in a variety of ways, more and more scorned and could barely object. The media would not allow it, it had been defined as a joke, millions of people liked it (they did) and thus its effects – whatever they are – cannot sensibly be discussed.

There is obviously a place for humour in democratic life, but perhaps, such is the sensitivity of the democratic edifice, there is a requirement that it be gentle, affected, even lame. A joke is a powerful thing, sometimes more powerful than a bomb. More than in other contexts, the joke cast at democracy or its institutions must be aimed with an awareness of what is at stake. Humour also has limits that are not often acknowledged by those who promote the quasi-moralistic value of laughter. The modern predilection for jokes, as the French writer Michel Houellebecq put it, is really evidence of an avoidance of more challenging forms of engagement: 'What is humour after all,' he asked in one of his published letters to the philosopher Bernard-Henri Lévy (*Public Enemies*, 2011), 'but shame at having felt a genuine emotion? It's a sort of tour de force, a slave's elegant pirouette when faced with a situation that under normal circumstances would evoke despair or rage. So, yes, it's hardly surprising that humour is these days rated very highly.'

It has also become fashionable for young people in modern democracies to imagine themselves the victims of malign dictatorships, which deserve in answer only ridicule and contempt. This largely inculcated response interestingly follows on the pattern laid down by the student rebellions of 1968: it is as though our cultures continuously seek to recreate that moment for its frisson of safe, comfortable dissent.

But there is a price to be paid. In his novel *The Joke*, Milan Kundera wrote that the tragedy of man is that, caught in the trap of the joke, he is deprived of the right to tragedy. This is a succinct summary of the condition of the modern politician. He cannot be taken seriously because every attempt at gravity becomes the occasion of laughter. In a culture of us-and-them, this can feel fine, but what it forgets is that the politician is not a dictator, but, in theory at least, the representative of those who line up opposite, laughing their heads off. The joke undermines the pretensions of the powerful and egotistical, but it also removes from the joker any possibility of an impact other than the achievement of a mutual alienation. A joke, unlike an accusation or a challenge, cannot be answered. It is like a full stop on communication, terminating the exchange in a mutuality of sullenness and self-righteousness.

What is at stake, then, is not something that belongs only to the target: it belongs to the joker as well, and so, the more 'successfully' he hits the target, the more damage he does to the life he has himself come to take for granted. The tragic element of the joke works both ways: once the barb is cast, it cancels out the grievance. By destroying the joker's claim to a tragic explanation, it makes him individually accountable for his role and place in the world. From its victim, the joke steals dignity, but from its perpetrator, for this very reason, it removes his own claim to victimhood.

Humour is among the most effective political instruments because it is impossible to respond to effectively except in its own currency, and somehow it is difficult to mint jokes in defence of existing values. The weapon of humour is always, therefore, going to be more adaptable to the needs of those who seek to usher in a new dispensation, rather than those defending the old. Conservatism has a greater need for seriousness; revolution has all the best jokes. Values, essential to the cohesion of human society, make for easy targets. On the other hand, a joke embraces multiple dimensions of meaning and one of its most effective functions is as counterbalance to the human tendency to see things straightforwardly as good-or-bad, black-or-white, for-or-against. In theory, humour should act as a defence, allowing in a sense of complexity and contradiction, thus safeguarding against populist sentiments, which naturally tend towards irresponsibility and anarchy. In practice, more and more, humour in politics has the opposite effect: it is the joke that simplifies and leaves the target struggling for words.

And the problem is not that the great questions of Irish society have suddenly begun to be expressed humorously or with rapier wit, but that the content of the humour has become a force of itself, being usually in the contentless languages of mockery or derision, cleansed of all political or intellectual content. Being 'funny' is regarded as representing an end in itself, and laughter the ultimate test of integrity. The kinds of energies which previous youth generations expressed through music, art or protest have in the younger generations of the present compressed into a single essence: a dissociated blend of ridicule and scorn that lacks roots in any form of empathy.

The problem, then, is not disengagement, but the nature of the engagement that occurs. The hackneyed refrain of the middle-aged and elderly to the effect that young people have become 'cynical about politics' trips rather too lightly off the tongue for us to trust its blanket prognosis. Cultures change for reasons, not accidentally or randomly, and usually they change because of some self-interested intervention by the powerful, who are well placed to cover their tracks.

Among the many negative aspects of Ireland's prosperity from the mid-1990s was that some of the worst aspects of British popular culture became translated into the small-town arena of Irish media. Many newspapers, magazines, and radio and television programmes adopted cruelty, mockery and spite as their chief codes of commonality. The inexorable encroachment of the internet through the same period contributed further to a fundamental change in Irish culture that, almost by definition, remained out of sight.

On the surface, the critical element appears to relate to technological change, and what modern idioms like Facebook, Twitter and the blogosphere now offer by way of access to public discussion. Debate has become less structured, less formal. It is possible to have your say nowadays by logging on to a newspaper site and responding instantly to an article or public event. But there is something at work here besides the convenience of the technology: there is also the congeniality of this arrangement to those who hold the power.

The internet, exponentially, reduces public debate to the level of a drunken argument, in which no holds are barred, in which disturbed or unpleasant people get to voice their ignorant opinions in the ugliest terms, in the name of 'free speech', but without giving their names. The internet seems to draw in such people, perhaps even nudging everyone who uses it towards the same disposition and mentality. To take a stab at naming it, you might call it the blurt of the impotent and excluded, who imagine themselves at last being listened to.

This is not democracy, but something else. When I go to vote, they ask for my name and check it against the electoral register. Many contributors of internet posts are pseudonymous, generally young men of similar outlook and mode of expression, recognizable for the most part as what journalists one time used to call 'the green biro brigade'.

The most interesting thing about such threads is the mob mind-set that seems to underlie them. They are not neutral conduits for spontaneous opinions, but channels dedicated to forms of disgruntlement which have, for what can often seem like good reasons, no other outlet. It is as if the assault, the ridicule, the sneer comes into being for its own sake, with the subject-matter being largely incidental. Something is targeted not because it has provoked a genuine response from an interested party, but because it provides an opportunity for a high-octane rant, which exists as a phenomenon in its own right.

Most contributors seem, above all, to want to draw attention to themselves. This would be unexceptionable if the web was generally regarded as some kind of effluent pipe of democratic discourse, redirecting the toxic waste to some safe area of disposal. It becomes problematic when these toxic responses are fed into public discussion as genuine perspectives, or even as fact, poisoning the groundwater of public opinion in a disproportionate and ugly fashion.

The web is only as good as those it attracts. And there is something about the nature of internet technology that not only attracts the more disturbed and disenchanted, but also draws from an individual the darker aspects of personality. This is in part to do with the anonymity the web affords, offering in effect a coward's charter to character assassins with an open mind only as to whom they may target next.

The individual user tends to come to the technology in a particular mindset and mood, in part created by the isolationism implicit in the nature of the technology itself, and in part by anticipation of a certain kind of group dynamic. It is as though the group's default mood is to be assumed as hostile, a fairly safe presumption in my experience. The interchange seems to operate around a principle of mutual anxiety, whereby each participant is on his mettle in order to demonstrate his capacity and willingness to be as unpleasant as everyone else. The individual user seeks to convey an impression of strength, cleverness or cynicism, by way of making headway in the group without inviting hostility or ridicule. This dynamic provokes contributions which are poisonous, aggressive, cowardly, vindictive and hostile, and ensures that ridicule, invective and ideological spite are the dominant notes.

The well-advised anticipation of a certain kind of group

dynamic awakens any sleeping neurosis in the blogger or poster, provoking a kill-or-be-killed disposition that inevitably creates extreme aggression and hostility. You find very little love or celebration of beauty on the internet, and for very good reason: anyone who did so would be trolled to death.

For this and other reasons, I treat the web pretty much as I would a dark alleyway at midnight. I make use of it, but do not dawdle or make eye-contact. Whenever I say something like this, someone always pipes up that there's 'lots of good stuff on the web'. This is true, but pretty much all the good stuff has been generated someplace else – in books, papers, articles. The amount of web-generated material exhibiting any intrinsic value is minimal.

The relationship of the newspaper industry to the world wide web seems, on the face of things, to be something along the same lines of that of the man to his gravedigger, and yet most journalists seemingly feel compelled to write and speak about the web as though it was an entirely benign and positive development. Any journalist who seeks to question any aspect of the culture of 'new media' is instantly labelled a 'Luddite' or worse, and not just by the bloggers, tweeters and posters, but probably more immediately by his own alleged colleagues in the so-called 'mainstream media'.

In part this is owing to the usual misplaced desire to be seen to be 'modern' in all things. Journalists appear to suffer disproportionately from this tragic ailment, which is why almost every broadcast media discussion about politics nowadays has to have some know-nothing blogger or tweeter. This is despite the fact that only a minority of people actually tweet, and none of these has anything to say. In fact, the only reason you would tweet in the first place is precisely because you have nothing to say, this being about the only thing you can say in the limited number of characters available.

In a decade or so, we will look back and wonder if we really could have been so stupid as to regard as a serious democratic phenomenon forms of communication that enabled anonymous assassins to pour vitriol and cynicism into cyberspace and attack named others with total impunity.

One of the most interesting characteristics of many contributors is their obvious lack of any memory-capacity: they react only to what is said or written in a particular context, rarely showing any awareness of the targeted author's positions on other subjects or even his history of commentary on the instant topic. They lambast for sins of commission and omission, haranguing the author for his failure to mention the few things they happen to know on the subject. It is as though a duty to inform themselves is regarded as some kind of unreasonable imposition. The basis of their comments is nearly always an obvious and hackneyed ethicality, of which any breach seems to send them into the emotional stratosphere.

There is a strange tone running through most internet blogs and posts, which assumes a high degree of cleverness on the part of the writer and other contributors, but attributes zero intelligence to the target, who is dismissed in splenetic and often personalized terms. Another strange phenomenon is that these assumptions seem to extend also to humour and irony, which are claimed as the sole properties of the bloggers and posters. If anyone they disapprove of makes a joke, or engages in any attempt to state something in a complex or, God help us, poetic way, the contribution is immediately subjected to the most forensic literalism and scorn.

Although I long since ceased reading such posts on my own columns, I would occasionally come across them at the end of other people's articles and sometimes would find myself caught up in some sense of a uniform tone that I recognized but could not name. Then, one day, it struck me: peevish teachers. Most of the comments were written as though correcting essays written by students. 'Not a bad article,' a post might begin. 'Nice to see some facts and figures for a change.' And so it would proceed, hectoring and lecturing, insulting and deriding. It was obvious that something other than an engagement was occurring – that, instead, what was happening was a kind of dance of envy, the plaintive keening of someone who felt they could write far better articles than the one they had just read, if only someone would give them a chance.

The reductionism of much web-based commentary is demonstrated by the following example of a post placed at the end of an *Irish Times* article in February 2012. One of just two added to this particular article, it came from a contributor styling himself 'Lord Jimbo', and started with a quote from the theosophist Krishnamurti: 'It is no measure of health to be well adjusted to a profoundly sick society.' Lord Jimbo continued:

> No wonder people aren't feeling well, they have to listen to political BS about the necessary short term pain, taking the medicine of recovery from people on €110,000 per annum plus expenses who have not a clue what is actually going on and may soon be overwhelmed by events. Meanwhile the government increases a range of stealth taxes making it even tougher for people on lower wages, in negative equity or unemployed. There is not an inspirational leader among them while the banks are allowed to carry on as if it is business as usual.

As may very remotely be detected from its opening sentence, this comment was posted in response to an opinion piece about mental health. The author of the article was Mary Donnelly, senior lecturer in the law faculty, University College Cork. Her piece was, in fact, a critique of the 2001 Mental Health Act and argued that Irish law continued to be in breach of the United

Nations Convention on Human Rights because of a failure to provide adequate provision for voluntary admissions to psychiatric hospitals. This, she argued, meant that many voluntary patients remained in psychiatric hospitals without the protections offered by external review procedures.

But as far as Lord Jimbo was concerned, she might as well have been writing about negative equity, politicians' expenses or the price of turnips. Bloggers and posters appear to see every opinion as an opportunity to declare their dissatisfaction with Irish politicians and the way Ireland has been run, and see no humour or irony in their one-dimensional response to Irish public life. It doesn't matter what the article is about – the important thing is the blank space which provides an outlet for venting.

But the most remarkable thing is that such posts are published, providing a kind of shop-window insight into what a visiting Martian would be forced to conclude was the outlook of the average *Irish Times* reader. It is impossible to avoid the thought that such interventions are actually being encouraged for some unstated cultural purpose.

The tone of detached, vacuous mockery that pervades the world wide web arises from a cultural stakelessness that unleashes a dull drone of hate-filled cynicism that is corroding the very fabric of modern societies, offering no benefit to the perpetrator but self-congratulation and the release of inflicting hurt. This is not accidental, but results from a kind of constructed alienation of the young by the not-so-young, and the internet is just one manifestation of this syndrome. Like the comedy obsession of recent decades, the internet fetish of the present is being consciously and calculatedly facilitated – even at enormous risk to the long-term health of the media.

The web is an interesting but essentially overrated channel of information, most of which, by definition, lacks the credibility of that published in an old-fashioned newspaper. Journalism, for all its flaws and limitations, is a professional pursuit, subject to laws, rules, checks and balances and basic values concerning truth and decency. Underlying the process of publication is (usually) a fairly thorough system of checking and verification, which bloggers and 'citizen journalists' are unable, under the headings of either training or resources, to match. There is therefore – and will continue to be – a major trust deficit in relation to what is conveyed in the newer forms. There will always be instances where the new technologies will enable the ordinary citizen to become a player in a particular story, but this is certainly not a phenomenon our democracies can rely upon. Far from becoming provoked and propelled into political engagement, the world is being pacified, distracted and waylaid into forms of pseudo-rebellion and mock-protest by a cultural development that in effect turns politics into an entertainment.

The argument frequently surfaces nowadays, particularly since the Arab Spring events of 2011, that the web functions as an instrument of democracy, enabling oppressed peoples to communicate and organize against their oppressors, fulfilling at a popular level, the argument goes, something like the function that samizdat (underground) publications played in the conniving of intellectuals against the Soviet Union. In China, Iran and the Middle East, we are led to believe, the internet is liberating the subjugated and downtrodden. For a fleeting moment, things might have appeared so, but increasingly it emerges that, on the contrary, it is repressive regimes that make the most of internet technology – to track subversives, gather intelligence, disseminate disinformation, attack potential enemies and effect misdirection. In his excellent 2011 book *The Net Delusion: How Not to Liberate the World*, Evgeny Morozov exposes the illusion of the internet mythology in this connection. He argues that the notion that the internet favours the oppressed rather than the oppressor is born of what he calls 'cyber-utopianism', defined as 'a naive belief in the emancipatory nature of online communication that rests on a stubborn refusal to acknowledge its downside'. His overall argument is succinctly captured in the chapter title: 'Why the KGB Wants You to Join Facebook'. Interestingly, he traces this phenomenon to the eruption in the 1990s of a kind of digital fervour inspired largely by former hippies, by then ensconced in the world's most prestigious universities, seeking to prove that the internet could finally achieve the objectives of the 1960s revolution. These 'cyber-utopians' had failed to allow for the differences between the cosseted West and the reality of authoritarian regimes elsewhere. Morozov pleads for a reinvented internet, which might yet move to combat these tendencies, but does not appear to be hopeful.

From the viewpoint of society, the relationship of the 'mainstream media' to the web is a bit like that of the dog to the flea. Until recently, there has been a tendency to see the internet as a competing source of information. Now, a different picture is emerging.

It's obvious, really. Imagine that you are ill in bed and have no form of diversion apart from the internet. Imagine, further, that, today and for the foreseeable future, all content deriving from what bloggers call 'the Old Media' – i.e. newspapers and broadcast organizations – has been blocked. There is nothing on the web except what is generated on it. There is plenty of pornography, advertising and poisonous invective about the fact that the main source of material has been closed off. There are some pictures of people tripping over their dogs. But otherwise there is nothing about what is happening in the world – no sport, no news, no politics. The only comment is about the fact that there is nothing to comment about. How long would you find this interesting? It is not just that, devoid of a mainstream to leech off, the web would become inaccurate, unreliable and lacking in authority. The point is that there just wouldn't be anything there.

Bloggers don't cover press conferences or football matches; nor do they much go in for the shoe-leather aspects of journalism, like following politicians around or ringing them up with questions. It's so much easier just to lift the raw material from professional sources, which you know are reliable because of the masthead they're presented under. Then, recycling the material, you calumniate those who generated it.

The arrogance and incivility of much web-based commentary tends to conceal the fact that blogging, posting and tweeting are almost exclusively parasitical pursuits: they depend on material provided by the 'mainstream media' to feed them. If or when they succeeded in fatally undermining the sources of their material, they too would perish.

Of course, many newspapers have, on the face of things, been unspeakably stupid in making their content available free of charge to the blogosphere. Consider this: if I am a regular purchaser and reader of *The Irish Times*, handing over my (guts of) two quid every morning at my local newsagent, and I wish to respond to something I have read therein, there is a clear and exacting procedure laid down for me to follow. I must write a letter, or, latterly, an email, giving my name, address and telephone number along with any comment I wish to make. To have any chance of publication, my letter must be short, pertinent and coherent. It must not personalize its arguments but must address itself to the issues at hand. If my contribution is considered suitable for publication, I will receive a phone call from the letters' editor, seeking to verify my identity. If there is anything personally abusive, blasphemous, defamatory or gratuitous in my letter, it will be edited out, and the letters' editor will inform me of these proposed changes in the course of our conversation. Then, all other things being equal, my letter will appear within a few days.

If, on the other hand, I do not buy the newspaper but choose to read it online, I can respond instantly to articles without giving any personal details, not even my name, and certainly not my address or phone number. Here, for some reason, there is a completely different standard. I can more or less say what I like, short of outright defamation, though sometimes even libels can slip through unnoticed. I can sneer, ridicule, abuse, dismiss. I can make references to details I know about the personal life of my target. There is no requirement for my argument to be coherent, pertinent or in good taste. Invariably, contributors are informed that a moderator will vet their posts for all kinds of things, but the evidence of such moderation is slight.

There is something odd about all this, about, for example, the fact that this form of dissent, which is so out of character with the conventions of media organizations, is nurtured and encouraged by conservative media organizations which apply quite different standards to other branches of their operations. It is as though the newspaper is produced for two categories of reader: one, the older kind, preserving some residual sense of the butter-box politics practised by Dan O'Rourke and de Valera; the other for those who regard politics as a kind of locus of entertainment and psychological catharsis, a kind of lions and Christians without much in the way of Christianity. Thus, *The Irish Times* in hard copy is one thing, and the web edition something else entirely.

But there is too a self-serving element: by creating an outlet for the rantings of bloggers, you cannot be accused of excluding the young from debate. It is impossible to avoid the thought that these new forms of dissent are encouraged because they relieve the generations-in-power – the 'regime' – of any responsibility to devolve real power downwards, or to absorb the thinking of the younger generations into their own mainstream.

And it is hard to avoid the further thought that this has to do with the convenience of this form of dissent, which functions as a kind of safety valve for youthful energies, enabling a shrill venting of rage and derision with minimal risk that the dissenters will seek an active involvement in the citadels of power or the ideological agenda pertaining thereto. Because those who emerged from the 1960s had been running everything, and refusing to provide space for challenging other perspectives, irony, humour and scorn have become, for those born after 1970 or so, the sole cultural outlets for their natural transformative energies. This is so convenient for the generations now in power that they are prepared to do almost anything, short of yielding power, to accommodate and appease this form of 'dissent'. In this way, the younger generations have been conned into collaborating with their elders in the usurpation of their capacity for idealism by the generations which immediately preceded them, and refuse to countenance that anyone can be more 'progressive' or engaged than themselves.

It is interesting, too, to observe that almost all of the content of these new forms of communication, in Ireland anyway, tend to adhere to the same ideological path as laid down by the post-Emergency generations now in power. The use of ridicule in this content is in general ideologically forensic. It seeks to target not the objectively observable foibles and absurdities of the political system, but more clinically those elements which are objected to by certain ideological interests and outlooks. In general, the satire and commentary on the web tends to follow a course set by the dominant consensus in the mainstream media, valorizing liberals and their causes and targeting anyone who questions these agendas. It is forbidden, for example, and therefore nigh on impossible, to use humour to target feminists or lobbyists for certain campaigning minorities, but it is acceptable to ridicule as a reactionary anyone who calls the spokespersons for such interest groups to account for themselves.

It is increasingly clear, too, that the 'old' media are rapidly becoming contaminated by the culture of the internet, with its no-holds-barred approach to public commentary.

During the May 2011 visit of US President Barack Obama, for example, an extraordinary episode occurred in which Taoiseach Enda Kenny was accused of 'plagiarizing' one of the visitor's own speeches, even though President Obama was standing beside him at the time. Anyone observing the saga develop from a perspective rooted in the 'old' culture of media and politics would have been mystified by what transpired, but written all over it was the 'new' style of commentary seeping into the core of society from the world wide web.

'If there's anyone out there who still doubts that Ireland is a place where all things are possible,' Mr Kenny declared when he introduced Obama at a public meeting on Dublin's College Green, 'who still wonders if the dream of our ancestors is alive in our time; who still questions our capacity to restore ourselves, to reinvent ourselves and to prosper, well, today is your answer.'

'Old' and 'new' media immediately went into overdrive, informing the public that this sentence was similar to a passage in Obama's acceptance speech on his election as US president in November 2008. A radio station got some of its grown-up staff-members to splice together sections from the Obama and Kenny speeches. One newspaper said that Enda Kenny had 'confessed' that the words were from Obama's victory address. Others published the quotations side by side and invited readers to 'spot the difference'. An *Irish Times* report forensically explained: 'The section of [Obama's] speech refers to the doubts of a people, to its dreams and possibilities and to overcoming the doubts. Mr Kenny's speech closely followed the words of Mr Obama's 2008 speech but with one or two small amendments, and the addition of a longer sub-clause.' The Taoiseach had to expend breath and time explaining to journalists that he intended the reference 'very deliberately' to be understood as a tribute, and that he thought the passage so well known that he felt no reason to attribute it. He, too, was required to be forensic in his self-defence: 'My speech was 470 words and the first forty were a direct quote from Barack Obama in 2008, putting in "Ireland" instead of "America",' the Taoiseach explained, ve-ry slow-ly, to RTÉ.

This had been obvious to any sensible person who had watched the event either on College Green or on television. It was crystal-clear that Kenny was engaging in a playful pastiche, speaking with a twinkle beneath his arched eyebrow, delivering a nod of tribute to someone he admired. But this did not stop this 'debate' going on for several days.

This literalism is interesting. Firstly, it seems to assume that subtlety, irony and nuance are the sole property of those who criticize from the sidelines. Only the critics and satirists can or should make jokes. But deeper down is the fact that this new climate appears to arise from a sense that public disquiet about politics and politicians has no limit, that almost any charge, however preposterous, can be levelled without compunction or consequences. The formless and directionless rage of the public has become such a reliable phenomenon that media people and internet bloggers alike seem instinctively to reach for anything they think will stoke it further, like idly throwing another briquette on the fire. Now, because it is so easy, they have become careless. Because there seems to be no limit to public rage, it really doesn't matter, most of the time, that the charges are spurious or trumped up. On the slightest pretext, people can be counted on to get wound up, and off we go again.

The obvious word for all this is 'cynicism', but somehow it seems inadequate, providing little insight into the true nature of the condition. The word 'cynic' has several popularly accepted, and somewhat different, uses. Firstly there is the sense of the cynic as a caustic, quick-witted individual with a sardonic view of life and other people's motivations. Nowadays, this incorporates, among other elements, a perspective on public life that is largely adapted from television and movies, in which the very identities of young people seem to rely on a sense of scepticism towards authority and a disavowal of sincerity in the public realm.

A more profound state of cynicism is characterized by a tendency to believe the worst of others, to see all acts of human beings as essentially self-serving. Beyond that there is the full-blown state of cynicism, exhibiting a contempt for accepted norms of, for example, morality, deciding that such strictures are invariably the impositions of a misanthropic and hypocritical authoritarianism.

Mixed in, too, is disillusion. The cynic most of us know may not be someone who instinctively scorns and belittles values and decency, but, on the contrary, someone whose high expectations of such values has been damaged by betrayal. Cynicism, by this light, is not an indicator of a disinclination to believe in what is good, but the product of too great a tendency to do so: the chagrin of the disappointed, the hangover from innocence, the resolve of one determined not to get fooled again. It goes without saying that this tendency, being ipso facto a function of youthful naivety, is prone to manipulation. Like all forms of cynicism, it has a concrete basis in reality, deriving from a deep sense of being 'left out', ignored, of being made the object of forces beyond your control. In a sense, what has happened to Irish independence in the past few years has rendered us all prey to such sentiments, because it has placed our ultimate civic destinies in the hands of outside agencies, who seem blithely unaware of our pain or anxiety.

Among the principal constituents of cynicism is the much-vaunted quality of irony, now supposedly all-pervasive in society. But irony is no longer what it was: a light coating of sarcastic humour to convey the opposite of a surface meaning. Irony as we know it today is one of the most destructive characteristics of modern culture: a capacity to express two meanings at once – one mock-sincere, the other satirical of that mock-sincerity, a double-speak that, culturally enforced, enables the development of ambiguity and avoidance. Nowadays, too, this public irony is almost invariably symptomatic of a cultural demand for the disparagement of values perceived as in some way inhibiting of modern freedoms. This characteristic can be observed in crude form in many popular TV shows, particularly comedy shows, cartoons and frothy dramas, but exists in diluted form in virtually all popular culture. At the back of it is an ostensible avoidance of sincerity or conviction, of any fixed or principled view.

In *Cynicism and Postmodernity*, Timothy Bewes advanced the theory that the rapidity and sheer overwhelming density of modern linguistic, commercial and rhetorical traffic 'has a deadening or decelerating effect upon society'. The relationship between the individual and objective culture, he argued, has become 'one of absolute alienation, such that the critical faculty has given way to stupefaction, a failure of engagement and, finally, a defensive strategy of cynical indifference'. To contemplate a culture infected with these characteristics is doubly disconcerting for those who become aware of the problem. On the one hand, they must perceive that the banishment of seriousness and engagement is both deeply problematic and also normalized to such an extent that it has become invisible. On the other, they become aware that, to draw attention to the problem, they risk bringing on themselves the full brunt of the awesome ridicule which this culture is capable of mustering against anyone who would question its ironic certitudes or wry complacency.

And yet, when things begin to go wrong, when the occasion of the certitudes is rattled, or the complacency becomes punctured in any way, the response is not irony or even ridicule, but outright rage. The mood shifts rapidly from non-engagement to an intense repudiation of events, behaviours and individuals. Then, in a further stage, the mockery kicks in again, but this time with a new and harsher edge, devoid of all irony and casualness, a venomous onslaught on that which is understood as having threatened the comforts that have been taken for granted.

It is easy to get swept up in this, to steer against the skid and thereby make the consequences worse. Confronted by cynicism, this is often the reflex response. But there is another way of seeing what is happening: that instead of sincerity having been destroyed, it has simply been driven inward; that, because our culture has been reconstructed to reject solemnity, those who have appeared to dissociate themselves through humour have rather been forced into this, to abandon seriousness for fear of ridicule. And this, to a greater or lesser extent, affects all of us within that culture. We express ourselves in the ironic idiom of the surrounding culture, not entirely because we share its apparent contempt for gravity, but because we do not want to expose our private sincerities to conventional derision. Because of this dissociation, it is difficult to say in what our culture actually consists.

From time to time, an event occurs which brings all this hidden ferment out into the open, by returning us briefly to the old way of seeing and being. One such was the death in 2005 of Pope John Paul II, after a period of illness that he made no effort to protect his people from. Having spent more than a quarter of a century teaching the world how it might live, he had spent a year or so teaching us how to die.

Here, I pause in relating this episode to observe that, immediately, by virtue of my chosen example, I have engaged the full antipathy of the culture I am seeking to describe in this chapter. To choose a religious topic in order to illustrate a cultural phenomenon is ipso facto evidence of reactionary tendencies. This, for the avoidance of doubt, is why I do it.

John Paul had been a deeply charismatic and much-loved figure, but his pontificate was by no means universally approved. He was presented in most media treatments as a deeply conservative and authoritarian figure, who sought to sweeten the pill of his uncompromising message with an avuncular disposition and a gentle touch. After years of hearing him spoken about in this way, few could claim that they had anticipated the outpouring of grief and affection that followed his death. Four million mourners gathered in Rome, with an estimated two billion people watching on television worldwide. Towards the end of the Requiem Mass, thousands of people in the streets of the Vatican City began chanting 'Santo Subito!' ('Saint now!') and 'Giovanni Paolo Santo!' ('Saint John Paul!') with an intensity that awoke in those watching something of the true depth of feeling that had lain dormant in the hearts of the billions who deeply loved this remarkable Pope. Few commentators were unaffected, except those who had written their scripts in advance. What emerged was the repressed gravity of our private thoughts, momentarily unpoliced by the cynicism of the public square. At such rare moments, it is still possible in our culture to experience, taste, a palpable suspension of the cynicism that has come to dominate and which, arrogating an unassailable morality to itself on account of its opposition to authority, gums everything up with scorn and disdain.

The main root of true cynicism is in a vacuum of belief, or at least of commonly held or commonly acknowledged beliefs, and this traces back to the loss of the primary belief in a Supreme Being, which once united humanity in a common sense of truth, value and meaning. The modern citizen-consumer is afraid to say how he really feels, and most of all is afraid of revealing that he, apparently uniquely, is at sea in a world with little meaning. And so he clings to the invented meanings supplied by conventional culture, while publicly joining in the disavowal of anything that might hark back to a time when that culture acknowledged a transcendent reality. Yet, deep down, he craves the old, publicly repudiated, meanings. In his heart he is on his knees, but in the public square he skateboards among the monuments of tradition and austerity, his apparent dexterity of disbelief arising from his terror of attracting in his direction the full brunt of the collective contempt.

The origin of the word 'cynic' is to be found in the Latin word for dog: 'canis'. More and more it is as though we have each of us sprouted one dog's ear to replace one of our human ears, which has atrophied and fallen off. All the time now what we hear tends to feed this dog's ear, but leaves the other ear, the God ear, famished for sustenance. A further problem is that each of us has only one mouth, so that, when we speak, we choose, more often than not, to speak what we have heard with the dog's ear. It is safer to do so. It draws less attention to ourselves, and therefore enables us to fit in better in a culture which increasingly seeks to detach us from our own passions, for fear that these might lead us to see how we have been betrayed.

Once upon a time, the Irish were a people who exhibited wit both in the sense of humorousness and cop-on, a cocktail that was not imported but very much the product of a history we have latterly been inclined to forget.

Garry Hynes, the director who first staged the work of the playwright Martin McDonagh with the Druid Theatre in Galway, told a journalist one time about a woman who came up to her after the premiere of *The Beauty Queen of Leenane*, wiping tears of laughter from her eyes, and said: 'I have a funny feeling that I shouldn't be laughing so hard.' McDonagh's plays, with their ironic twist on the established forms of Irish drama, offered a recreation of the experience of traditional theatre with a permission to stand outside it and see the characters as, in some sense, unreal.

I always think a great writer carries an emblem of his overall genius in the very first words of a piece, and McDonagh achieves this in the very first exchange between mother and daughter in

*The Beauty Queen of Leenane*:
  Mag: 'Wet, Maureen?'
  Maureen: 'Of course wet.'
Maureen's answer is both fatalistic and angry: fatalistic towards the world and the weather, but angry towards her mother on account, perhaps, of it all.

That woman who came to speak to Garry Hynes in Galway encapsulated the attitude of a lot of Irish people towards McDonagh and his work. They find his plays funny, because they find themselves funny. But they also possess a degree of sentiment for themselves and their ancestors which he, as a kind of intimate outsider, understandably, and probably happily, lacks. This means that Irish people are perhaps worst placed to judge McDonagh and his work. To enjoy his plays, we have not simply to achieve intellectual distance, but also to withdraw sympathy from ourselves, to join in the laughter of the ages, created precisely to numb ourselves, or those who begat us, against the pain of reality.

It seems somewhat indecent to voyeuristically enjoy that humour deprived of its catastrophic context. Critics often said about McDonagh's work that his characters weren't real, but this is like saying that Beckett's tramps weren't real, when most of us spent our childhoods meeting them on the roads. The characters in McDonagh's plays are actually all too real, but it is equally true to say that they have had their feelings removed, or at least removed beyond a humorous pane. We watch them in their misery and meaninglessness and can only laugh. As children in the West of Ireland during the second half of the twentieth century, we saw, met and knew them also: bent men cycling into town in new caps, bearded ladies limping along windswept boreens, desiccated spinsters with their dreams behind them, unwashed drunks on their knees in public houses on dole day. These people existed all right: they were our neighbours, our grandparents, our uncles and aunts. They lived next door or on the edge of towns or in houses with the doors open from which the smell of life emanated as you passed. These were lives which happened, as opposed to being constructed in the mythological imaginations of cultural critics and commentators. These were lives which seemed to the gaze of the modern eye to be without meaning or architecture. Their existence is not the issue. The issue is why their lives have come to seem more funny than heartbreaking.

Partly it is because the world they inhabited, and which seemed to trap them, was also a world saturated with reimported nostalgic meanings deriving from the now detached imaginations of those who had gone away. They remained in poverty, but occupied a place which, in the memories of the departed, had a connotation of Paradise. Thus their poverty was reinvented as kitsch and their misery became indistinguishable from a picture postcard. Their imprisonment in it was partly as a result of a desire to retain the image which so pleased those who occasionally returned. I remember a returned Yank aunt who came to visit us once and left a week earlier than planned, and being convinced that it was because we did not, at the time, have an indoor toilet. And yet, if we'd had one, I knew she would have complained along the lines that we were losing our 'authenticity'. This is the tragedy of Ireland, which as Patrick Kavanagh implicitly predicted, is now turning into comedy.

The charge has often been levelled that Martin McDonagh has no compassion for his characters, and in a certain sense this seems to be true. But he neither laughs at his characters nor invites us to do so: the humour comes by virtue of his faithful observation of the characters and their language. McDonagh has been faithful to the way our ancestors, who inhabited the worlds from which his plays sprang forth, used to laugh at themselves. Many of the jokes in McDonagh's plays relate to the imprisonment of his characters in one world while another seeks to encroach. The existence of familiar items of modern living, like Tayto Crisps and Australian soaps, in the lives of people who are in some ways recognizable as our own aunts and uncles, creates a tremendous poignancy and pathos. We might well cry because this is all they got of the harvest of modernity; and also because the imagined purity of their previous existence had been sullied in this way. But perhaps we laugh instead because this is the only way of protecting ourselves and the choices we have made or been denied.

You might conclude from this that perhaps the Irish have always been heartless, two-faced bastards, laughing up their sleeves at one another's misery. But the more interesting insight is that, to protect ourselves from the psychic disintegration which would have followed from a genuine encounter with our own sense of the sadness and despair of our fellows, we turned ourselves into comic figures. We laughed at our fate, not to mock but to protect ourselves from what we imagined must be the griefs that begat us. We laughed at those whose lives we would prefer to forget, because to do otherwise would make the whole thing unbearable.

Humour is really a layer of gristle between bones which would otherwise grind into one another to the point of seizure. The humour in McDonagh's plays, then, is not a literary humour, but an organic comedy harvested from real contact with the homeland of his work, and of course also with its inhabitants. The Complan, porridge, pisspots and brutality in the plays would be unendurable if they were not funny. The stories Martin McDonagh creates, as tightly sprung as rat-traps, are undeniably beautiful creations, but the clarity of the humour is not a product of his imagination but of his ear for the altered reality of the places in which he spent, by all accounts, a great deal of his childhood. He is, in a sense, a satirist. But his satire is beyond mere attack, having mutated into a kind of kiss-of-life. The humour, being born of the most unimaginable kind of horror, is not the dried tinder of so much modern comedy, but the purest, hardest, blackest anthracite, mined at the deepest level of the human soul.

In the bleakness of McDonagh's visions is a profound comedy, the fruit of the necessity to protect ourselves from the abyss we cannot remember, but which threatens these characters at every turn. Only by virtue of their being, to an extent, cartoon characters, dissociated from reality by a sense of 'postmodern' surrealism, are we spared their despair.

This enables us to see something of the relationship between Irish society and its past, its sense of humour and its present tendency to regard this as simply a local version of something we observed in the knowing nonsense of imported comedy and slapstick culture.

The Irish sense of humour used to be droll and understated, seeming to float above things as though only barely noticing them. The joke would come a little late, a throwaway that was the more enjoyable for seemingly having almost been missed. We didn't have to try to be funny: we just were.

Neither did we need everything explained to us. We understood understatement and irony, and knew the difference between allusion and larceny. We did not take things literally. We had a lightness of touch that was second nature. We 'got' things and assumed other people would 'get' them as well. We nodded and winked and allowed ambiguities to lie unmentioned and undisturbed. Common sense was common. We may have been simple but we weren't stupid. Now, we awake to find that the raillery of our ancestors has been obliterated and everything that is not the object of splenetic, crude lampooning is received with a moralism that is literal, leaden and clunky, and where the point of virtually every analysis of public phenomena is the levelling of an accusation, the unearthing of the 'sin', the locating of the theme that enables the accusers to gain the readiest access to the high moral ground. We congratulate ourselves on having shaken off the humourless judgementalism of 'traditional' Irish Catholicism, seemingly unaware that the worst aspects of this former dreariness have transmogrified and reasserted themselves in more banal and toxic forms.

There is a time for joking and a time for sincerity. No culture can survive without seriousness. Indeed, one of the things we have observed in the Ireland of recent years is how serious people tend to become when things go wrong. It is like one of those episodes we remember from childhood, when a responsible adult joins in with a game being played by the children and is having great fun until something happens – perhaps a broken window or some similar calamity – and suddenly there is a complete change of mood. The ball is confiscated and everyone is required to come indoors for the day.

So it is, now, with the public square. While things go well, the mood is one of devil-may-care levity; when the effluent hits the extractor, everyone loses their sense of humour and begins to vent a previously unimagined rage at the nearest scapegoat to hand.

When you look back at the recorded words used by those who might be called the architects and midwives of Independent Ireland, the first thing that strikes you is their unremitting seriousness. These men and women may have been among the most amusing people ever born, but such aspects of their personalities are largely lost to history. By all accounts, Dan O'Rourke was an extremely witty man, who devoted much of his energy to the development of sporting skills among the young, but when he spoke about Ireland he left all levity to one side, adopting a profound solemnity that everyone seemed to regard as appropriate and correct.

This solemnity was perhaps not a difficult tone to strike, since O'Rourke was of a generation of men and women who had very recently endured the unhappiness and humiliation of living in a country denied its right to self-determination. It was easily improvised, too, from the briefest dipping into the many pages of doleful history recorded as the story of Ireland's long experience of occupation and radical interference.

In times of peace, prosperity and optimism, although continuing to be essential to the health of the public realm, this tone becomes difficult to achieve. The better things get, you might infer, the less serious everyone becomes. Extended peace and tranquillity causes the people to lighten up. Their leaders, if they are to survive, must acquire not merely a sense of humour, but the talent for demonstrating this in public. It is no longer appropriate to be all the time banging on about the national soul. The urgency for patriotism recedes as a cultural priority, and considerations of survival and liberty, previously in the balance, come to be taken for granted. Then, in a further stage, patriotism becomes something slightly embarrassing, especially if there are unreconstructed elements still carrying out unspeakable actions in the name of a patriotism they seem incapable of articulating beyond the conventional language of self-interest and parochial grievance.

But the problem is that the business of summoning up a sense of public-spiritedness, or of concern for and interest in the public realm and in the workings of the State, or perhaps even of a fascination for the condition of the collective or national psyche, is just as essential in times of calm and stability as it is in times of conflict and disruption. This is why States develop rituals of remembrance: to enable the memory of historical experiences to be re-entered periodically, so that the people do not start taking their freedom for granted. Inevitably, these rituals come to be seen in a slightly schizophrenic way: on the one hand, they are taken literally, entered into with solemnity and sincerity; on the other they are quietly ridiculed, being out of context in the present. But this is what a public ritual amounts to, and makes it essential: an enactment of a process of remembering that, by virtue of being ritualized, enables us to participate without awkwardness in something that it would embarrass us to do on our own. Mass communications have demolished the necessary distinction between private and public responses, rendering many of the most vital procedures, observances and ceremonials of a nation more difficult to stage and invest with an authenticity that might serve to enable belief.

A further process occurs also. It is as if the seriousness itself comes to be associated with the past misfortunes and miseries that had made it essential. It comes to be seen as 'old-fashioned', as though the necessity for seriousness could somehow be consigned to the past. A non sequitur appears to enter in, whereby the very language that is essential to the construction and maintenance of public values and institutions comes under cultural fire because of the associations it has with times of calamity, chaos and deprivation. It is as if the people really begin to believe that the seriousness that appears to go hand-in-glove with matters of civic importance is something superfluous and therefore dispensable, to be associated with men in dark suits and with grey hair, something that belongs only to the dark days of the past. It is a small step from here to imagining that the seriousness was the cause of the darkness.

Some commentators cite in this connection what they deem the appalling example allegedly set by leaders such as Charles Haughey, who they say have damaged public faith in politics. But it was not Haughey who destroyed public faith in politics: it was the people themselves who invested in a particular idea, admittedly sponsored by Haughey, and then found themselves disappointed when things didn't work out as well as they imagined they would.

You might say that what we need is a different kind of leadership. But any present or future leader, before he or she would utter a word, would have to deal with the difficulty of plucking words from a damaged culture to speak to that culture about things that no longer exist for it. To speak as Dan O'Rourke was able to speak so effortlessly in the Treaty debate of 1922 would be to set oneself up as the butt of jokes and ridicule.

There is no point in seeking to set the morality of Dan O'Rourke against some moral vacuum existing today. This is the trick everyone plays now, as a way of avoiding the issue. Yes, there have been moral failures in the creation of the modern Irish State, although these are not confined to those listed by the champions of the modernizing project. The point is that, for this moral slippage to have brought about the entire dereliction of a culture, other processes would long before have needed to be operating at a deep level – in language, thought, art, texts, speech, memory, in the intimate crevices of each citizen's relationship with the public realm. Something had to have happened long before to destroy the very fabric of the culture of which Dan O'Rourke was speaking and addressing so knowingly and with such acuity.

This is more serious than a moral vacuum. The deeper problem is that certain qualities existed in our culture then, which Dan O'Rourke was able to call into his self-explanation, which today are not available. The real problem is not in the absence of men like Dan O'Rourke, or of the capacity to speak of great things, but in the total devastation of the culture into which he spoke so fluently and with such a confidence of being understood.

To simply repeat the words and concepts on which Dan O'Rourke was able to rely absolutely would today be to descend immediately into parody, and to invite cynicism and scepticism in reply. But this is because the very air through which such words might have to travel has been changed, infected with a virus capable of instantly shooting down and obliterating words of sincerity, passion, patriotism, loyalty and true hope. And because this virus exists, and its existence is known at an intuitive level to everyone, nobody speaks like that any more.

What should concern us is not just that there is nobody left to honour the values that men like O'Rourke could take for granted, but that these values can no longer be articulated or awakened. They are dead to us. Not only can we not imagine the idea of being prepared to fight and die 'for Ireland', but we are unsure where, or if, this entity called 'Ireland' is to be found. We no longer speak about Ireland as an imagined or imaginative entity other than in the context of rugby or soccer matches, an irony providing little grounds for laughter.

When patriotism is invoked in a political context in our culture now, it is as an instrument of moral blackmail rather than a call to a genuine common purpose. When words have been abolished as carriers of value, they can be recast as weapons. When someone is accused of unpatriotic actions, the underlying implication is not that he has put his own interests before his country, but that he has put his own interests before some competing interest, usually that of the accuser. Nobody knows what the words 'my country' means, only about the functioning of 'the State' and the needs of 'society'.

Some time in the nine decades since the Second Dáil, patriotism died, and was reborn as an empty notion, a husk of an idea. The problem is not that we cannot find someone to speak of morality. There is no shortage of such humbug. The problem is not even that morality has been lost to us. The problem is that we have nothing to be moral *for* – no entity, concept, quality or quantity that might be placed at the centre of an endeavour recognizable as patriotic action. It is pointless to speak of the need for a return to values like 'morality', 'ethics' or even 'patriotism', when there is no foundation on which to lay any of this. When, as Pearse cautioned, everything has been reduced to interests, there is nothing but interests on which to build, and interests will always be in competition with other interests.

We may have more motor cars today than we had when men

like Dan O'Rourke strode the land, but we have lost many more important things. 'Patriotism' is just one of the concepts that exist today as mere ghosts of qualities that once stirred the hearts of Irish men and women. O'Rourke came from a generation of great people, but he was not a superman. In many respects, he was an ordinary man. What we need to understand is that people who thought, spoke and acted as he did were commonplace back then. Now, were they still with us, even they would find it impossible to touch the greatness in themselves.

There is, in such discussion as nowadays occurs about the collapse of public engagement with politics, invariably a presumption that it is some kind of temporary state, to do perhaps with either a somewhat mysterious failure of politicians to inspire the people, or perhaps with the seductiveness of all kinds of distractions with which politics is for the moment unable to compete. This sense is accompanied by a hope that public cynicism is some kind of intermediary stage on the road to a new enlightenment, that we will shortly break into a new compartment in which idealism and ironic knowingness will exist side by side.

It is a vain hope, not helped by the fact that its advocates seem not to have the remotest notion of what such a new dispensation might, in practice, consist. This is one of the great ironies (hah!) besetting postmodernism – that, whereas it clings to some flimsy notion of accidentally ringing a new set of changes, its very ideology acknowledges, as one of its central tenets, that cultural possibility is limited to the constant recycling of a finite number of existing elements. This suggests that political passion is possible only in roughly the form it took in the past, and that political rhetoric will again become inspirational only if it strikes a note similar to that which, in the past, ripened in the hearts of the young the seeds of a genuinely patriotic dissent. Thus, leadership becomes acting.

Recent events, including markedly what is remembered as

'9/11', tell us that the principal threat to Western democracy emanates from quarters not noted for their grasp of irony. But perhaps this nagging new narrative is telling us something else: that human life, requiring a degree of passionate absolutism, even fanaticism, will find some way of turning these qualities on those elements which threaten their survival. For the very elements – irony, relativism, apathy – which we in Western societies have nurtured to save ourselves from self-generated passions and to avoid responsibility for the future drift of our societies, have become the red rags which provoke rage in the hearts of outsiders who do not share what they see clearly as our lack of beliefs.

# 7

## *Autopsy of a Party*

IN SLIGO, WHERE MY FATHER COMES FROM, THERE SEEMS STILL TO BE a healthy disrespect for Anglicization. There is, for instance, a certain studied casualness about the way they spell some of their placenames. Rathcormack can also be Rathcormick or Rathcormac, and Drumcliffe can have the 'e' or not, depending on, it seems, the mood or time of day.

Another occasion of such confusion is Ballisodare, or Ballasadare, or Ballysadare, where William Butler Yeats wrote 'The Salley Gardens', a place which for me is forever associated with the mounting excitement of the approach to Sligo from Roscommon, although in recent times bypassed by the new, improved N4.

I remember in the 1970s, when I first started to go to Sligo, the sense, when you hit Ballisodare, of having arrived in another place, different, more exotic, laden with feeling and history. On a clear day, you could see Ben Bulben from the top of the Curlews, or Curlieus, not far beyond Boyle, but the world's most evocative mountain disappeared from sight until you'd passed Collooney and Ballisodare, until, finally, the mountain's stunning profile stood proudly against the horizon.

There was a mood of expectancy that struck when you turned

the corner into Ballisodare, down the main drag and past the disused, distinctive old mill on the Owenmore River, that loomed high and majestically on the left-hand side as you picked up speed again on the way out the Sligo road. There was a sense about it of the darkness of a troubled and enigmatic history, somehow rendered safe, approachable but still present. I don't expect everyone, or indeed anyone, to share this feeling with me, but it has remained. Sometimes, since they did the road and the bypass, I have from time to time peeled off the N4 to take the old road and feel the mood rise up in me again, a mood almost Proustian.

In recent times, however, Ballisodare is a different place. In 2004, the mill was demolished and the site developed as a five-storey apartment complex, comprising seventy-five units with car parks on the ground floor. Back in 2005, the Mill Apartments had been developed at an estimated cost of €12 million and promoted as 'a property that simply has it all', with two-bedroom apartments selling from €320,000. The apartments were fitted for broadband and boasted ash-veneered doors, granite kitchen worktops, first-class tiling and intercom systems.

The brochure had trumpeted:

If home is what you make it, then you couldn't make it better than this. At home in the Mill, Ballisodare, you're surrounded by unspoilt natural beauty. Whether you're buying your first home, planning to invest, looking for a holiday home or simply looking for a taste of the good life, at the Mill you'll be rewarded with a property that simply has it all.

Imagine walking to the sound of the falls. The salmon are running and in moments you'll be in the thick of it. Waders on, a smooth cast and you feel it. A touch! Just minutes from your place and you've already got one hooked. What's more, Lough Arrow,

Lough Gill, the River Easkey and many more small lakes are still just a short drive away. For bigger game, hit the bay and you can hunt shark or even the mighty blue fin tuna. If you like fishing, you'll love Ballisodare.

It should have been a showcase development, modern housing in an exquisite location steeped in history, but it didn't work out that way. There was talk of subsidence and damp, which, together with, it was said, shoddy building standards, made the apartments uninhabitable. The complex remained largely unoccupied and, as time passed, it deteriorated into an alarming state of dereliction, with late-night cider parties and hooliganism finishing off what nature had begun. By 2011, the complex sported numerous broken windows, and vandals had wrecked many of the apartments and scattered glass and debris all around the complex. Many of the doors and fittings had been removed, the water tanks ripped out, the windows smashed and the partitions kicked in. The large car park was empty and had all of its wiring and cables stripped.

In May 2011, a local newspaper, *The Northwest Express*, ran a front-page feature on the deteriorating complex, proclaiming it 'a look inside the belly of the dead tiger'. The only sounds, it said, were of 'dying batteries in the smoke alarms'. A local blogger, Lenny, had provided photographs of the decaying complex: the wrecked apartments and stairwells, the electrical fittings torn from the partitions, the shiny lift doors looming incongruously over the littered, filthy floors; the hallway floor covered with unopened mail.

Accompanying each photograph was a chunk of the estate agent's blurb from five years earlier, the words as teasingly reminiscent of the dream as the images were evocative of the nightmare it had turned into:

Look out your window and bathe in the breathtaking beauty of the Ballisodare River. With its abundant supply of wild salmon and bubbling rapids it's a magnet for anglers . . . relax over dinner and let your thoughts drift with the current of the river.

All of these apartments have generous living areas and cleverly laid out kitchens . . . Whatever shape or style of apartment you'd like, you'll find it at the Mill.

They say God is in the detail and here attention to detail is second to none . . . At the Mill quality is everywhere you look. And that quality is protected by a 10-year home bond guarantee.

It is strange to contemplate how the same events can, at different times, be regarded as entirely different phenomena. What was once benign, or virtuous, can later become questionable, even bad. What was at one time evidence of increasing modernization and progress, is later something else. A house, a building, can be either a promise of Paradise or a vista of Hell, depending on the context in which it is presented or received. It was indeed a vivid glance inside the belly of the dead tiger. But it was just one of hundreds of such phenomena, widely termed 'ghost' estates, by then littering the country.

The frenetic building that took place during the Tiger years had a different meaning then. It was part of the culmination of all the promises we had been made about what Ireland could become if we nurtured the right attitudes and did the right things. I remember very clearly the sense of bemusement we felt when first we began to notice the extent of the transformation, and then the reassurance we got, and then the feeling of comprehension, relief, that arrived when we had digested the error on which the initial doubt had been based. This was a different Ireland – ah yes! – not the hopeless one we'd grown up in, not the Ireland where everything was shite.

\*

In my home town, Castlerea, there was an even more startling transformation.

When we were boys, we created our own soccer club in the commonage between our houses on Main Street and the River Suck. It was a wild place, where once upon a time there had been neatly maintained vegetable gardens but now there was nothing but an unfenced wilderness, and below that Roddy's Field, which used to flood sometimes in the winter. On the river was a long sliver of an 'island', an extraordinary other world, which was really not an island at all but ran into the old mill at the millrace near the Father Michael O'Flanagan Bridge spanning the River Suck as it brushed past the western extremity of Main Street.

We called the club Hackers Lane. It was really just a small patch of reasonably level ground, which we tamed, mowed and picked the stones off. We built a 'clubhouse' out of branches and sheets of rusty galvanize, to run to when a shower fell. Others might have been content to use jumpers for goalposts and argue about scores, but Hackers Lane had real goals, real flags and real markings. To this day, I find myself drawn to those bins you see in sports shops full of Premiership quality footballs – just to check the price. Most of them are now cheaper than the leather football we all chipped in for back in, I'd say, 1970, which cost us £5. When it was wet it was like kicking a large, round stone.

The goals were about three feet high and four feet wide, precise miniatures of the goals on any professional soccer pitch, carefully constructed from lengths of timber 'borrowed' from my father's shed, with proper joints and bolts to hold them together. The nets were made from onion bags from Egans' shop, sewed together with twine, and these were held in place over iron bed-ends we found in Roddy's dump. The posts and crossbars were painted white. The pitch was always marked with sawdust from Connolly Brothers or Beirnes' joinery. We erected a sign, which proclaimed in white lettering on a brown background: 'Hackers Lane FC', with no apostrophe, like *Finnegans Wake*. There were no goalies, and a special rule about not being able to enter a sawdust semicircle around the goalmouth, unless the ball was in there first. We played games of fifteen minutes a half, a departure from the previous tradition in the town, where games were played on Saturday nights in the Fair Green, between teams of maybe twenty boys a side, until it got dark or everyone had gone home. These games were played in the big cattle pen, when only the dry cow-dung saved you from coming to serious grief on the concrete floor.

The life of Hackers Lane coincided roughly with the interregnum between the World Cups of 1966 and 1970, and then died away as we became more interested in other things. We played leagues and knock-out competitions between teams as carefully seeded as the pitch, and occasionally hosted 'internationals' between Main Street and Ballindrimly or Knockroe. Generally we could beat anyone on our own turf, but got hammered when we ventured away from Hackers Lane. This was because we were used to the carefully kept pitch. I remember one time holding Knockroe to a nil–all draw at Hackers Lane and then getting beaten six–nil on the pitch beside Gannon's house in Knockroe, which had not a blade of grass from one end to the other. Football boots were banned at Hackers Lane, and anyone wearing them, as Seanie Connell and his team were that day, could run rings round us.

What strikes me most forcibly about this time, looking back now, is the way we were left alone to our childish fantasies and dramas. The place where we played was just behind the houses where several of us lived, but it might have been a thousand miles into the wilderness. Adults rarely bothered us or even acknow-ledged our existence except sometimes to wander down and watch one of the games. The ground was commonly owned, but nobody could remember exactly which piece went with which house, and it had been decades since anybody, apart from myself and my uncle Martin, had tried to fence or cultivate any of the gardens. In summertime, the area around our mowed pitch would flame up with weeds, which had the appearance of a vast forest. As you passed on the nearby roadway, the 'backroad', you would be unaware of our presence except for the occasional shouted obscenities and the dull thud of leather on leather. If you wanted, you could slip away from the game, run across Roddy's field, tiptoe over the felled tree across the narrowest section of the Suck as it negotiated around the 'island', and lie in the long grass on that independent republic listening to the shouts and cheers of your friends.

The ground we played on had no value. Nobody wanted it or bothered about it. For miles around there was nothing but wide open spaces, untilled fields and vast stretches of bog. Years afterwards, I would go back and stand looking at the space where Hackers Lane used to be, now again overgrown, absorbed back into the wilderness from which we had reclaimed it.

Today, what was once Hackers Lane is called Riverwalk. It is a block of apartments, perhaps a hundred of them. It was built at the height of the Celtic Tiger, incentivized by Section 23 tax reliefs. It is strange to see it now, its four storeys looming high over what used to be our pitch, like one of those stands we created in our fantasies while we played there forty years ago. It is surreal.

It's true that it's no Ballisodare. The apartments are well kept, although many of them appear to be unoccupied. At any given time, a dozen or more of them appear to be available for sale or rental. There is no sense of a community there, of the kind of activity you would expect in a complex designed to house two or three hundred people. In the beginning there was a gym and a restaurant and talk of a boardwalk, but that's all history now. Now there's just the apartments and the stark question: why?

Back in the time of Hackers Lane, if you'd asked us, we would have asserted with certainty that this was the last field in Ireland on which anyone would seek to build.

When the builders moved in, three decades later, some of us who had played there in the 1970s occasionally went down to watch. It was like watching someone bulldozing your past. Even leaving nostalgia aside, it seemed mad that this could be happening. But it was – which meant that you had to keep your sense of the madness of it to yourself, for fear of showing up your ignorance of the way things were now. It appeared to make no sense, and I met nobody who seemed convinced that it did, or had any clue as to why it was happening. I remember, a hundred times as the apartments were being built, asking people and being asked by people: why? A hundred new apartments in Castlerea, a town of 2,000 inhabitants, was like overnight increasing the population of Dublin by, say, 150,000. People would say that it was 'great for the town', as though assuming that, once the apartments were built, someone would come to live in them.

This phrase used to come to me, one I'd heard a million times growing up, from my parents, aunts and uncles, neighbours: 'Live horse and you'll get grass.' But nobody said it now: they just assumed that everybody else knew something they didn't, that someone, somewhere had a plan, which would one day be revealed in all its glory. As in the wider context, there was this sense that scepticism was something to be left unvoiced, lest the speaker indicate a lack of faith or understanding of the possibilities of the new Ireland. Somehow, most people seemed to become convinced that their deeper sense of pessimism was the thing they needed to look at, to interrogate with a view to establishing why they were so downbeat about everything, and this caused people to stop saying how ridiculous it was to build a hundred apartments on a swamp on a piece of ground that, ten years beforehand, you couldn't have given away.

\*

As these examples indicate, at the heart of the Irish experience of prosperity, between the mid-1990s and the late Noughties, was a delusion that is a little tricky to pin down. It had elements of a belief in the free lunch: the idea that past poverty had simply been the outcome of not understanding how the game was played. We smiled condescendingly at the primitive efforts of previous generations to achieve material self-realization, when all you had to do was jettison all those old-fashioned notions about sovereignty and independence, and sign up to the modern way. Now that we had shaken off our immaturity, we smugly told ourselves, all that was behind us.

There was also this half-blinkered approach to the idea of self-sustenance. Although almost nobody seemed to have the faintest idea how or why Ireland had suddenly become prosperous, there developed this idea that such things did not need to be understood except by those with responsibility for ensuring that prosperity continued. Economics, insofar as it was a matter of public contemplation or discussion at all, was regarded as a kind of modern juju. If you believed in it, it continued. If you started to doubt it, it might crumble and disappear.

In 2005, three years after the introduction of the euro, I wrote an essay for a BBC radio programme about how it was affecting the psychology of Irish society. My main point was that the euro was, in effect, a technology for throwing your money around. In retrospect, this verdict appears somewhat tautological: I should really have said that the euro was a technology for the enablement of economic incontinence.

At first, the new currency presented us with challenges from which we feared we might never be liberated. The government even distributed free electronic calculators to assist the public in making an easy transition from monetary backwardness to the modern world. Not only did these not help, they made things worse by suggesting the difficulty was purely of an arithmetic nature, whereas in truth the relationship between the departing punt and the shiny new euro was attended by sundry factors of a cultural and existential nature.

It never occurred to us that a currency could change our way of thinking about everything, including, eventually, the totality of our relationships with reality. Comparing the punt with the euro was like comparing an apple with an orange. We had become convinced that the euro would somehow make our lives better. We didn't know how this was supposed to work, but we did not doubt it, and were therefore unsurprised when it started to happen.

Then there was the inscrutability of the new currency. Shortly after the introduction of the euro, I remember feeling an escalating sense of despair about ever again being able to intuit the value of anything. Before that, I had been able to look at an object of my desire in a shop window and have a general sense of its worth. Sometimes with certain brands or labels, I would be way off the mark, but in general I had a sense of the correct balance to be maintained in the relationship between the product and my desire to have it. The euro caused this facility utterly to desert me.

Nobody had ever explained to us that a currency becomes internalized in the human being, its logic soaking into everything that drives us: confidence, hope, aspiration, ambition, desire. It was like a foreign language had suddenly been imposed, taking away from me many of my previous understandings about means and worth and forcing me to accept at face value a totally new version of reality. Presented with a putative transaction, I was reduced to ploddingly working out the fundamentals, mechanically and without any intuitive sense of value. If I looked at a pair of shoes and thought them worth about £35, my calculation, with or without the aid of the government's calculator, might have led me to expect them to retail now at between €40 and €45. But when I checked the label and found that the shoes now cost €75,

I immediately put this down to my own inadequate sense of the transformation that was occurring.

Something was happening to me that arithmetic could not touch. Because I had significantly more euro than previously punts, I began to feel richer in a way that, for all its irrationality, seemed to infect my sense of confidence. Where once I might have earned, say, £2,000 a month, now I was pulling in €2,500. I was quids-in, except that nobody seemed sure if you were allowed to call them 'quids' any more. Eventually, we decided that you could, which copper-fastened the sense that what had happened was merely a transition from an awkward, lumpy currency which inculcated a sense of caution and negativity, to one – having the same functions and capacities – which made you feel confidently part of something much bigger and primed with potential.

This sense that the euro had opened us up into some vast new reality brought with it suggestions of endless possibilities. Not alone did the euro whisper to me that I needed to shake off my former prudence and live a little, but it also confided that this prudence had been morally dubious, a brake on my potential to grow and be happy. This created in me a kind of recklessness, I have often thought, changing my character in some fundamental way. My initial confusion was replaced not by clarity but by a kind of indifference. In a short time, realizing that I no longer had recourse to any reliable instinct about the likely cost of anything, I stopped trying to work things out and simply surrendered to the change that had occurred. I invested the euro with a faith that had no rational basis other than that there was no alternative. I no longer knew how much money I had to spend or how much of it I had already spent. €50 became the new £20.

The consequent imposed recklessness involved also an awareness that the new money was less durable than the old. A €20 note looked like real money, but seemed to become dog-eared and tatty much more quickly than the punts had seemed to. This fuelled a growing sense that the new money was for throwing away, as though it had been designed to promote a casual attitude towards income and expenditure. You went to a cash dispenser to withdraw some spending money, with only the foggiest notion of how much you'd need. Experience was already telling you that adding 25 per cent to what you might previously have withdrawn in punts was as meaningless as withdrawing twice or three times as much. You just thought of a number, doubled it and added a tenner just to be sure. And when you came to the till or check-out counter, you just put your hand in your pocket or your purse, scooped out a mess of notes and change, held it out to the assistant with a nonchalant, 'Take it outta that!' Still, you never seemed to have enough, so you always ended up going back to the ATM with what would once, not long before, have seemed like wild abandon. If you thought about this, which generally you didn't, you quickly dismissed any misgivings by reminding yourself that the new currency represented a new dispensation, in which old frugalities and cautions were not merely pointless but possibly dangerous.

In the Tiger years, many of us didn't so much spend money as give it away. We loosed our hold on previous inhibitions and reservations. Much of the time, we had little idea how much we were spending, where it was coming from, how much we had left, or how much we were being ripped off. We stopped counting. Occasionally, when a bank or a credit card statement came in, we sneaked a look and recoiled, horrified. It was like the miracle of the loaves and fishes, and if we thought about it at all it was to think that here, at last, was the payoff for our faith and willingness in the matter of becoming outgoing and mature. We felt like kids just out of school, in our first jobs, with money jangling in our pockets. Many of us, psychologically speaking, were returned to that moment in our own lives, when, with money to spend for the first time, we felt entitled to a bit of a blow-out before knuckling down. Except here there was no question of knuckling down: only pessimism could kill this and the best way of keeping pessimism at bay was to carry on spending.

Whatever defences we might have had against these currency-induced tendencies were undermined by a related shifting in our sense of the value of bricks and mortar. Because property-owning was for many Irish people an unfamiliar experience, owning your own house or a piece of land had acquired almost sacramental characteristics in the Irish imagination. The unacknowledged racial memory of hunger and want held to the connection between these experiences and propertylessness. We had long believed that value and security could best be maintained in fields and sites and bricks and mortar. In the late-Tiger years, this totemic belief contrived to convince us that our outward recklessness was being underwritten by something as ungainsayable as the earth's core. Every other day, we awoke to newspaper and radio headlines informing us that the value of the house in which we lived had increased by some incredible percentage since the last time we had thought about it. This fuelled our nascent sense of property as possessing some almost transcendental capacity to hold and enhance value. Our houses, which had hitherto rested with their solid foundations plunged into the ground, started to detach themselves from any basis in three-dimensional reality, becoming instead the repositories of an escalating sense that prosperity had, all the time, been a simple matter of doing things correctly. Every day, as we pulled our hall doors behind us, we delivered a metaphorical pat to the pine on account of the way this edifice of concrete and timber and glass was somehow managing not just to store up all the value we had invested in it, but to multiply it even as we spent our days working for a more modest return. This meant, among other things, that anything we ourselves earned in the course of this modest day's endeavour could be regarded as mere pocket money, to be disposed of with a sense of impunity. Income was icing on the cake of prosperity.

In March 2008, *The Irish Times* published a peevish review of my book *Lapsed Agnostic* under the headline: 'Forgive Us John, For We have Become Prosperous'. This will tickle me until the day I die. The implication was that I thought prosperity a bad idea. In fact, as the book made crystal-clear, I had come to see prosperity as an illusion prone to seducing me as much as anyone. A whole section of the book was a reflection on my flirtations with materialist satisfaction, through the mediums of shirts and cars.

Yes, I, too, was caught inside the Celtic Tiger bubble. Despite the fact that I was one of those who at a professional level remained sceptical almost to the end, at a personal level I was lured into the state of collective delusion that gripped Ireland in the Tiger years. I, too, would sometimes sit daydreaming about how much the value of my house was going up while I was day-dreaming about it. I, too, took myself down to my financial adviser, who showed me how to renegotiate my mortgage to conjure up a new kitchen or automobile. I, too, was 'guilty'. This is the truth of it.

But being truthful is a dangerous business in a society where everything has become literal and where the main activities are scapegoating and finger-pointing. The above paragraph, with its self-deprecation and irony washed out, could be reduced in a tabloid headline or a tweet to: 'Waters says he's to blame for Tiger excess.' Thus, our picture of what happened in the Tiger years remains incomplete. We hear mainly from those with grievances, those looking for scapegoats, those seeking to forget. Everyone else keeps shtum. Among the likely consequences of this behavioural pattern is that it takes a long time before the truth begins to be understood at the level of culture.

In time to come, future generations may arrive at some clear understandings of the condition of delusion that gripped Ireland in those years, especially in the middle years of the Noughties, when Irish self-confidence seemed finally to break away from the binds of history. At the time, there was no objection to talking about how well 'we' were doing. Since the meltdown, however, the word 'we' has been banned – forbidden as unjust to those who did not participate. The conventional piety has it that these were the 'most vulnerable in society', but mostly the ones we were hearing from were those who lived through the Tiger years as if nothing was happening, good or bad, turning their backs on anything resembling optimism or enjoyment in the certain knowledge that it would all come to nothing. These would be the statues in Glasnevin Cemetery, I guess, and possibly the occasional Trappist monk.

While occasionally someone still speaks of 'we', there is this palpable sense that everything happened to – or was caused by – a tiny minority of other people. Often it sounds like what transpired was nothing to do with whoever happens to be speaking at any particular time. Like little boys seeking to divert enquiries about a broken window, most people, in discussing the meltdown, revert to the frugalistic moral logic of the pre-Tiger period, applying a post-Famine asceticism to a post-mortem of other people's foolishness. Politicians who have occasionally sought to allude to the more widespread nature of the madness are immediately jumped upon and accused of 'blaming the People'.

Still, there was a 'we', a category of Irish people who, for the first time, thought they glimpsed the possibility that history might not hold against them a permanent and unyielding grudge. For centuries our people had contemplated the wealth of others and imagined that poverty was a condition tied to Irish destinies as though to a conjoined twin. Then, one day, for no reason that anyone could think of, it seemed that history had had a change of heart.

Media, like water, tend to follow the path of least resistance. In the Tiger years, this meant following the logic of prosperity and suppressing any contrary impulses. In the wake of the collapse, it has meant stoking public rage and directing it towards a handful of high-profile potential targets, who have been lumbered with most of the blame. The subtextual idea is that 'The People' are entirely innocent of all charges. A frequent theme of commentators nowadays is that there was no 'we' who 'partied' during the boom. But the truth is that, although there may be some rare souls who can claim to have got nothing from the boom years, the vast majority of citizens enjoyed some benefits.

And yet, underneath the surface cacophony of rage and recrimination that has defined the Irish public conversation in recent years, it has been possible to detect another chord – of self-blame on account of having 'lost the run of ourselves'. Nobody says this too often or too loudly, but it remains a tiny trace element in the public conversation, and contains just enough substance to have kept most of us off the streets in spite of what has often seemed like extreme provocation. People talk a good riot on the radio phone-ins, but when the demagogues summon them to action, they stay home and wait for the revolution to come on TV. As politicians implemented swingeing cuts under direction from their IMF and European masters, the expected public backlash was largely confined to the radio phone-ins. There were enough guilty secrets out there to guarantee the relative passivity of the Irish public as at least a decade of austerity was ushered in.

Take Special Savings Investment Accounts (SSIAs), one of the most extraordinary bonanzas of the Tiger period, whereby the government topped up savings accumulated under the scheme by 25 per cent, to the tune of about €4 billion. There were approximately 1.2 million SSIA accounts, which means that roughly half the working population benefited. The top-ups were provided with borrowed money, which the general taxpayer was obliged to pay back.

Again, it is an element of the story that now seems slightly dreamlike, but for several years there was almost continuous and celebratory media coverage of the SSIA phenomenon. At the time, it was a matter of not inconsiderable shame to admit you didn't have one. People would smile condescendingly at you and secretly think how thick you must be. Later, when it all went wrong, you might be forgiven for thinking nobody at all had had one. In this and other ways, the SSIA episode enables us to see in microcosm the psychology that governed the boom years, and how this has shifted subtly in the years since the boom ended.

SSIAs were intended to encourage saving and curb consumer spending, but ultimately provided a classic example of private virtue becoming public vice, with the matured accounts feeding into the economy at precisely the wrong time. Just as we should have been hitting the brakes, a rogue foot was put on the accelerator. Maturing in 2006 and 2007, the SSIA accounts contributed enormously to the overheating of the economy. Without the expectation generated by them, the property market might have peaked several years before it did, with far less serious consequences.

In advance of maturation, motor dealers, mortgage lenders, technology stores and furniture outlets were extending credit on the back of SSIAs, although the rules specifically forbade this. As the economist David McWilliams pointed out, the SSIAs were really a tax that penalized all taxpayers for the benefit of approximately 50 per cent. He wrote in the *Irish Independent*:

When it comes to spending the SSIAs, it is psychology that predominates – because to rate in the New Irish Dream, to achieve parity of esteem, you have to have it all and have it now. No one can overshadow you, and if they do, it can't be permanent. If it is permanent, you are a loser and therefore not worthy. So the collective psychology of the nation is one of anxiety: where everything one person does, buys, wears, learns or accomplishes, sparks a reaction in others. Not only because these things look, feel and smell better, but because they confer status. This psychology impacts on the economy in a simple way.

And here I have to own up to recognizing myself in this broad description. I did not have an SSIA, but this apparent restraint did not arise from any moral virtue: I simply didn't have any spare cash. And the reason for this is that I had other uses for whatever financial resources came my way.

Although more than 100,000 Irish people bought properties abroad in the Celtic Tiger years – in Spain, Portugal, Bulgaria, Croatia and other exotic places – the only talk about this now is the occasional coy mention in the newspapers about the comparative rate of decline of property prices on the Costa del Sol or the Adriatic. Listening to the outrage that flows incessantly over the airwaves, you would think that only a handful of people bought such properties, just as you would think that nobody had the faintest idea what an SSIA might be.

We don't talk about this too much. You vaguely remember those intense conversations you had with your neighbour round about 2004 – about the comparative joys of Andalusia and the Algarve, and then, a few months later, him excitedly telling you he opted for a nice place in Sandanski. He never mentions it now, and neither do you. It's like having a relative who's doing time. It is not considered polite.

I have my own foolishnesses to account for. First among these is my little house in Spain, which I bought at the height of the boom. In the circumstances in which I found myself, I might have bought it anyway, but that is neither here nor there. Folly is folly, and this one at least affords me some emotional access to the collective psychology of the delusion that landed us in the economic do-do. (It also tempers my indignation about the errors

of those now fingered as the main culprits in our national undoing, but in this respect I am definitely in a minority.)

It happened like this. In the late 1990s, I became friendly with
an Irishman who owned a house on the Costa del Sol. I call him
'my Tiger friend', although we were never exactly friends, but
simply had occasion to meet from time to time, usually by
accident, and would get to talking. He had a way of almost
caricaturing the conventional notion of a Tiger arriviste and playing up to that, mocking himself and taking himself seriously at the
same time. Then he bought a house in Andalusia and immediately
began to think of himself as having joined the big players.
Sometimes he would call me from the roof terrace of this house
and describe the mountains and the village and the sunshine,
languidly teasing me about the rain that he could correctly guess
was hammering upon my window. He would tell me about how
much his house had grown in value in the few months since he had
bought it. It was a no-brainer, he used to say: only idiots remain
under-borrowed in a boom, when debt is a sign of courage and
wisdom. 'We're the boys!' he would declare if I showed even the
merest flicker of doubt or dissent. I swear: he exists.

In 2001, I won a significant amount of money in a defamation
action. My Tiger friend called me immediately and said I should
buy now before the prices went up again. He introduced me to a
man from the Spanish town adjacent to his own house, who
would, he said, take care of everything. The genius he introduced
me to specialized in renovating old houses and undertook to find
me a property, deal with the planning issues, carry out the 'reform'
of the house and handle all the legalities. I went over to meet him,
went to see a few properties in the same village where my Tiger
friend had his house and more or less bought the first one I
viewed. It was an old three-storey house in a tiny square off the
main town plaza. It was cheap by Irish standards, but when you
considered all the costs of reconstruction, probably not such good

value as it first appeared. Note the 'probably' there? Denial is a difficult condition to shake off.

And in the spirit of continuing partial denial, I intend to gloss over the details for reasons not entirely, you understand, to do with space. It was, I now freely admit, a disaster. For several years, I seemed constantly to be sending money out to my man in Spain, eventually losing track, not entirely without premeditation. The house became a bottomless pit for money. Every year a new disaster seemed to strike: collapsed ceilings, crumbling plaster, burst pipes. The paint peeled everywhere because there wasn't enough ventilation. Our man installed some air-conditioning, at vast expense, but the timer never worked, so the problems grew worse. Once, we arrived for our summer holidays and found a large hole in the floor of the lounge. In the end, it turned out that we didn't even have planning permission for the changes to the house, including the addition of a room to the third storey, which was already illegal.

I next came upon a quixotic Mancunian, since dead of a drug overdose, who made his predecessor look like Antoni Gaudí in the matter of both saintliness and building skills. The next time I arrived, expecting to review my beautiful new roof kitchen, I found a hole where my roof had been. In the end I went around the streets stopping perfect strangers until I encountered an honest Englishman who saved the house from collapse or/and almost certain seizure by the authorities. But maybe I'm still in denial.

Yes, of course I am.

My Tiger friend, meanwhile, couldn't be seen for dust. It turned out that his own house was worth about half what he'd paid for it. I'm still trying to figure out whether he was as stupid as myself and looking for another mug to make him feel better. It doesn't matter: all education is an expensive business.

When I was dreaming it all up, I convinced myself that I would go out to Spain perhaps a dozen times a year, at least once a month and maybe – why not? – for the whole of the summer. We ended up going for a fortnight once a year, and for several summers had to rent an apartment because the house was uninhabitable.

It wasn't greed, but fantasy, that did for me. OK, perhaps a little bit of greed, there being a certain attraction in the notion that you could overnight become a cute hoor and strike a killer deal to provoke a murmur of respect when you entered a room: 'Smart boy, Waters: bought himself a nice pad in Spain when they were cheap.'

Mainly, though, it was the fantasy. I remember mine with the utmost clarity, because a friend and fellow-prospector in the Spanish property goldrush spelt it out in graphic detail one evening as we planned our coup. It involved a sunset, a balmy terrace from which you could reach into the sky; a copy of Camus' *The Myth of Sisyphus* or Dostoyevsky's *The Brothers Karamazov* cast lazily aside as you looked up to welcome a lithe lover in a light cotton dress; a jug of sangria waiting on a cool marble table. Even the nagging awareness that I hadn't tasted alcohol for more than a decade did not alert me to the intrinsic insubstantiality of this tableau. I was hooked.

It took some years to discover the obvious: that you don't need to own a terrace to read Camus on one, and lithe lovers come and go, regardless of material circumstances. I have yet to taste sangria, and only occasionally think that if it tastes half as good as its promise it might be worth a wet brain.

What the fantasy causes you to end up with is a piece of property in a foreign country which needs to be maintained when you are reading Camus back home. There are times of the year when even the Spanish sun does not shine as brightly as in the 3D Technicolor of the selective scenarios we construct out of our infinite desires for something or other. To walk across the Balcon de Europa in Nerja at 7 p.m. on a Wednesday in November is one of the loneliest feelings in the world. All the lithe lovers have departed and only the crones and domino-playing pensionistos remain.

But the strange thing about fantasies is that, though they never come true in literal detail, they rarely lead us entirely astray. In a convoluted way, our Spanish odyssey has actually delivered. When, in years to come, I look back on the past decade of grief and guilt, I will remember it fondly, though not for reasons I fantasized about in advance. Instead of comprising merely hot August nights and tranquil moments gazing across the Mediterranean, our memory-book of Spanish adventuring includes also a series of what we have come to call 'surprises' – usually arising from collapsed ceilings, sweating walls, burst pipes and rising damp. We have yet to have a holiday in which we have not shared our house with tradesmen of various kinds, who work assiduously, messily and loudly while we are there and leave when we do.

And yet, when we are old and grey and full of sleep and prayer, our Spanish 'surprises' will dislodge in us the most laughter and remembered fun. Our house in Torrox is always with us, even in the deepest Irish winter, when the Spanish storylines continue. It has been a tragi-comedy peopled by characters more colourful and fantastic than even Dostoyevsky could conjure, and a series of plot-twists that in other people's language are termed catastrophes but in our family saga have become embellishments to the blossoming legend of Torrox. We fall around laughing at mention of the architect who spent the first four years of the third millennium in a Spanish prison, but whom the local authority of Torrox insisted we must continue to use in order to avoid a fine for his failure to submit a proper planning application. These experiences are as much a part of our Spain as flamenco and sun-shine. If you remain half awake through life, you eventually figure out that the purpose of fantasy is to provide inspiration to keep the human mechanism ticking over. It rarely works out, but, if you don't take it too personally, you find the outcomes amusing in their way. Reality has a mind of its own and there's no point in being too sore about it. Life is a succession of foolish errors followed by death. What we think we desire is not what we really long for, so the greatest pleasures and happiness arise from letting go of the fantasies that started us off on a particular path and opening our eyes to whatever life decides to drop in our laps. Out of the calm that follows the tearing out of the last hairs on our heads, there emerges a different kind of satisfaction than whatever we anticipated on the basis of our desires and imaginings.

You wouldn't plan our Spanish adventure the way it's turned out, but it is what it is. We pay taxes and water charges in return for sunshine and a pocketful of memories. We endure the administrations of the most bureaucratic officials on the face of the planet, and make ourselves available to the shysters and parasites which said officialdom appears to maintain as part of the system of exploiting *extranjeros*. The mention of Torrox never fails to bring a smile to the lips of anyone who has gone there with us. And when, one of these years, we come to Spain and find our Spanish house exactly as we left it, unyielding of 'surprises', unsweating and fragrant, I know that, contemplating a sun-filled fortnight without Paco or Mauricio to talk to while we're there and reminisce about afterwards, we will feel deep inside just the tiniest lurch of emptiness and regret.

The Celtic Tiger came about through the interworking of illusion and desire. Underlying this process, which in turn led to the sclerosis of the banking system, was the desire to cheat reality. Having always been poor, we became dizzy at the thought that poverty might be banished for ever. Did we lose the run of ourselves? Of course. Did we come to believe in the free lunch? Yes, we did. Was there a 'we'? Yes, there was.

229

In *The Great Crash 1929* John Kenneth Galbraith identified the main cause of that catastrophe as 'the desire to get rich quickly with the minimum of physical effort'. If we are honest, we will admit that this desire gripped us too. So intoxicating was the fantasy that we abandoned all prudence. The banking system, though presumably managed by people who know how these things go, spiked our drinks. The government of the day, though it might be presumed to know a thing or two about the price of lunches, didn't want to call time. Galbraith describes this phenomenon also: 'The signal feature of the mass escape from reality that occurred in 1929 and before . . . was that it carried Authority with it. Governments were either as bemused as were the speculators or they deemed it unwise to be sane at a time when sanity exposed one to ridicule, condemnation for spoiling the game, or the threat of severe political retribution.'

Ireland in the Tiger years was as susceptible to facts as a drunk with a crate of whiskey. The idea that our dreams could end in tears seemed not merely impossible, but illogical. As Galbraith advises, the only antidote to the kind of delusion that gripped us is what he calls the immunizing memory, the capacity to recall previous events dictated by the immutable principle that what goes up must come down. But, because we had never been there before, we had no memories to prompt us. We imagined we could escape from drudgery and create a space for ourselves where economic insecurity would be a thing of the past. We thought that, since our ancestors had already paid our collective dues many times over, it was no more than our entitlement to be rich for a change.

Now, we are observing how reality works: there is no free lunch, no gravity-defying strategy, no magic way of cheating reality. Now, we are as expert in slumps and recessions as we used to be in booms. We are learning that there is an unacknowledged law-of-life that will eventually strike at attempts to shore up against the fear of want, insisting, 'Thou shalt not accumulate, or at least not with any certainty of success.' We are not squirrels or magpies. What we have for sure is what we stand up in, right now. What we own is our capacity to create wealth in the future. True wealth, as Patrick Kavanagh said, is potential. I have my skills, talents, energies and with these I have the means to feed, house and clothe myself and my dependants, day to day. I can try to skim off some of the fruits for the rainy days ahead, and from time to time may strike lucky, but generally such endeavour will be subject to the enormous risk of depletion – unless you happen to be a German bondholder, boom-boom. Our pension funds, which we nursed so lovingly for the joyful decade of the Tiger, are in such ribbons that we are unable to look at the bottom line without experiencing a profound melancholy akin to that of Kafka's Gregor Samsa on the first morning of his metamorphosis. Our houses are the same edifices of bricks and mortar they were before – having, it seems, been swollen and reduced as though by some cosmic practical joke. We stand and look at them and find they have not changed at all. Something in us changed, and then, painfully, changed back again.

We start over, chastened but wiser. It seems unfair, but there you go. Life is life and love is love, and money can buy you neither.

# 8

# *Because I'm Worth It*

IMAGINE THAT IN A FEW YEARS WE WERE TO LOOK BACK AT THE crisis enveloping us in recent times and realize that it was but a symptom of another, much deeper malaise. If so, what might be the true nature of the malaise?

We have fallen into the habit of defining the present difficulties as economic phenomena afflicting 'the country'. But it should be obvious that 'the country' is the same as it was before. If you drive around a bit you will notice that the topography of the Irish landscape is largely unaffected by the arrival of the bailiffs. Indeed, it is possible to tap into a similar constancy that preceded the boom and remains after it.

For example, in my twenty-odd years of going up and down from Castlerea to Dublin, I've used three different routes, one in the beginning, the others in more recent times. Twenty years ago, the route that suggested itself, without any real competition, was Enfield, Kinnegad, Mullingar, Ballymahon, Lanesboro, into Roscommon town and home via Ballymoe. But the changing infrastructure of the midlands more recently suggested, indeed imposed, a new route: Kinnegad, Edgeworthstown, Longford, Strokestown. The roads became better, having had the full benefit of the structural funds bonanza, and took perhaps an hour or more off the journey time. Even more recently, the building of the M4 has offered an even faster alternative: the motorway to Athlone and then a moderately rough ride via Roscommon to Castlerea. But the 'old' route remains as it always was. And, whereas the 'new' route is in many ways emblematic of 'modern' Ireland – wide, straight lanes, flyovers, American-style road markings and 'gasoline' stations – the 'old' route via Ballymahon retains many of the qualities of Ireland as we remember it. To drive between Mullingar and Lanesboro is to go back twenty or thirty years.

I find it good to take that road now and again, to allow myself to meditate upon the true nature of change and to reflect on something that you might miss from listening to the radio every day: 'Ireland' is not in crisis – its people are.

Yet, no physical calamity has befallen us. We breathe and walk and laugh as we always have. As human beings we are changed in just one tangible way: we are more afraid.

Why? Because the systems we have created for conducting exchanges in the material realm have ceased to function as they did.

If your car refuses to start, you call a mechanic or the Automobile Association and expect to be back on the road within hours. But the system failure that currently confronts us is not purely mechanical. Some elements are technical, but far more critical is understanding what has happened to the 'human component': how it used to operate within the system but no longer does.

Listening to the conversations that repeat and repeat themselves on these topics, one might jump to the conclusion that what is at stake is something akin to the weather. We talk about restoring 'the conditions' for recovery, improved growth etc. For each of us, individually, such an analogy may be approximately useful, in the sense that each of us depends for his economic security on factors generated in the thoughts and activities of others, rendering things outside our individual control much as the weather is. But each of us is also part of the 'human component' of the system which has disintegrated precisely because of that human quotient.

The crisis that confronts us has been generated not by leaky gaskets or an occluded front, but by something out of the ordinary occurring within human responses. By 'out of the ordinary' I mean in terms of what we had become accustomed to, rather than something absolute and totally unpredictable or definitively catastrophic.

A market system is not powered by steam or internal combustion, but operates on the hopes and desires of human beings. We can talk all day about economics, but really the centre of the problem resides in the human heart: in the quality of hope, desire, faith, confidence and determination that may be available to the community in crisis.

Our banking system, for example, being based on the principle of fractional reserve lending, has been operating off an illusion sustained only by the quality of human hoping – a faith-based system. Typically, we tend to talk about the banking problem, too, in technical, legalistic or ethical terms; but if a faith-based system has ceased to function, perhaps it is because the quality of faith itself has been damaged?

Perhaps the economic system is really collapsing because human beings sought to find through it an answer for their longings that cannot be found in this way?

One implication of the recriminatory discussion that has ensued since the beginning of the disintegration in mid-2008 has been that we might have continued to pursue our desires as we had been doing – presumably to a successful conclusion – had a few bankers and politicians not torn the bejaysus out of it. More recently, the discussion has been dominated by those who tell us that, by effecting this or that ethical or mechanistic adjustment, we can restore the system to balance, with human beings once again snug and well adjusted at the heart of it. Thus, all discussion is predicated on the idea that, had we done things slightly differently, we could have preserved our illusions.

What passes for sanity in our present discussion, therefore, is really a kind of existential cute-hoorism that still seeks to cheat reality by insisting that human beings can create systems to cater for all their wants. A further irony is added by the fact that this very conversation, imbued as it is with fatalism and rage, is preventing any reinvigoration of the human qualities of hope and confidence without which the system cannot be rebooted.

Certain ineluctable characteristics define us: we need to eat, to sleep. Here's another: we cannot be satisfied by anything this dimension has to offer. Time and again, we observe that, sooner or later, an apparently functioning system becomes subject to the unlimited nature of human desire, which blasts it asunder like a tornado ripping through a church fete.

We have spent four years talking economics. Perhaps, before long, we might spend a short time talking about the nature of humanity and what it is we expect? What if we had become incapable of hoping because we had rumbled the tricks that enabled the maintenance of a faith-based economic system? What if something has been happening to the very desires that get us out of – or sometimes into – bed?

Back in 2010, a friend sent me a copy of the latest Italian 'Censis' report, which is an annual state-of-the-nation summary of the essential patterns and issues affecting the collective well-being of the nation. You would expect such a document to outline growth projections and possibly issue dire warnings about negative indicators such as unemployment and increasing borrowings. You would hardly expect to find an existential analysis, and certainly you would never do so in the Irish equivalent, whatever that might be. The Censis report combines elements of demographic survey and social analysis, and claims to describe Italy 'in its most intimate essence'. In 2010 it found a society possessed of 'a collective unconscious without any law or desire'. It was so gnawingly evocative and yet such an unusual way for a modern society to be described by the technocrats appointed for this purpose that it caused me to think a little deeper about the problems we had been experiencing at home.

Italian society, the Censis report outlined, 'slides under a wave of disorderly instincts', becoming 'dangerously marked by emptiness'. The report spoke of 'a painful alienation'; of a 'flattened society', dazed and disoriented; of nihilism and of the weakening of the individual citizen's sense of connection to the public realm. It identified profound patterns of cynicism, indifference, passivity, and excessive enslavement to media perspectives and prognoses, which condemned the population 'to the present without possibility of going deeper in the memory and in the future'. Trust in long-term drifts and in the effectiveness of the governing class was declining alarmingly.

The picture of a nation less willing to grow, to build, to look for happiness is one that resonates with that of other European societies including – jarringly – our own. The characteristics described, when we come to think of it, are true of possibly every country calling itself 'modern' today. And yet, what a strange idea for us who have been bombarded with economistic prescriptions and information: that, underneath all this palaver, the reason for everything may be that our societies have been misunderstanding human desire. This is doubly strange because desire is perhaps the thing our societies pride themselves on understanding better than anything else, on catering for and pandering to absolutely. Desire: the driving agent of our markets, our consumer culture, our media, our individual 'mechanisms' as 'components' of our societies and consumers of the products and services that keep the wheels of progress turning around.

In the late spring of 2011, the Irish people received their first formal analysis of what had befallen them, when Peter Nyberg, a Finnish consultant who had been commissioned to investigate the nature of the banking collapse, reported his findings. By then, we hardly needed to be told that a 'herd instinct' had taken over our banking system, that our economy became subject to an 'exceptional financial mania', that 'irrational forces' took hold; that 'contrarian views' had been rubbished or ignored, that we had had insufficient checks and balances and had lost sight of the purpose of regulation. Indeed, much had already been made since the disaster hit of the failure of regulation as a key factor in our undoing. In one sense, this is a fatuous and somewhat tautological proposition, since rules and laws on their own are insufficient to damp down the unstoppable energy of human desiring. But in another sense the absence of adequate regulation may be germane: in the sense that 'rules' are a way of making other people's experiences available as a form of collective memory. Such a memory bank is especially vital in a time when surfeits of optimism and complacency are prone to inculcating an inadequate capacity to remain cognizant of how things tend to turn out.

It is impossible to analyse the recent Irish economic madness without understanding and taking account of the national personality, which Nyberg appeared to treat as a neutral factor in the disaster. He used the language of psychology, but had insufficient knowledge of the underfoot conditions to come up with anything more than technocratic clichés. It is odd that we gave the job of analysing us to a Finn. We have lots in common with the Finns: they too were subject to occupation (by the Russians), had a famine, declared Independence just a few years before us and afterwards experienced a bitter civil war. But the average Finn emerged from this history quite differently from the average Irishman. Finns, in general, are reserved people, not tending towards outward shows of emotion. They work hard and drink harder. For some reason they have not taken the burden of their history upon themselves as we have, but appear to have achieved a solid sense of self-confidence. They are not as given to romanticism as we are, nor indeed to lamenting and complaining. They get on with things. Any more than an Irishman trying to figure out Finns, a Finn trying to figure out Ireland just wouldn't have a clue why we ended up so different after such similar experiences.

If we wish to embark on a psychological analysis of the reasons for the catastrophe, we need to go right back into the particularities of Irish history on a mission to understand our relationship with optimism, good fortune and prosperity. The underlying Irish personality has not for a long time been a sunny one, except with a modicum of chemical assistance. Normally we are gloomy and pessimistic, a disposition soundly based in a miserable history. Our natural response is to be fearful of outcomes, to see the glass as half empty, to expect the worst, to believe that reality is essentially hostile, to think that not much is possible. But we are also relatively accepting of hardship and misfortune, tending to resort to a kind of ironic resignation when things go badly, to count our blessings and acknowledge that, no matter how bad things seem to get, they 'could be worse'. This natural state of affairs is not pretty, but it has long had the unacknowledged virtue of keeping us safe from other elements of our personality, such as a tendency to go crazy at the drop of a green furry hat. It has functioned to hold us back from risk, which, while protecting us from disappointment and even possibly certain categories of misfortune, also ensured that we rarely took the chances that might have led to us achieving by our own lights.

The purpose in Irish culture of the begrudger was to spot any incipient signs of people getting potentially disruptive notions above their stations and to nip things in the bud. And this, paradoxically, helps to explain why we become so excited whenever an Irish person, say a sportsman, a writer or an Irish fly climbing up a distant wall, achieves anything abroad. For a long time, 'abroad' was the only place such a thing could happen, because anyone who tried to make anything of himself at home would be buried under an avalanche of cynicism. What overcomes us on such occasions is not admiration but a kind of wonder that this individual had somehow managed to shake off the national torpor and give foreigners a run for their money.

But these conditions pretty much ceased to exist during the second half of the Tiger years. After an initial period of widespread caution, the national mood-barometer swung completely in the other direction, and the Irish went from a nation of doomsayers to a nation of hyper-optimists. The glass, far from being half empty or even half full, was overflowing. The begrudger, who had previously patrolled all aspects of Irish endeavour, fell silent over his pint or sometimes threw himself into the party in the confidence that his genius for amnesia would stand him in good stead in the event of things going wrong.

In a strange way, this shift was given an unexpected impetus by an enhanced awareness of our previous pessimism, which entered the equation as a spur to increasing confidence and self-belief. There was a growing sense that we had been misreading reality, that it was not hostile to us after all, that there was no reason Irish people could not do things better than others. The arrival of cheap money when we joined the euro added fuel to this developing sense that our reading of history had been completely wrong.

The new logic went something like this: 'OK, so we've always been poor and we don't quite understand why that's no longer true, but everybody else seems to be happy and positive, so maybe everything really is changed and what you need to do is stop being such a mope and a killjoy.'

In these dizzying years, protecting Irish prosperity became a matter of keeping your doubts to yourself. The flip-flopped national historical memory led us to regard anyone who threatened to pull the communication cord as mean-spirited and unpatriotic – people who had allowed themselves to become downcast by the weight of Irish history, who could not see the dawn even when the sun was shining up their backsides. Peter Nyberg called it 'a misplaced sense of optimism', but it would be more accurate to say that it was a compensatory optimism to counteract the cultural effect of the centuries of pessimism that had gone before.

Perhaps the discipline we needed was not psychology but psychiatry. You might say that what happened to us in the boom years is that our condition shifted from what a psychiatrist might have diagnosed as straightforward depression to what the psychiatric profession nowadays identifies as 'bi-polar disorder', the primary symptoms of which are dramatic and unpredictable swings between depression and mania. Symptoms of mania include excessive happiness, excitement, irritability, restlessness, increased energy, reduced need for sleep, racing thoughts, high sex drive and a tendency to make grand and unattainable plans. Does that sound like 2004 to you? A 'manic episode' is a 'period of abnormally elevated mood, accompanied by abnormal behaviour that disrupts life'.

Depressive symptoms, on the other hand, include sadness, anxiety, irritability, loss of energy, uncontrollable crying, changes in appetite, increased need for sleep, difficulty making decisions, and thoughts of death or suicide. Doesn't that sound like Ireland between 1982 and 1995, and again between 2007 and the present?

The story of the Celtic Tiger is of the triumph of instinct over memory, of the pursuit of immediate gain without any accounting for the likely consequences, of a collective loss of the sense of what human happiness really is. In our desire to repudiate the failures of the past, we sought to dispense with all warnings that human nature has certain characteristics that do not change much in the short run. Peter Nyberg's analysis reminded us that, perhaps over a period as short as a few months, we erased from our immediate consciousness virtually the entire race memory bequeathed by our ancestors.

Sigmund Freud wrote that if you would understand what happiness is, put your foot outside the blankets on a cold night, leave it there for a few minutes and take it back in. Happiness is not something to be pursued in a linear, relentless way, but occurs as a relative phenomenon in a life of pain and pleasure, effort and reward, sacrifice and occasional satisfaction, ebb and flow.

Something Nyberg did not emphasize is that, in a capitalist system, misunderstandings of happiness are both inevitable and essential. When people seek happiness by buying things, it is probably that they don't understand, or have forgotten, how life really works. Capitalism, indeed, depends on such misunderstandings.

Ireland is a relative newcomer to the capitalist mainstream, having for centuries been a dependency with no capacity to further its education by dint of hard experience of the kinds of risk involved. Perhaps, then, we were not to know that growth is an illusion that does not satisfy, or that materialism does not deliver in a linear, exponential manner, or that bricks and mortar are not coherent repositories of material value, or that boom is always followed by bust. But, still, there is something unforgivable in the way we seemed to forget some of the earliest lessons we received. Every Lent and Easter of our childhoods we were taught that self-denial is the best way of enhancing enjoyment of life, that the point of forgoing the things we immediately crave is not self-punishment but achievement of an understanding of our desires. This is the lesson we awoke to every Easter Sunday morning, discovering that chocolate tastes better when you've had none for a while. Because we had come to see such propositions as arbitrary impositions on our capacity to enjoy ourselves, it was probably inevitable that we would kick over the traces the first chance we got.

We had, over the previous couple of decades in particular, fallen into a way of seeing ourselves that identified all difficulties arising from progress as transitional and discountable. An acquired belief in the unqualified benefits of progress caused us to ignore the connections between change and emerging dissonances, seeing only those aspects of progress which seemed unambiguously beneficial. Indeed this was part of the pattern we had imitated from elsewhere: for decades, Western societies had adopted an ideologically motivated ostrich-posture towards inconvenient or incoherent drifts within themselves, and, although these were now bursting out in all kinds of unexpected ways, we were still refusing to make the most rudimentary connections. Even after the onset of the catastrophe, although we talked and talked about what had befallen us, we still spoke of the symptoms in reduced and boxed-off contexts, describing the difficulties in ways that implied that they were the inevitable consequences of ancient repressions, and assuring ourselves that they would ultimately yield to technocratic manageability.

In cultural terms, we tend to think of desire either as something abstract or as something optional that can be summoned up in human beings by an advertising campaign. Culture persuades us to forget that human desire is a pure energy, and that when it cannot achieve correspondence for itself, it does not simply remain static, waiting. It has a life of its own and that life continues as best it can.

We Irish have mistakenly tended to identify such characteristics as moral failings. We talk about the 'spiritual vacuum' and how the 'consumer society' has led us to become so accustomed to having our desires satisfied in a certain way that we can no longer get enough, cannot even decide what we want, have 'lost the run of ourselves' and so forth.

But there is a further stage that we do not appear to have considered: human desire answered in the wrong way starts to atrophy. Failing to find some true path forward to an object equal to itself, it either turns inwards and begins to destroy the human being, or becomes flattened, reduced by persistent disappointments to a crushed husk of itself. The result is cynicism, disillusionment and alienation. When a whole society does this, it loses the will to grow and build.

The problem, as the 2010 Italian Censis Report made clear, exists in the collective unconscious. The failure to define human desire within an absolute framework, in which satisfaction is something to be achieved over the long run, creates an implosion of human energies which in turn sets off a crisis of hope. Disappointment with outcomes in the economic sphere, the report elaborates, creates a 'flattening' of faith in future development, and increased cynicism about values and tradition. This accelerates an erosion of faith in all of the former repositories of moral or judicial order and unleashes a 'widespread and disturbing instinctual disorder', with individual behaviours increasingly born out of a 'self referential and narcissistic selfishness': gratuitous violence; an impulsive tendency to commit misdemeanours; casual sexual behaviours; the pursuit of personal satisfaction through shopping; a quest for excessive external stimuli that make up for the subject's interior emptiness; and a 'demential quest for experiences that challenge death'.

It should be obvious that the existential and anthropological crisis outlined in the Censis report was not confined to Italy. Irish society, too, had increasingly been yielding up the same symptoms, at the core of which could be detected the same depletion of desire, which had been reduced by the recurrent inadequacy of materialist answers.

We think desire is something that belongs to our time, almost as if we invented it. We are prepared to accept, in an abstract kind of way, that our grandparents came together out of some kind of desire, but we don't tend to dwell on this. We think of them as having been too easily satisfied. And here we encounter what for us may be the most sensational idea of all: that they desired far more than we do. We think of the religious demeanour that seems to have defined our societies until relatively recently as simplistic and deferential, an instrument of social control. We do not often think of the trajectory of human desire under the influence of a religious culture. But our condescension now reveals itself as misplaced. For what we see, when we imagine such a phenomenon, is a near perfect arc of desire – liberated from distraction and misdirection, human desire led out from its point of origin into a flight-path where it can project itself towards something beyond, and thus is enabled to avoid collision with things which, not being its equal, tend to sap its energy.

This is the ultimate shocking conclusion for our societies: that the pursuit of a religious idea is ultimately the only way in which a whole culture can free up the human desiring of its members in order fully to realize itself. Religious-minded people understand this implicitly, but even they often seem to understand it in a different way: that the religious idea is a kind of contract not to give human desire full rein. The opposite is true: only by allowing it to pursue unfettered what it intuits to lie beyond does human desire become really free. One problem with modern cultures, which have swung from religion to secularism, is that, in pursuit of individualist solutions, they forget the necessity for collective understandings of objective focal-points, such as the idea of God once fulfilled in, for example, Irish society. This tendency has unleashed an opposite reaction, whereby the resolutely – and increasingly defensive – 'religious' mentality insists upon the continuing recognition of a God who in reality is no longer a cultural phenomenon, but has become just as individualized as the secularized logic that denies Him.

244

*

One of the things that has delighted and amazed me in recent times has been the way that, notwithstanding the constant flow of bad news in the public domain, Irish people continued to describe themselves as happy and contented, certainly by comparison with other peoples caught up in similar circumstances. Survey after survey came to the same conclusion: in spite of the state of the economy, and even contrary to the daily evidence of radio phone-ins, we were still counting our blessings and perhaps reminding ourselves that things 'could be worse'. Of course, in assessing such data, one needs to be mindful of the Irish capacities for self-delusion and calculated duplicity. In many respects, the picture emerging from various surveys of the post-apocalypse Irish personality contradicts both the historical profile and the evidence of public venting in the years since the Celtic Tiger headed off into the sunset. But let's hear the evidence at least, before we own up to its incomprehensibility.

One such survey, conducted by Gallup late in 2010 – before the 'bail-out' but after more than two years of relentless bad economic news – found that Irish people continued to describe themselves as among the most fulfilled and optimistic in the world. Ireland came tenth in this global poll, with nearly two-thirds of Irish people apparently describing themselves as 'thriving' and 'contented'.

A March 2009 survey, six months into economic Armageddon, found that we were still 'the happiest, healthiest and most satisfied people in the EU'. A September 2010 study placed us as 'among the happiest and most charitable people in the world', while another, a month later, informed us that we were less likely to be sick or depressed than our European neighbours. In October 2011, a Eurobarometer survey found that some 90 per cent of us are 'very' or 'fairly' satisfied with the lives we lead.

This picture is occasionally challenged by what seems like its opposite. In January 2012, the National Consumer Agency highlighted what appeared to be acute financial worries among the population, with one in three Irish people concerned about not having enough money to meet everyday expenses. Such contradictions seemed to come down to what question was asked – and perhaps who was asking. Confronted by a question about how 'happy' we are, we seem immediately to categorize the issue as either 'existential' or 'political/economic', and answer accordingly. That Eurobarometer survey also indicated that, when people were asked questions clearly relating to the economy, their responses reversed those given to the general questions. Just 4 per cent of respondents said they were satisfied with the national economy, compared to an EU average of 30 per cent. And yet, asked a more general question about the outlook for the next year, only 9 per cent of us expected things to get worse, placing us just marginally below the EU average of 14 per cent.

There are different ways of interpreting these anomalies, but to me it seems that people divide their responses between what they have been conditioned to think as a result of tuning into the everyday collective discussions, and what they really feel, looking at their lives in a broader context. Economically we are inconsolable; existentially we are happy enough, perhaps because history has inculcated in us a talent for not expecting much except misfortune.

But even more interesting are the often convoluted attempts at explanation conducted in the national media, which persists in treating this as a mysterious phenomenon meriting some kind of complex explanation. Some newspapers carried lengthy analyses of the 2010 Gallup survey, exploring every conceivable aspect of its findings with the exception of the most obvious. They consulted economists, sociologists, psychologists, philosophers, and even occasionally self-styled 'metaphysicians', but carefully avoided discussion with anyone in the habit of looking at Irish society without a secular-approved ideological viewfinder.

Often, in such ruminations, you find that two diametrically opposing concepts of life and the world are being offered, as though on a pick 'n' mix basis: on the one hand, the idea that, recession notwithstanding, human happiness continues to relate to positive growth figures (i.e. a comparative index that, because of the continuing success of the cuckoo-in-the-nest economy, places Ireland still among the richer countries); on the other hand, a sense that there seems to be some mysterious quality of resilience in the human spirit that is mobilized by adversity itself.

What nobody ever mentions is that Ireland, in spite of everything, remains a Christian country. If religion is considered at all in such analyses, it is the subject, invariably, of some colossal reduction – to 'community' or 'values' or 'consolation' – and always referred to with the sneakily not-quite-articulated undercurrent that any adherence to such concepts of reality is outmoded and in contravention of 'rational' principles.

It is quite shocking to observe the construction and phraseology of such analyses lately and note how they now implicitly exclude or rule out all consideration of Christianity as a contributing factor to human happiness. The favoured terminologies refer to 'happiness indices', to 'psychological well-being', to 'meaning of life indicators', even, by way of acknowledging the downsides or limits of technocratic solutions, to addiction, suicide and self-harm. Rarely if ever do they allow for consideration that happiness, where it exists, draws its rationale from an absolute perspective, understood in the Irish context in Christian terms.

If you delve right into the anatomy of this type of discussion, something deeper strikes you: there is an implicit comparison being made in all this, which is very likely based on a fallacy. The comparison, invariably, is with some posited notion of how Irish people 'ought' to be feeling, as a result, presumably, of objective circumstances as described, one intuits, by those doing the interpreting. In media terms, these 'objective circumstances' seem defined overwhelmingly by the continuing financial crisis.

What the science tells us is that money is only an indicator of happiness, which diminishes the more money comes to be considered the most important thing. In other words, the more emphasis people place on money, the more reduced tends to be their sense of well-being, and this is liable to be true whether they end up rich or poor. And this syndrome is observed more acutely among people who use money as a means of alleviating self-doubt. The relationship between money and happiness is graphically captured by what is called the 'Easterlin Paradox', named after the economist Richard Easterlin, who, in a groundbreaking piece of research in 1974, found that the relationship between money and well-being was not as conventional wisdom tended to present it. He discovered that whereas up to the level of basic economic security, people with above-average incomes tended to describe themselves as happier than those below the average, there was a tipping point beyond which this apparently self-evident formula ceased to apply. Easterlin discovered that once a country had moved beyond the point where basic needs were met – food, shelter, energy, etc – happiness rates did not increase in tandem with incomes. After this, money ceased to have a direct accelerating effect on human happiness. Once basic needs are met, the next phase involves unhealthy comparisons with how other people are doing, and these inevitably make everyone less happy.

In his fine 2009 book, *The Value of Nothing*, Raj Patel analysed recent data and, echoing Easterlin, decided that having more money is more likely to make a people less happy. But he also observed that, while it is possible for a country to increase its happiness using money, the cost of doing this, beyond a certain basic level, is unexpectedly high. Beyond the level of basic human needs, the relationship between income and happiness ceases to be arithmetic and becomes exponential. 'So to go from one to two units of happiness might take ten dollars, but after hitting the point at which our basic needs are met, to go from two to three units of happiness would take one hundred dollars, from three to four would take one thousand, and so on.'

Even if we had never heard of the Easterlin Paradox, we would probably intuit that the relationship between money and happiness is not straightforward. Most current affairs discussions, however, seem to assume that the relationship between money and happiness is absolute. It is important, then, to retain a basic understanding about all this: that it is the media – and only the media – that persistently assume economics to be the best or sole measurement of human happiness. And it is important, too, to be aware that this is not a natural or objectively justifiable way of understanding reality in its totality. This is the thinking that lured us into the current calamity, and so is unlikely to lift us out again.

Even a short time spent monitoring radio or television programmes dealing with what is called 'current affairs' leads unavoidably to the conclusion that the version of the world being offered derives from a mindset intent upon spreading anxiety and pessimism. Minute to minute, we are told how worried we should be and what we should worry about next. If you listened a lot, you could easily get to thinking that the future is irredeemably bleak and that everyone else seems to realize this except yourself. And yet survey after survey tells us otherwise.

The scope, influence and usefulness of journalism comes down to the range of words it is capable of using. If you listen to the average edition of *Morning Ireland* and give any thought to what you are experiencing, you realize very quickly that the range of words is very narrow, that the version of the world you are being offered derives not so much from a certain analysis as a certain mindset. You note that what is being elevated is what is measurable, countable, provable. If you tune in at any time other than during the sports section you will all but certainly hear, within the first thirty seconds, one of the following words: 'cash', 'levy', 'redundancy', 'cost', 'tax', 'payment', 'credit', 'liabilities', 'income', 'bail-out', 'revenue', 'compliance', 'growth' or 'bankrupt'. It is possible, in this way, to provide what seems to be a description of reality. But it is at best a partial, and more likely a skewed version of human reality that reduces everything to earnings, outputs, profits and deductions.

Listening to such current affairs programmes, you might be forgiven for imagining that perhaps 87 per cent, or 92 per cent, or 95 per cent of objective Irish reality is defined by economics. These past four years, the menu of topics for such programmes appears to have remained unchanged: banking, budgets, bail-outs, cutbacks, forecasts. If we were to imagine this to be a coherent and reliable description of reality, it is unlikely that many of us would describe ourselves as 'happy'.

But, judging from the aforementioned 2010 Gallup survey, and indeed from simply walking down the street, you gather that most people listening to this purported representation of reality seem to retain, in spite of it, an intrinsic sense of reality as something utterly different to these descriptions. Most people are reasonably healthy, have a job, friends, loved ones. Most people have a sense, when they stand up from the table after breakfast, that they are not defined 95 per cent by economics, but 99.9999999 per cent by something else. Yes, I may have financial difficulties, but I still have my life, my consciousness, my hope, my spirit. The sun shines, from time to time. Reality remains resplendent with shimmering strands of optimism that no sociologist is capable of describing. Even if I do not, at any particular moment, have a job or an income, as has happened to most of us at one time or another, the objective reality of my life is rarely overwhelmed by the resulting challenges, but also holds within it a hope that is greater than any economic or social fact. Most people, in other words, have a sense of Providence, which has been with them for as long as they remember.

Journalism by nature requires figures, measurements, statistics, in order to present what seems like an authoritative view of what matters. Economics, however discredited as a science or interpretation of reality, provides a relatively convenient way of describing what seems to be happening in the world.

People, though, are not so easily 'described', in the totality of their humanity and desires. Underneath the surface guises – 'consumer', 'commuter', 'worker' – behind the economic categories headed 'bed-nights', 'absenteeism' and 'footfall', other things are going on. And journalism, for whatever reason, seems increasingly ill-equipped to describe what these 'other things' are.

It is important to retain this awareness, as you listen yet again to some doleful, desperate account of the future from some jargon-spouting latter-day Jeremiah, remembering that the way the media represents reality is the function not of objective understanding but of ideological and semantic convenience. These 'descriptions' of 'reality' are rendered inevitable by a new public-square logic, increasingly dominating all aspects of our public life. This logic relentlessly insinuates a way of comprehending reality from which the languages and thought processes of religion and authentic art – art as a means of awakening deeper awareness of human responses – have now been almost utterly cleansed. Thus, what were once everyday understandings have been replaced by reductive languages and reduced forms of public reasoning by which all things must be measured, weighed, accounted and 'proved'.

More and more, the words and constructions capable of summoning up broader understandings are being removed from public earshot, to the extent that it now sounds strange if a voice on the radio begins to speak of the future with no mention of growth projections, but rather in terms, say, of beauty or hope or desire or goodness. Sooner or later, he will be asked something like: 'But what is your prognosis, going forward?'

But even more galling is when, by way of a break from their routine daily efforts to redefine the humanly desirable, these same media technocrats set aside huge tracts of weekend space to discuss how it is that, in spite of the 'reality' they have spent all week describing, human beings still find reasons to believe in life's possibilities. In these explorations, everything conceivable will be considered except the hippopotamus in the hallway: the fact that, for some 1,500 years, Irish society has been vivified by the idea of Christ, and that, in spite of the relentless efforts of the technocrats, campaigning secularists and self-styled rationalists, the hope extended by His proposal still endures in the very DNA of most Irish people.

One of the great clichés of the Tiger period was the idea that we had replaced the zeal we once displayed towards Godliness with a fanaticism for materialism. There was something in this, but we need to be more precise and forensic. What really happened to us in the Tiger period was that we let out the throttle on the materialist experience, just to see what might happen. We had moved from a culture in which the idea of happiness was bound up with the next life to one in which the idea of happiness had boomeranged back and begun to hover around ourselves and how we might look, feel or be.

Still, the lesson is hard to absorb. It is a slow process of experiencing, observing, re-experiencing, making the same mistakes over and over, and finally coming to terms with what is staring you in the face.

In the autumn of 2008, just after the crisis first broke, I noticed that it was becoming even harder than before to find a parking place at weekends in the car park of the Dundrum Town Centre, the capital's largest and most patronized shopping mall. Inside, similarly, I found the place was thronged with people, which seemed to go against the prevailing mood of advancing austerity.

But when you looked more closely, you noticed that people weren't carrying as many paper bags as they used to. A management source told me that, once the recession hit, the footfall shot up but the receipts went down.

I began to watch things more carefully. And, sure enough, things were just as busy as before but it was obvious that much less real business was being transacted. The punters were walking around, window shopping, trying things on, talking things over with their hunting companions, going away to have coffee, coming back and trying things on again – in short, enjoying the entire process just as before but nearly always cutting just short of the money shot. And this told me that, already, we had begun to suss that the satisfaction of shopping is about 90 per cent ritual and 10 per cent tied in with the tangible benefit of the goods you might buy. (In fact, if you factor in the post-purchasing guilt and the almost inevitable realization that no purchase will ever satisfy your deepest cravings, you realize that you can enjoy virtually the entire experience of shopping without buying anything at all.)

During the January sales in 2011, I accompanied my girlfriend while she hunted for shoes in the same shopping mall. We fetched up in House of Fraser, where there was a small mountain of footwear on the floor, like so many grouse brought down by bloodthirsty women. I sat for a while among the menfolk, heads in their hands, looking at that heap, thinking of it as a pile of disappointments, ill-fits and unrequited desires. If I am ever asked to conceive a monument to the Celtic Tiger, I shall propose a sculptured mountain of women's shoes.

To 'shop' – to really make a verb of the word – is to engage fully with the illusion created by human desire. There are few things within public sight that enable us to see our desires in action like the floor of a busy department store. It goes far beyond the sway of shoes, garments, objects. Buying things, especially things intended to be worn, is a way of storing up the future, of identifying and entrapping a perfect moment to come, in which all desire might be fulfilled. Once you understand this, you understand why they call it 'sales fever'.

Pure materialism is not merely an excess of spending; it is a different way of seeing reality. When we succumb to it, the things we buy ourselves to wear or drive are no longer about looking good for ourselves or even about making us more attractive to others, but a way of reinventing ourselves in accordance with a utopian fantasy of earthly potential. Shopping for clothes or shoes or cars is a way of reconstructing – perfecting – ourselves. A pair of jeans or a Mercedes is not simply something to wear or drive, but part of a technology of being. This is the nature of the fever: to come across something that really speaks to me of my innermost earthly fantasies is to encounter something literally breathtaking. On encountering the object of my desire, I am thrown into a conflict with my rationality, my sense of value, prudence and balance – and reason is doomed to lose. To want something you do not really need is to meet something in yourself that you cannot fathom or control. This is why the L'Oréal slogan 'Because I'm worth it' was such a brilliant marketing ploy: it justified the unjustifiable and put an end to all reasonable argument.

When we are able to be really truthful about the Celtic Tiger, we will perhaps come to admit that it left most of our desires unfulfilled while filling us with the sense that satisfaction was always just around the corner. For a brief time, it enabled us to look better on the outside while inside feeling even hollower than before. And afterwards we grieved for something that, deep down, we knew we could never have attained in the way we pursued it.

In one of his writings, Pope John Paul II told a pointed story about two priests emerging from a church and being visited by the striding presence of a beautiful woman going by. One looked instantly away, recoiling from the temptation. The other looked squarely at the woman and even turned to admire her further as she passed. John Paul asked: which priest acted properly? His answer was that each had done the right thing for himself: one, being immature, had rightly avoided the danger of looking at the woman in a reductionist way; the other, having arrived at a point where he could see her in all her created beauty, was able correctly to enjoy this fine example of God's handiwork. The meaning is powerful, but a little opaque: nothing is sinful in itself, but can become so by unreadiness. In the end, if we are capable of understanding who we are and what makes us human, nothing can lead us astray.

For more than a decade, we laboured under the collective delusion that the Celtic Tiger would deliver the outright satisfaction of our desires in every context. For four years in the wake of its departure, we have fallen sway to the further delusion that this promise would have been delivered on had the politicians and bankers not screwed it up. A moment's reflection should jerk us back to reality: we created the illusion of a utopia by plundering the future. We lost sight of the infinite nature of our desires and thought they could be sated with things we could eat or drink or wear or drive.

The past four years, by contrast with the Tiger decade, have seen the emergence of a form of dystopianism, a reaction to the surging utopianism of the preceding period, combined with an incipient sense that it is only because of the flawed nature of its personnel that the political system failed to deliver the satisfactions we craved. We react with rage to the discovery that – surprise surprise! – human beings are weak and flawed, and man-made systems have not made us safe and happy ever after.

We use the word 'hope' a lot nowadays, probably far more than it was ever used before, and it is difficult to avoid the thought that we do this because, at a public level, we are no longer allowed to think much about what 'hope' really means, or where it comes from. Perhaps we use it so much because we have, publicly at least, forgotten what it means.

Our public thinking process, more and more, belongs to what is called secularism. Even the words we use to think inside our own heads – long before we open our mouths – are given to us by a culture which has already decided everything, even if this culture has not chosen yet to make these decisions explicit. This is the core difficulty of retaining not merely a religious faith, but also a transcendent hope, in our cultures now. To hold on to faith and hope, we have to be fully aware of the forces operating to prevent us from doing so, and be determined to overcome them. But it is almost impossible to be so aware, or at least to retain awareness, moment to moment, because, precisely, the language we depend upon to think with in the first place is not designed for this purpose. Indeed, it is designed for a contrary purpose: to convince us that 'reality' comprises only the material, the visible, the measurable and the provable.

There is only one kind of hope. It is not divisible into economic hope and political hope and religious hope. Most of us, whether we are aware of it or not (mostly, we are not), hope for something eternal, if only in the sense that we discount the idea of death as so remote a prospect in the future as to be irrelevant to how we feel now. Meanwhile, we attach our hopes to more immediate prospects: love, pleasure, wealth, friendship, the weekend, the summer holidays, a business deal, a cup of coffee with a friend. Whether we are conscious of it or not, the propulsion mechanism that drives us forward is connected to a complex inter-working of such hopes. The problem is that, unless these hopes are sustained by something that ultimately supports them all – an ultimate, 'bookend' hope which, as it were, holds the others upwards – these lesser hopes will ultimately collapse like a row of dominoes once we have observed for a time how well or inadequately they serve us.

This is one of the things our post-Christian culture does not elect to tell us about the consequences of present drifts. The increasing despair of our society is connected to this phenomenon. We have lost our sense of a Loving Father, and so wander blindly about a desert of sensation and adventuring which only teases our desires with the absence of what they crave. When it goes wrong, the advocates of this approach simply tell us that we have been doing things wrongly, or too quickly, or too greedily – never that the entire enterprise might be misguided.

For the moment, we have what might be termed the 'luxury' of explaining the present chaos of pessimism and anxiety in our societies as resulting from an economic crisis only. What this explanation tends to forget is that the economic collapse was made inevitable by the level of borrowing that preceded it. We need to be clear about this and what it means. Right across the Western world, human beings have been trying to cheat reality; or, to put it another way, to compensate for the elimination of transcendent hope from our cultures by borrowing vast amounts of money in order to create new kinds of hope to sustain human optimism. But it takes a hell of a lot of borrowing to replace God, which is fundamentally, so to speak, why our nations are now all virtually bankrupt.

Since so much of what happens in the modern public square seems concerned with satisfying human desires for pleasure and happiness, it is easy to forget that the desires themselves are not necessarily connected to the things on which we fix them. Our culture seems to believe that it has invented human desire, that peace and happiness are add-on benefits that can be generated out of human genius and activity. Embedded deep in our collective conversation is the delusional notion that human life continues in the manner of the machine, requiring only the correct fuel and adjustment to drive it onwards to new frontiers. But, inside his own skin, each human being knows that this is wrong, that there is no default state of ease and sufficiency, from which he can only grow happier and more fulfilled. He knows that, deep in his heart, he is confronted by key questions and unavoidable facts. He wonders why he is here and where it will all end and why he should bother getting out of bed in the morning. He knows that the human 'mechanism' is a delicate, mysterious entity, depending for its propulsion on some deep-set sense of meaning.

Human life needs more to sustain it than what mankind is capable of imagining, proposing or generating. Ultimately, all we can create for ourselves are false hopes that sustain us for an instant and then dissolve, leaving us grasping for the next. What gets us out of bed on any given morning may be identifiable as the promise of progress, the lure of money, the call of duty, the prospect of love, the imminence of spring, the sight of a new sunrise, the thought of a fix. But ultimately all these will lose their power. If our hope for the future remains exclusively rooted in such phenomena, the process of anticipation followed by disappointment, occurring again and again, will lead to a dwindling enthusiasm.

We speak of certain phenomena associated with 'modern' reality as intrinsically connected to a mechanical idea of human society. Thus, for example, we identify suicide as being connected to recession and unemployment, or the breakdown of a romantic relationship, as though these connections were absolute ones, rather than simply the expression of the extent to which hopes have been redirected by our culture to things that are by definition transient and incapable of being guaranteed. Hopelessness, then, becomes an individualized phenomenon. Everything is pathologized, which is to say reduced to a mechanical understanding of humanity. In the individual, we call the diminishing hope of our societies by a catch-all name, 'depression', and treat it with medication, which takes the burden of hoping off the shoulders of the human being but also plunges him further, albeit this time anaesthetized, into the pit of despair.

*

For related reasons, we see the present moment of economic disintegration across the civilized world as an aberration, when in truth it too is inevitable. All human systems are prone to failure, because man is flawed and doomed to misuse his freedom.

We are beginning to perceive that existing words, like 'downturn' and 'recession', are inadequate in conveying the precise nature of present events. For what is emerging seems not so much a periodic dip in economic fortunes as a self-inflicted wound arising from the fear and insecurity of human beings. Because we could not trust the future, we have destroyed even the present. This, then, at its roots, is a human crisis rather than a merely economic one, and it flows directly from a collapse in our understanding of our own natures.

In a rather simplistic sense, this arises from the loss of what used to be conveyed, however clumsily and ineffectively, by religion. Because of the corruption of our public thought, the very phrase 'return to God' conveys merely the idea of rushing to a spurious form of consolation because reality has started to collapse. What is collapsing, however, is not reality, but the flimsy construct that man engineered out of his own desire to replace the Loving Father on His throne. What we need, then, apart from fixing the broken systems, is to become conscious again of the essential nature of humanity: mortal, dependent and primed with desire that nothing on earth can satisfy.

Once, the human hoping of Irish people was generated from a consciousness of the workings of Providence, from the promises of Christ and the evidence of the oversight of the Loving Father over the frailty and littleness of human lives. Now, one might often imagine that our hopes are self-generated, that they emanate from no more than a sentimentality generated by a process of self-suggestion. Hope, one might think, is something germinated out of chance and random possibility. We repeat the word 'hope' and, by a kind of self-hypnosis, seem to imagine the phenomenon itself manifesting in front of our eyes.

No human life can fully blossom without a hope that is transcendent. And hope is a strange entity: the very idea implies the presence of its opposite: despair. God, as John Lennon observed, is 'a concept by which we measure our pain'. Hope tends to flourish in inhospitable conditions and often appears redundant when things appear to be going well. As it approaches its goal, it blurs into certainty, and then abruptly turns to despair when the mirage of satisfaction dissolves. But then, after a period of grief, hope reappears like a new shoot from the dying seed.

Hope is the core of the Christian message, but the power of this concept has been dulled in our time by virtue of the success of mankind in creating systems that appear to answer human needs far better than the kind of society we 'remember' as having existed before. This is fine for as long as it continues working, creating an approximation of satisfaction that operates by stealing from the future. But while the limits of the illusion may be hidden for a while, even a long while, they can never be eliminated.

We look condescendingly backwards at the lives lived by our parents and grandparents, wondering how on earth they endured without the freedoms we take for granted. Nobody reminds us of two essential truths: (1) these 'freedoms' do not satisfy or sustain us; and (2) one way or another, these freedoms have to be paid for.

All of us are now exposed to these new realities, and an individual faith is no longer sufficient to sustain any of us. Here as elsewhere, we underestimate the extent to which we become puppets of the common mentality. I may 'think' I am thinking, but the culture is doing the work for me, directing me always towards concepts that belong to the shared mindset of the society rather than to my own human nature and needs. This 'given' form of

thinking tells me what is 'true', nudging me away from unapproved forms of understanding.

This is the nature of our crisis. It is not an economic crisis, nor
a 'moral' crisis, in the conventional sense. The problem is anthropological, which is to say human. We are losing our sense of how
to live, because we have forgotten what we live for.

It should be obvious that the 'bookend' Hope cannot be
regenerated by politicians or economists or bankers or even priests
or artists. Hope cannot be expected to emerge from man-made
places or sources other than on the same temporary terms as it
seemed to exist in the past – and has now been exposed as fragile,
false or fleeting. Hope, really, knows but one true essence: Hope
with a capital H, Hope directed at the eternal and infinite.
Anything less reduces man and condemns him, sooner or later, to
despair.

Pope Benedict XVI wrote in *Spe Salvi* that the distinguishing
mark of Christians is that they know they have a future. They may
not know the detail of what awaits them, 'but they know in general terms that their life will not end in emptiness'.

In recent times, our culture has sought to supplant the eternal
Hope of man's most profound longing with lesser, intermediate
kinds, supplied by economics and consumerism, which enable
society to function, after a fashion, and allow, too, lesser forms of
hope to be marketed to populations from whose sight the Great
Hope has been removed. But, inevitably, the day dawns when the
illusion does not work any more. Perhaps that is the day we have
now arrived at. Had we any means by which to comprehend this,
it would not be a bad thing.

The founding fathers of America set about their task of construction with little to work with apart from a belief in Providence
and their own determination to be its enthusiastic agents and to
inspire their people to similar endeavour. They drew their hope
not from a manifesto but from a belief in a higher order, in which

the ultimate hopes of mankind were reflected as a glorious story.

We, the people, want more than we can give ourselves.

Perhaps the next stage of our national education is coming to understand the structural disproportionality between our wanting and what any man-made system, political or otherwise, is capable of delivering.

What we should require from our leaders – beyond the obvious role of managing and representing – is not the deliverance of a system that will solve our problems, but the inspiration that will communicate that everything depends on each one of us equally, on our human capacities and desires, and on the strength of the hope that each of us can discover in his or her own heart.

# 9

# Believing Backwards

There has been nothing more terrible in Irish history than the failure of the last generation. Other generations have failed in Ireland, but they have failed nobly; or, failing ignobly, some man among them has redeemed them from infamy by the splendour of his protest. But the failure of the last generation has been mean and shameful, and no man has arisen from it to say or do a splendid thing in virtue of which it shall be forgiven. The whole episode is squalid. It will remain the one sickening chapter in a story which, gallant or sorrowful, has everywhere else some exaltation of pride.

This is the opening salvo from Padraig Pearse's essay, *Ghosts*, published in 1915, just a few months before Pearse and his comrades embarked on the historic mission that would lead to their deaths at the receiving end of firing squads.

For some years after I became a columnist with *The Irish Times* in 1991, I would quote frequently and liberally from this and other essays of Pearse, desisting only after the roars of the Celtic Tiger drowned out all such reasoning. How, after all, could one talk of 'failure' at such a crowning moment of Irish Independence?

In truth, mentions of Pearse had tended to go down badly even in the more modest economic conditions of the early 1990s. A series of factors, including both a retreat from what was termed 'insularity' and a repugnance of the appropriation of 1916 by the blood-soaked Provisional IRA, had rendered unmentionable everything Pearse had uttered or written. He and the other leaders of 1916 had come to be blamed for the outbreak of conflict in Northern Ireland in the late 1960s – the main 'evidence' in support of this charge being that this occurred just a few years after the fiftieth anniversary celebrations of the Rising in 1966. It should go without saying that the 1969 uprising in the North did not occur as a result of northern nationalists rediscovering some 'myth of destiny', but because civil rights protestors, seeking to draw attention to the wholesale discrimination against Catholics in Northern Ireland, had been brutally stamped upon by the unionist establishment. But sometimes things become axiomatic by virtue of their repetition.

Latter-day analyses of Ireland's historical condition mostly have in common that they blame 1916 for everything that came after it, while extending no credit for its achievement and no consideration for the fact that most of the leaders were in no position to control what happened afterwards.

In truth, the main shortcomings of the 1916 Rising were: that it was truncated; that the imaginative project envisaged by the leaders was short-circuited by their deaths; and that the job of Independence-making was inherited by lesser minds. It is arguable that what was celebrated in 1966 was a counter-revolution, a travesty of the Republic proclaimed at the GPO. At a time when we might otherwise have been examining how poorly the Irish State had come to resemble the vision of Pearse and Connolly, the quarter-century war in the North caused this analysis to be stillborn, making way for the conclusion that the revolution itself was at the root of our dysfunction. As part of a developing repugnance, a rather attractive analysis was offered that it might be possible to slip the reins of history altogether, that, really, Ireland was less joined to its insular past than its global future, and what the hell was Ireland anyway?

Pearse, in particular, has come to be a much caricatured figure in modern Ireland, his understanding of the nature of freedom being largely unappreciated by those who inherited that freedom and frequently took it for granted. This vision is to be found in many of Pearse's poems – now disparaged by the modern literati – and other writings.

Much more worrying than the threat of political violence, for those who would discredit 1916, has been the notion, central to the philosophy of the 1916 leadership, that the battle they fought was for the Irish national ideal, what Pearse called 'the national soul'. This, we have allowed ourselves to be convinced, was narrow, insular, even racist, and therefore ought to be left behind on the scrapheap of history. IRA violence played into this agenda, by giving a figleaf of morality to the repudiation not just of gunmen past and present, but the entire baggage of ideas and beliefs which had motivated the long fight for Irish freedom.

The principles on which the 1916 Rising was conducted, as expressed in the Proclamation of the Irish Republic, were in tune with the most progressive ideas in the Europe of their time. It is clear from what the 1916 leaders wrote and said that they saw themselves as the creators of what they wished to be a pluralist Ireland. Freedom was for them, in the words of Wolfe Tone, 'the rights of man in Ireland'. Pearse, in his essay *The Spiritual Nation*, defined Irish nationality as 'an ancient spiritual tradition'. He did not, contrary to the distortion imposed by the intelligentsia of more recent times, say that it was an 'Irish Catholic tradition', or 'an Irish Catholic and Gaelic tradition'. His view of nationhood was based on that of Thomas Davis, the Protestant ideologue of the Young Ireland movement, who held that nationality was a spirituality, a power alive in the land, into which all those who lived in that land could become connected. By Pearse's definition, this did not exclude anyone who wished to bear it allegiance, although this did not mean that it was simply the postmodern sum of influences brought together in the population. It was not confined to Gaelic Ireland, though Gaelic Ireland was its cornerstone.

In this, as in so many of his other writings, Pearse was acknowledging the contradictory nature of nationhood: on the one hand it had to be rooted in something pre-existing, on the other it depended for its life on interaction and cross-fertilization with the external world. He cited Davis:

> This country of ours is no sand bank, thrown up by some recent caprice of earth. It is an ancient land, honoured in its archives of civilization, traceable into antiquity by its piety, its valour, and its sufferings. Every great European race has sent its stream to the river of Irish mind. Long wars, vast organizations, subtle codes, beacon crimes, leading virtues, and self-mighty men were here. If we live influenced by wind and sun and tree, and not by the passions and deeds of the past, we are a thriftless and a hopeless people.

In the series of essays that included *Ghosts*, written just before the Rising, Pearse outlined in detail the specifications of true freedom, and the process by which it would have to be attained. In one of these, *The Murder Machine*, about the effects of the English education system in Ireland, he outlined the precise nature of the psychological effects of the colonial process in Ireland. This was several decades before the groundbreaking works of the great Caribbean-born psychiatrist Frantz Fanon, who exposed the interior workings of the colonial machine in his classic works about the effects of French colonialism in Algeria. Pearse perceived that the 'murder machine' had, in effect, created in Ireland the conditions of slavery: 'Certain of the slaves among us are appointed jailors over the common herd of slaves. And they

266

are trained from their youth for this degrading office. The ordinary slaves are trained for their lowly tasks in dingy places called schools; the buildings in which the higher trained slaves are trained are called colleges and universities.' The murder machine, he contended, 'aimed at the substitution for men and women with "Things". It has not been an entire success. There are still a great many thousand men and women in Ireland. But a great many thousand of what, by way of courtesy, we call men and women, are simply Things. Men and women, however depraved, have kindly human allegiances. But these Things have no allegiance. Like other Things, they are for sale.'

On Thursday 11 November 2010, the day the representatives of the International Monetary Fund arrived in Dublin to take charge of the Irish economy, *The Irish Times* carried an editorial headed 'Was it for this?' The title, of course, was a line from the poem 'September 1913', by William Butler Yeats:

> *Was it for this the wild geese spread*
> *The grey wing upon every tide;*
> *For this that all that blood was shed,*
> *For this Edward Fitzgerald died,*
> *And Robert Emmet and Wolfe Tone,*
> *All that delirium of the brave?*
> *Romantic Ireland's dead and gone,*
> *It's with O'Leary in the grave.*

The writer of the editorial began by acknowledging the monumental irony of that newspaper framing the question in such a way. The leader began:

It may seem strange to some that *The Irish Times* would ask whether this is what the men of 1916 died for: a bailout from the

German chancellor with a few shillings of sympathy from the British chancellor on the side. There is the shame of it all. Having obtained our political independence from Britain to be the masters of our own affairs, we have now surrendered our sovereignty to the European Commission, the European Central Bank, and the International Monetary Fund. Their representatives ride into Merrion Street today.

The editorial went on, more predictably, to excoriate Fianna Fáil for having failed in one of its primary missions 'to maintain the status of Ireland as a sovereign State'. It cited Eamon de Valera, a man unspoilt by favourable commentary in Ireland's 'newspaper of record', speaking in his inaugural address to the newly founded Fianna Fáil in 1926 of 'the inalienability of national sovereignty' as a fundamental belief of the new party. The leader-writer declared: 'The Republican Party's ideals are in tatters now.'

The desire to be a sovereign people, the leader continued, 'runs like a seam through all the struggles of the last 200 years'. The theme of self-determination had persisted from the United Irishmen to the Belfast Agreement and continued to resonate. But: 'The true ignominy of our current situation is not that our sovereignty has been taken away from us, it is that we ourselves have squandered it.'

It was a powerful and apt summary, and thus managed to justify what was, in fact, the extraordinary liberty of invoking a history of struggle for self-determination that *The Irish Times* had largely looked at askance while it was happening. Roy Greenslade, writing in the *Guardian*, declared: 'The fact that Ireland's premier newspaper was prepared to wring its hands and draw on a revolutionary history that it used to decry was a truly significant step.' A poster, MarkCou, added at the end of Greenslade's commentary: 'Even more significant as *The Irish*

*Times* has historically been "west-British" newspaper of Dublin's dining classes. For them to ask what was for that [*sic*] the revolutionaries died . . . well . . . indeed, powerful stuff.'

In the wake of the Easter Rising, *The Irish Times* came out strongly against the rebels, declaring that 'an attempt has been made to overthrow the constitutional Government of Ireland'. It referred to the Rising as a 'desperate episode in Irish history' and avowed that it could 'have only one end'. That leader-writer hoped for a 'speedy triumph of the forces of law and order'. Meanwhile, readers were advised to stay at home and read Shakespeare until things calmed down. A further editorial, entitled 'The Insurrection', decried the 'record of crime, horror and destruction' by the rebels, but praised the 'many gleams of the highest valour and devotion' by the 'gallant soldiers' who had put down the insurrection. The writer did 'not deny a certain desperate courage to many of the wretched men who today are in their graves or awaiting the sentence of their country's laws'. The editorial continued: 'The State has struck but its work is not yet finished. The surgeon's knife has been put to the corruption in the body of Ireland and its course must not be stayed until the whole malignant growth has been removed.' If this was a demand for the execution of the leaders of the rebellion, the paper got what it wanted, and its main rival, *The Freeman's Journal*, interpreted the editorial in this way, declaring it a 'bloodthirsty incitement' to the authorities.

*The Irish Times* had undergone many changes in the ninety-five years between the two editorials. By 2011, it was on its second Catholic editor, and had, in a series of deft moves, shifted its position from peripheral unionist to mainstream liberal, acquiring a central influence in the affairs of what it persisted in referring to as 'the State'. Although a reasonably broad church in terms of commentary (it has tolerated me as a columnist for twenty-one years, though sometimes it's been a close thing), it had never, in its view of Irish nationalism and the historical struggle for Independence, strayed too far from the tenor of that 1916 editorial. Suspicious of nationalist sentiment and rhetoric, it had been central to nurturing the revisionist mentality that developed in post-1960s Ireland, and most of its commentators would have been of the view that 1916 was at best the misguided and undemocratic act of reckless men.

The odd mixture of aptness and incongruity to that November 2010 editorial arose perhaps because it gave voice to something underlying the revisionist positions for which *The Irish Times* had long been a cheerleader. The anti-nationalist sentiment that had become especially fashionable in the wake of the outbreak of the Troubles in the late 1960s was transparently a present-connected construction designed to distance the intelligentsia of the Republic from the violent extremism of the Northern conflict. A horror of Provo brutality had driven many of the newer generations into the intellectual embrace of a pseudo-unionism, leading them to excoriate the motives and actions of the founding fathers and sneer at what were dismissed as their pretensions and delusions.

But underlying this, and sometimes equally transparent, was a neurotic attachment to the idea of the Irish nation and its heroic mythology and stirring passions. It was strange that it took the arrival of the IMF to bring it out, but out it certainly brought it. On the other hand, those readers cursed with long memories might briefly have lingered on the irony that a newspaper that had been to the fore in urging Ireland to cast off its insularity and embrace the new European dispensation should now be invoking the spirit of the founding revolution as the edifice of its modernizing project fell about everyone's ears.

The historian, wrote Friedrich Nietzsche, looks backwards, and in the end believes backwards. Perhaps this sentence provides the clearest means of understanding what, beneath the babble of superficialities and resentments, has happened to Ireland: we believe backwards. All our understandings, being constructed to achieve something in the present, are upside down. We do not trace our understanding of events or the lines of our reasoning from their sources in time or fact, but instead trace our thinking back from some need or exigency in the moment, forming our understandings of past events on the basis of today's perspectives and desiring. Those who would have us ignore what Thomas Davis called 'the passions and deeds of the past', and live influenced only 'by wind and sun and tree', have put everything back-to-front: it is not that our dark, heroic past is a dangerous incitement in the present, but that present requirements often dictate whatever colour and meaning we ascribe to history.

There is undoubtedly more than a grain of truth in the idea that the initial attempt at reconstructing the Irish nation after Independence was deeply flawed. Irish people of a certain age have strong memories of the clumsy efforts to create and preserve a notion of Irishness that was bogus, impracticable and un-attractive. There is no doubt that, albeit arising from the best of intentions, but informed by a deep and basic insecurity, the post-Independence leadership of Irish society began to think that if the Irish people were to preserve their cultural heritage they needed to maintain it in sterile conditions. This idea was based on a pro-foundly pessimistic view of the quality of Irish culture – in fact, on the colonizer's view of that culture. In much the same way, the reaction that followed from the 1960s tended to elevate the external and the imported, casting the indigenous, whatever it was, on the tip.

From the moment of Independence, Ireland got itself wrong. Failing to understand that it couldn't extricate itself from an identity forged in the historical embrace with its neighbour, it firstly sought to expunge from its culture all traces of alien influence in favour of a crude 'authenticity' with no actually existing reality. Then, over-correcting this error, it sought to remove evidence of its native culture so as to present itself as thoroughly modern in every way. This failure of self-understanding is at the core of Ireland's recent problems. What emerged was a mishmash of an identity, embracing self-congratulation and self-parody in equal measure.

Ireland had once been one of Europe's most endowed civilizations. Despite its turbulent history, it had many things going for it: a small population and considerable resources of tradition, culture, soul, education, and physical attractiveness (of the landscape) – not to mention the potential for the most viable 'green' brand in the world at a moment when green economics was threatening to inherit the earth. It seemed almost impossible that such a bountiful land would be incapable of sustaining itself. But the unfolding story of Irish self-government reveals a consistent pattern of self-delusion, myopia, inferiority complex, bravado, defeatism, cynicism, sentimentalism and conceit. We went from the paranoid insularism and cultural myopia that followed national independence, through the post-1960s obsession with a faux 'self-confidence' based on borrowed ideas, to the final, salutary meltdown of the Celtic Tiger.

The text of *Ghosts* proceeds from the opening given at the start of this chapter: '"*Is mairg do ghní go holc agus bhíos bocht ina dhiaidh*," says the Irish proverb. "*Woe to him that doeth evil and is poor after it*." The men who have led Ireland for twenty-five years have done evil, and they are bankrupt. They are bankrupt in policy, bankrupt in credit, bankrupt now even in words. They have nothing to propose to Ireland, no way of wisdom, no counsel of courage. When they speak they speak only untruth and blasphemy. Their utterances are no longer the utterances of men. They are the mumblings and the gibberings of lost souls.'

There are few passages from Irish literature that could be

reproduced now and provoke such a potent effect of identification in the modern reader. At the time, the words referred to the relatively modest failures of Pearse's own generation, and perhaps the preceding one, characterized by what he saw as compromise and moral cowardice. Now, though, we can see them, clearly and correctly, as pure prophecy of a final culmination of what Pearse perceived as the mistaken drifts of his own time, continued to disaster a century later by a generation in retreat from such passionate proposals as Pearse himself outlined. And yet, their remarkable pertinence notwithstanding, it is impossible to imagine an Irish political leader today uttering sentiments remotely like these.

The failures of his own time, Pearse believed, had been a failure to conceive of Ireland as a spiritual entity.

They have conceived of nationality as a material thing, whereas it is a spiritual thing. They have made the same mistake that a man would make if he were to forget that he has an immortal soul. They have not recognized in their people the image and likeness of God. Hence, the nation to them is not all holy, a thing inviolate and inviolable, a thing that a man dare not sell or dishonour on pain of eternal perdition. They have thought of nationality as a thing to be negotiated about as men negotiate about a tariff or about a trade route, rather than as an immediate jewel to be preserved at all peril, a thing so sacred that it may not be brought into the market places at all or spoken of where men traffic.

He who builds on lies rears only lies. The untruth that nationality is corporeal, a thing defined by statutes and guaranteed by mutual interests, is at the base of the untruth that freedom, which is the condition of a hale nationality, is a status to be conceded rather than a glory to be achieved; and of the other untruth that it can ever be lawful in the interest of empire, in the interest of wealth, in the interest of quiet living, to forego the right to freedom. The contrary is the truth. Freedom, being a spiritual necessity, transcends all corporeal necessities, and when freedom is being considered interests should not be spoken of. Or, if the terms of the counting house be the ones that are best understood, let us put it that it is the highest interest of a nation to be free.

Such words still have the power to move us, but in a way that should provoke even more grief than if they could not. For they sound to our ears like something from the script of a great movie, devised in order to depict some inconceivable passion, rather than the thoughts, insights, of a real man. The Pearse who wrote them emerges from them as a man of extreme poetic sensibility, with a tortured view of reality. There is, we admit, something beautiful in the flow of those words, but they remain just words, an effusive outpouring of sentimental hyperbole, an aria composed by an over-active mind. It is impossible for us to imagine that, in writing those words, Pearse was writing for the benefit of people who, though lacking his talent for words, did not lack his ability to feel and understand things as he did. His essays were exceptionally beautiful in their time, but they did not sound crazy, as they do now.

What we have to ask ourselves is this: does this hint of craziness reside in the words that Pearse wrote, or is it something added by the present? Is it a function of some objective condition of his proposals, or a subjective quality infecting our apprehension of what he said?

I believe the latter. The idea of becoming impassioned to the point of blind hatred, or bedazzled to the point of enchantment about a political vision such as he articulated, is now, literally, laughable. There is, of course, a widespread belief that this is a good thing, because such passions are nowadays deemed dubious and dangerous. Conventional wisdom holds that we are all the better off for their being extinct. But on what basis do we decide such a thing? How, surveying the landscape of the present, can we conclude that what Pearse wrote was mad, whereas we in our present disarray and confusion are sane?

Once, an Irish politician could, in addressing an Irish audience, rely on the existence of some deep attachment to the idea of 'Ireland'; now he or she can rely only on the hope that people will be swayed by the promise of a cent or two off their taxes. Pearse's core theme, of the nation as spiritual entity transcending all physical needs and interests, is nowadays alien to our collective thinking processes. For a modern political leader to speak of the ghosts of the dead asking big things, while addressing what we still anachronistically call 'the nation', would be like a teacher talking about the birds and bees to a tittering roomful of twelve-year-olds. The words would provoke only confusion, dismissiveness and ridicule, because the cultural context on which their meanings depended has been obliterated.

This is no minor adjustment in thinking, but the encroachment of an entirely different way of seeing. Intrinsic to this change, and hermetically sealing it against interrogation, is the idea that present-day thinking is self evidently superior to all previous forms. The new thinking has clearly failed – and its failure may yet prove total and fatal – but the accompanying hubris renders it impervious to the proposition that important understandings have been lost on the way to thinking as we have come to. We have forgotten that the issue of national identity is not merely ornamental – it is of utilitarian and psychological and of manifold other practical importances. It has to do not just with how we might live, but what we might live on.

In evoking the nation, Pearse was addressing a peasant culture with a simplistic view of Christianity, but he did not preach simplistically of faith and spirituality, nor seek to valorize a particular dogma. Rather, he spoke of spirit as a shared, inherited space in which a people might live and love and hope and reason, precisely on account of a shared inheritance, which he called 'the nation'. Nowadays, when we refer to the question of nationality, it is as an awkward and largely undesired heirloom, filleted of practical meanings. Mention of 'spirituality' signals, usually, the avoidance of the specifically Christian. Our leaders tend not to be poets or thinkers who speak of lofty things, but functionaries who string together technical phrases in the manner of middle managers or accountants. And this too is regarded as emblematic of progress: an advance from romanticism to technocracy that ignores the underfoot debris in its determination to approve of itself.

On the face of things, it appears coincidental that Pearse's reputation went into decline some time before the advent of the Celtic Tiger. But it is interesting that this phenomenon anticipated the hubris arising from the apparent successes of attempts to achieve self-realization by bartering resources and independence in a new and purportedly voluntary dependency. The complacency thus generated in the hearts of new generations – untouched by the consciousness of past national struggles – unleashed a condescension that, while taking the achievement of independence for granted, heaped ridicule on the supposed naivety of the liberators. The dogged, holistic dreams of these visionaries stood as obstacles to the building of a prosperous Ireland on the basis of traded sovereignty and waived assets. There arose, then, a cultural imperative for the dousing of concepts of nationhood and spirituality in vats of irony and scorn.

We assume, because the outward appearances of political phenomena remain ostensibly as they were, that the phenomenon of politics has remained more or less intact, while we, in our sophistication or cynicism, have grown bored by it. In truth, politics today is not politics at all, but something more like management of a minor company with an uninteresting product, and politicians are no longer politicians, but middle-ranking executives seeking to use the theatricality of what was once a quasi-artform to communicate their dull ideas to a virtually comatose public. Political gatherings have turned into a sort of shadow-play, in which the rituals of the one-time Art of the Possible are enacted in a kind of emotional neutral gear, and the buttons of previous passions pressed in a manner which dimly excites the memories of past glories and triumphs. The heroic, epic, utopian models of politics have been dismantled, and in their place we have a banal mid-afternoon soap opera, with cardboard sets and bad scripts. As we approach the centenary of 1916, Ireland has been reduced to a counting-house in which nobody is able to count.

Our present-day political leaders are distinguished mainly by the fact that they have succeeded in remaining standing after riskier-looking personalities were eliminated. The constant eye that must be kept to the quark of public opinion represented by the single transferable opinion poll ensures that safety is the primary value.

Public opinion has replaced communal passion as the new god-head of politics. The problem is that, even though the version of public opinion on which the political culture recreates and re-invents itself is, in some sense, a true representation of the public political mind, it is not satisfying to those whose sentiments it is supposed to depict. We miss something but have no idea what it is. In its heart of hearts, public opinion is unsettled by its own lack of authenticity, and craves the brave and radical public enactment of something it has been taught to fear and disapprove of in itself.

We keep hearing about patriotism, but have this uneasy feeling that such a quality is no longer available. The word persists, but the thing itself has disappeared. Since the implosion of the Irish economy in 2008, there have been innumerable attempts by politicians to invoke the quality of patriotism, to ask people to make sacrifices for their country, to place their own interests behind the common good.

Instead, what we observe is an Ireland in which every citizen speaks on behalf of his own interests. Sometimes the contributions are couched in pious terminologies about the 'most vulnerable' or the phenomenon of 'inequality', but most of the time it is possible to discern that the speaker is either expressing some personal gripe or using some easily recognizable victim as a shield. Trade unionists threaten to bring the country to its knees; public service workers make it clear that no one can expect any sacrifices from them; senior civil servants retire under the weight of extraordinary pension packages, and so on.

To define the problem correctly, you have to leave self-righteousness aside. It is not a question of judging, or pointing fingers, but of seeing clearly. It is not simply that people are unpatriotic but that the quality of patriotism is no longer available. People genuinely do not know what is meant by the word or how it might relate to their relationship with Irish society or the State.

I will not labour the issues of corruption, greed and feather-bedding that have bedevilled our politics for a generation. Of course, some of the blame must be laid at the door of our political system – at the quality of leadership it throws up and the way it has reduced the public square to a flea market. But there is a deeper problem: we can no longer imagine ourselves as a people. When we try to do so through the medium of a political personality, it always seems to go wrong.

Nearly a century ago, when Pearse was writing *Ghosts*, there was no indigenous government. Thanks to him and his martyr comrades, we have had our own government for nearly nine decades, but have about as much regard for it as Pearse had for the English Crown. Ireland has failed to become the spiritual entity he envisaged but has been reduced, as he and Davis feared, to a 'sand bank', a 'caprice of earth' in which freedom has been corrupted, squandered and defiled.

Perhaps part of our problem is that 'tribe' has become a dirty word. When we think of ourselves as a community we seem to want to do so in terms that won't threaten or offend anyone. We define ourselves as a 'people', but it fails to move us. We call ourselves a 'community' but it doesn't ring true. The word 'nation' has become pastiche. A 'tribe' is an unthinkable, unmentionable thing – a dark rabble of malevolent elements, looking warily at outsiders from the introversion of its cocoon. The approved ways of seeing ourselves as a collective tend to be the innocuous, and therefore useless, ones – precisely because they lack power to move or mobilize, whereas the dangerous ones are avoided for fear of the evils we have associated with them. Only political extremists, who nowadays seem to be very stupid people, appear willing to pick up the smoking emblems that have united us in adversity and fear. The concept of Irish national identity has itself been demonized – not because of anything intrinsically evil about it, but precisely because timid men and women have run away from it in fear. Why should we be surprised when the fanatics steal it away, rendering us not only bereft but also guilty by association of the crimes they commit under cover of our banners and symbols?

Words like 'race' or 'tribe' are, as Pearse insisted, but the surface representations of a much deeper, spiritual process, taking place within a collective as a result of a common culture. Just as the birth of a child represents the unity of two souls to unleash a third, the interactions and fermenting of human cultures creates spiritual entities, which demand to be acknowledged. A nation, tribe, race is a collective imagination, and this, rather than the superficial aspects like blood, colour, religion, is what is most important about it.

\*

Pearse's writings contain much that we might have found useful had we been less neurotic and superior in our treatment of him. The idea has taken root that, rather than a vision, they represented a narrow, xenophobic squint of fear towards the wider world – positing a reactionary, Gaelic, Catholic Ireland to the exclusion of outside influences. This is, to say the least, unfair, but mostly it is unfair to ourselves. I defy anyone to find in the works of Padraig Pearse a single racist or xenophobic sentence. He cited Davis, with approval, demolishing in advance the simplistic argument that Ireland needed to dismantle its aspiration to nationhood if it wished to become a modern republic: 'He who fancies some intrinsic objection to our nationality to lie in the co-existence of two languages, three or four great sects, and a dozen different races in Ireland, will learn that in Hungary, Switzerland, Belgium, and America, different languages, creeds, and races flourish kindly side by side, and he will seek in English intrigues the real well of the bitter woes of Ireland.'

I can assure those who have refused to read these essays for fear of being contaminated by their reactionary content that there is not a single paradox or complexity of present-day discussions about race, tribe and identity that has not been anticipated by Pearse himself, or Davis, Tone or Lalor, whom he quotes liberally in his texts. The banal arguments which, in our present-centred hubris, we imagine have only occurred to us in our new-found enlightenment, are here debated and outlined in the most eloquent and illuminating fashion imaginable.

The iconography of patriotism was so strong in Ireland up until the present generation that it is almost impossible for those who experienced it to agree about the essential nature of this country with those who did not. Most of us who went to school during the 1950s, 1960s and 1970s were imbued – mainly by teaching priests, nuns and brothers – with a profound sense of patriotism, and moreover, with a very distinct image of what that patriotism might look and sound like. As a result, those of us born before the early 1960s have one version of Ireland; those born afterwards, if they think about 'Ireland' at all, think about an entirely different entity, and it is often difficult to work out what that entity might consist of.

When you begin to think about it, you realize that, for example, the present-day leaders of Sinn Féin and those who have so robustly opposed them in the past are cut, in a sense, from the same cloth. The 'Republican' leaders, in the way they dress, speak and carry themselves, resemble self-created latter-day versions of the signatories of the 1916 Proclamation. More correctly, they are like composites of our present-day understanding of what those seven men might have been like. Gerry Adams, for example, has the stern, avuncular asceticism, with the merest hint of zealotry, that we might ascribe to a Padraig Pearse, as well as the sense of engaged energy and keen political intelligence we'd maybe associate with a James Connolly and the literary ambition identifiable with a Padraig Pearse or Thomas MacDonagh. For all that the 1916 leaders have been dehumanized by decades of mythologizing and revisionism, Adams could sit down in the midst of our image of them, and seem quite plausible. It is as though we have created him, and he has created himself, in the stereotypical image of Irish patriotism.

But the astonishing thing is that the same might be said about those who have set themselves so trenchantly against republicanism with its present-day capital 'R'. Media commentators of his approximate age-group, whether opposed to or supporting him, resemble Gerry Adams much more than they resemble young Irishmen born since the middle-1960s. I include myself in this navel-gazing analysis. Those of us who were inculcated with the values of the Irish revolution, and had our belief-systems consolidated by the anniversary celebrations of 1966, hold in common certain concepts of patriotism, loyalty, solidarity and heroism which are utterly alien to people a decade or two younger than us. Take at random a number of the names of those who have engaged in these debates about the legitimacy of revolution now or in the past – myself, Kevin Myers, Tom McGurk, Fintan O'Toole, Eoghan Harris, Damien Kiberd and Eamon Dunphy – and reflect on how closely such a group might resemble an unconsciously imagined recreation of the group which signed the Proclamation. We have in common a deep seriousness about the importance of these matters, a strong sense of an ideal which is either elevated or debased by various events or actions, and a demeanour of earnestness which makes us all appear at least a little ridiculous in the eyes of younger people. In a sense, then, those who purport to address the new, post-1960s Ireland rather than the old one they claim to be detached from, are fooling nobody, perhaps not even themselves.

All of us who become embroiled in these controversies seek to resolve the same conundrum: how do we reconcile our acquired understanding of nobility, honour and patriotism with what we have witnessed during the decades of conflict, punctuated by the frequent barbarism of the IRA? In seeking to square this circle, some took the path of rationalization, others that of renunciation. If the Provos had never happened, all of us might in the past four decades have been united on a single platform, extolling the virtues and majesties of the Irish revolution, safely removed from it by the guts of a century. But the IRA campaigns had so contaminated the legacy of Griffith, Pearse and Collins that the tendency of many public figures was either towards selective silence or a generalized disavowal of the historical project of Independence. I always believed such responses mistaken, because they delivered ownership of that project into the hands of those who sullied it.

Nevertheless, I defended Sinn Féin frequently during the 1990s, believing that coaxing it into the mainstream was vital to any prospect of peace. I expressed, I believe, the perspective of a significant section of the Republic's population who had lived through the earlier part of the Troubles, holding, at the time and long afterwards, that the Provisionals' response was in some respects legitimate and unavoidable. As a teenager down West, I had collected money after Bloody Sunday for the families of the dead.

I did not offer support to the Provisionals for their indiscriminate slaughter of innocent bystanders, but I can see why some saw this as a semantic evasion. Many of us who offered comfort to the Provos, in whatever degree, believed not so much that the actions of the IRA were legitimate but that, since this was how many Northern nationalists saw it, we, not being in their shoes, could not rush to condemnation. We wished and prayed it would stop, but could not go further without distancing ourselves from our own history and leaving Northern nationalists isolated and more desperate than before. I have written several times before of what I called 'talking the Provos down from the ledge', by which I meant the attempt to convince the extremists that they would not lack support if they laid down their guns. If the killing could be stopped by bringing 'our' side in from the cold, then surely it was better that we offer them solidarity if they stepped back from the brink and handed over their hostages?

What we call 'the Troubles' seeped into every facet of Irish life for the bulk of all our lifetimes. By dictating the essence of the plot by which public life was governed, they influenced every major political development in the Republic, and moulded our understanding of all our major political figures. They also provided the moral gearbox of southern public life, dictating that, almost every time a mouth was opened in public, the issue of 'where you stood' was uppermost in the mind of speaker and listener. Were you 'sound' on the National Question? Were you a quisling or a snakin' regarder? Were you a republican or a revisionist, a fellow-traveller or a neo-unionist, a Sticky or a Provo?

These questions resulted in the obliteration of clarity from Irish public life, rendering nearly everyone afraid to speak. Everything that we knew of ideals was rooted in what we had to throw out in order to stop the killing. Before, there had been certainty: the revolution, Independence, the Free State, the Republic, all these stages, for all their attendant limitations and ambiguities, allowed for moral clarity in one direction or another. But the questions about the Troubles withheld any hope of clarity, and therefore tore the public imagination apart.

It is, in retrospect, understandable: a conflict that seemed rooted in who we were, which made it impossible to feel morally clean about involvement or morally certain about repudiating it. Could you claim to be Irish without supporting the IRA? Could you be human and support them? Was the very idea of Ireland somehow a source of succour to the murderers of children? Most of us needed to feel that there was something glorious, something morally irrefutable, to be found on one side or the other, and that we could choose it and feel better. But there was only ambiguity feeding into our ambivalence, feeding back into the problem.

Everything since seems to have been dictated by the moral inertia arising from that irresolvable conundrum, and from the limits it placed on thought and talk. Denied an expression of our own sovereignty, and lacking a clearer reason to merge with the rest of Europe, we did it for the money. Lacking a self-confident political philosophy, we acquired off-the-peg models from else-where. Our economic fortunes seemed to ebb and flow not from our own energies or ambitions, but in accordance with external phenomena. People came to live here because they chose to, not because we chose them to. Things happened to us; we didn't make them happen. Much or all of this occurred because of the immobilization of national thought as a consequence of the running sore of the Troubles. Because we couldn't pick through the ambiguities, we allowed ourselves to be bullied into silence, and that silence pervaded everything.

The Provisional IRA came draped in the iconography of all that was glorious that we had been taught to believe in. Only now do we perceive that these pseudo-republicans never possessed the vision of national realization for which some of us sometimes pardoned them some of their sins. What they were involved in was a local faction fight, a turf-war, in which the nearest they came to a republican philosophy was the phrase 'Brits Out'.

But we may soon also come to perceive the limits of arguments that sought to have us condemn not merely the IRA but everything the IRA said, invoked, employed or abused – the baby, bathwater, bath and kitchen sink of all we were, felt and thought. Perhaps as time passes and the bloodshed of the past generation recedes from public memory, our children will begin to see the repudiation of our history and its heroes as motivated by less elevated considerations than we have imagined: post-colonial forelock-tugging, self-abasement in the absence of coherent public thought, or, at the very best, fear of the conflict spilling across the border. All of it understandable, but not especially noble, and certainly an insufficient basis for relinquishing our right to speak of who we were.

It is not that I lack an intellectual understanding of the impetus and objectives of the broad sweep of thinking and talking that has occurred under the banner 'Revisionism'. In its own moments it was a necessary and virtuous undertaking: to snip the cultural wires which brought unthinking support to the depraved activities of the IRA. In its present-centred imperative, it was an honourable, vital response. The problem is that it became ideological, not merely pitting itself against the immediate quarry – the Provos – but turning the full brunt of its armoury on anything from which this contemporary nuisance looked for succour or sustenance. Seeking to put the fire out, the revisionists destroyed the house with their water hoses, when a more judicious aim might have enabled much of the contents to be saved.

Thus did Ireland become an absence, a vacuum, a blank space, the hole in the cultural doughnut. The truth of it is that, for nearly half a century prior to the arrival of the IMF in Dublin in 2010, the implications of that arrival had existed in potential form by virtue of the treatment accorded to each and every aspect of Ireland's once vast reserves of wisdom and tradition within the modern voice-box of the supposed Irish nation. Virtually every public conversation had as its basis the question of removing this or that residual influence of Irish nationalism, Catholicism, Irish culture, the Irish language, Irish ways and laws. The logic of these exertions was precisely that Ireland by its nature was problematic for its own people. But whatever else it was, it can hardly be called surprising that, finally, the literal notion of Ireland as a going concern in the world was suspended while outsiders came and told us how to run our country. This eventuality had been preceded and implicitly announced for many years by the relentless onslaught of key members of the Irish cadre delegated to talking about Ireland, its past and future, its prospects and desires, with the vast majority of these voices spending their waking hours berating their own history, values, traditions, symbols and heroes. The IMF's arrival in Dublin was no more than a formalization of the position, an inevitable outcome of years of self-disparagement, self-repudiation and self-deconstruction.

In an intriguing article, 'Making Ireland Unlovable' – examining the persistent media onslaughts on the very idea of Ireland and Irishness – and published on his website in 2011, the veteran Irish observer and philosopher Desmond Fennell wrote:

> The evidence of this fifty-year-old phenomenon, from its tentative beginnings to its present climax, is there in the archives of the

national media for our historians to research. Their task and purpose would be to produce a structured account of its origins and development, together with an explanation of how its successive agents saw what they were doing. Obviously the reduction of a loved Irish identity to an unlovable nothing is of equal historical importance to the construction of that same identity which nourished the Irish Revolution.

For his trouble in saying such things, Desmond Fennell has found himself increasingly marginalized. Despite having published a lengthy shelf of books and innumerable academic and news-paper articles, he is nowadays absent from public discussions and most of his recent books are self-published. One of the accusations levelled against Fennell was that he was a parochialist, a reactionary nostalgic, yearning for and seeking to recreate the conditions of Ireland past.

Yet one of the most common questions asked since the implosion of the Irish economy has been: why did dissenting voices not emerge and make themselves heard? And here is the answer: the only forms of 'dissent' that are permitted in the governing conversation are those readily rebuttable by the regime. We in Ireland have this rather self-congratulatory idea that nowadays we have intense, passionate debates about everything, when really we have dramas in which one side, representing the orthodox view, seeks to consolidate its hold on the public mind. Across a broad spectrum of vital matters – economics, European affairs, national questions, social issues – we have surreptitiously replaced the concept of free, open debate with a kind of ritual in which the prevailing consensus pits itself against unapproved ideas and invites would-be dissenters to have a go. Underlying this process is an ideological subtext, which elevates the idea of 'progress' over all others. Adherents of the approved orthodoxies regard it as self-evident that what they speak is the total truth about everything, and that their perspectives are incapable of either refutation or refinement.

Towering overhead is a moral totem pole, casting a long shadow. The dominant ideology creates discussions in an ostensibly democratic fashion in order to dramatize its own goodness. Hence, to dissent from orthodoxy is not merely to be wrong, stupid and perverse – it is to be, in a precise cultural sense, bad. Because the dissenter is fundamentally questioning the very essence of progress and its capability to deliver to humankind all that is possible, it is necessary for such a troublemaker to be ritually shamed as a lesson to others. To volunteer as a dissident across a range of issues – social affairs, family questions, immigration, etc. – is therefore to court not merely disapproval but a withdrawal of affection in the public realm.

The core, deeper-down reasons for Ireland's present predicament, then, include the following: the loss of a ready and communicable concept of patriotism; the undermining of all forms of conventional authority, especially of the fatherly and divine kind; the cultural disparagement of age and sincerity; the replacement of a transcendent form of reason with a positivist model which demands literal and verifiable proofs for everything, preferably of the statistical kind; the replacement of existing and long-accepted norms for family life and human relationships by a new dispensation – known as 'equality', but actually its opposite – in which minority behaviours became elevated above those of the majority; the marginalization of analyses capable of penetrating the topsoil of the emerging culture, in case old ideas might thus be enabled to reassert themselves. This list is not exhaustive, but it conveys the general sense of the broad drift of things.

At the core of these failings is one that, in a sense, captures them all: a failure to define an Irish identity that could survive under assault from external forces. The love of Ireland exhibited by such as Dan O'Rourke and Padraig Pearse was of a deep-seated kind, devoid of selfish elements. It did not confuse love of nation with self-interest or personal grievance, and this is something that modern culture does not allow citizens to achieve. In some ways, the loss of this vital ingredient had its roots in other losses: of the language, the Christian faith, the sense of Ireland as a civilizing force in the world (the 'Island of Saints and Scholars' of inherited mythology).

Over the full course of the twentieth century, a struggle persisted between those who unwittingly clung to a colonized mentality and those who erroneously tried to go back to the pre-existing culture. This became visible mainly in terms of a debate between modernity and tradition. The full truth resided with neither side, but the clash resulted in the inertia which inevitably results from a collision between an unstoppable force and an immovable object. Since the 1970s, there has been a sustained attack on values and ideas identified as relating to a past form of cohesion, and therefore representing a threat to the achievement of new freedoms. The objective outcome of this process has been the obliteration of previous ways of seeing and understanding, and their replacement with nothing or very little. Through the decades of this battle, the collective conversation was at the mercy of an unhelpful pendulum swinging back and forth between two equally obsolete extremes. This threw up, in turn, traditionalist hostility to the colonizer, revisionist hostility to tradition, and post-revisionist hostility to the post-colonial revisionists. It is difficult to say where we are now, or indeed if we are anywhere worth naming.

It should hardly escape the attention of even the most doggedly 'modern' in outlook that the elimination of notions of spirit, nation and attachment to tribe tend to promote the idea of consumption, under various headings, as a way of achieving happiness. This is not a new idea, nor does it suffer in today's

Ireland from a dearth of articulation. Nowadays, indeed, the urgency of our becoming 'less materialistic' in outlook is frequently proposed, but invariably without any accompanying idea of what this might look like. It has become an empty mantra, a phrase that causes people to nod and clap their hands, but which has no attainable meaning in a culture from which all options to materialism have been eradicated.

Despite our repugnance of sincerity, and both despite and because of our present-centred hubris, we are left with fundamental unanswered questions: What is Ireland? Why has it been decided that it no longer exists? By whom, in fact? Why does it wish to celebrate the cultures of all other people but place its own in sackcloth and ashes? And so forth. If we are perturbed by these puzzles, we may approach the next most fundamental question: where is the essence of a once-colonized and unreintegrated people to be discovered? Is it to be found in the past, in the culture of the colonized, in some fusion or hybrid, or in a complete wiping of the slate to invite some form of postmodern reconstruction? For the moment, we appear to have adopted an ostrich-posture in relation to this question: let's just wait and see what turns up.

These are no mere intellectual diversions, any more than they are the province of fanatics and psychopaths. We are talking here about survival, not merely in the Darwinian sense, but in terms of the psychic health which flows from coherent identity, and in the inter-relationships that grow from cross-fertilization with other people and cultures.

In the Tiger years, which coincided with the ending of the Northern conflict, these questions for the most part went underground. This is because money distracts, and because it stores up life to be lived later. Those years were, in a sense, a period of national unconsciousness, as we tried to catch up on everything that we imagined history had withheld from us. The period of apparent prosperity also created the illusion that such discussion had been rendered irrelevant by virtue of our having arrived where we wanted to go without recourse to such talk or ideas. We forgot, or for understandable reasons did not appreciate, that money can disappear, whereas self-knowledge survives great wants and calamities.

# 10

# *The Harp That Once*

IT IS ALWAYS HARD TO ARGUE WITH MONEY. YET, BEHIND THE NEW, allegedly self-confident self-images of the modern entity we still call Ireland, some unsettling questions remain. Like, can we look with satisfaction on the way our globalized economy has become as dependent as it has? Or, was there really no other way that Irish society and its economy might have developed?

One of the things that often strikes me about the way we talk about things is the underlying assumption, always, that 'progress' is ipso facto founded on more 'rational' assumptions than things that happened in the past. I have come to suspect this notion, because increasingly it seems to me that, whereas its proponents invariably dismiss or disparage what they term 'traditional' forms of belief, what is called progress simply requires a different type of faith-system to be imposed by the victorious power elites of a new era. When you get right into it, you get a clear sense that it is often to be regarded as actually no more rational than ways of thinking overturned to put the new dispensation in place. The logic of modern capitalism, for example, is frequently presented as epitomizing reason and coherence, but is based on a faith that has no more positivist basis than any of those now decried as superstitious and obscurantist. In fact, capitalism depends on a belief-system not exceedingly dissimilar to those of the religious tradition. It involves the creation of money *ex nihilo*; it requires a deep faith (confidence) in the workings of the system; it demands tithes to be paid to the State, which has become as the new church of Mammon.

I often think how strange it is that, while working tirelessly to eliminate from our culture the idea of a God who watches over everything, we have recently replaced Him with something far more irrational. Nowadays, what keeps watch on our every move is not a deity but something called 'the markets'. But the erosion of belief in a transcendant Being has led in turn to an erosion in the metaphysical relationship between mankind and land, earth and nature, resulting in the collapse of moral perspectives of the old and trusty kind. Without these, we are at the mercy of forces far less merciful than any deity we might imagine.

The markets never sleep. These ghostly entities sit night and day in front of computer screens, observing trends and reading minds, weighing up the fates of peoples, anticipating Greek confidence, dictating the value of Irish bonds. Nobody seems to know the names of these beings, or where exactly they sit and watch, or what they look like. But constantly we are reminded of their watchful presence by the new ordained, some of whom are called 'bankers' and others 'economists'.

The bankers, especially, are blessed with exceptional powers, being the ordained ones who create money out of nothing. Strangely, despite recent chastening experiences of the evils that can sometimes rise up in people accorded unearthly powers, it rarely occurs to us in this context that allowing mere mortals the right to turn paper into treasure, or create wealth in the flashing pulse of a computer cursor, might be fraught with dangers.

To listen to our public conversation about economics is to suspect that almost nobody understands what's happening. Those charged with explaining things are almost invariably engaged not in making things clear but in sending 'signals' to 'the markets'. As a result, there is almost universal confusion about the meanings of events. There is nowadays a widespread sense among people that such matters are somewhat beyond them – and, interestingly, their confusion mirrors the economic state-of-affairs. Mostly we just pay our taxes and levies and get on with things. We accept that, somehow or other, we must have sinned, and therefore deserve our punishment. Like the Holy Trinity, 'the markets' are a mystery beyond the comprehension of mortal man.

But economics, properly understood, is as simple as two-plus-two. When I was a boy, my sisters and I spent summers in our grandmother's house, in Cloonyquin, County Roscommon, next door to where the great songwriter Percy French grew up. My grandmother kept cows, sheep and hens, grew her own vegetables, baked her own bread and made her own butter and jam. We called her butter 'country butter', to distinguish it from the 'town butter' you bought in a shop. Thus, almost everything that was needed on a day-to-day basis was produced on the farm. Every Saturday night, the travelling shop from Brady's of Elphin pulled up outside the gate, and my grandmother brought out two trays of eggs which she swapped for tea, sugar and a few other essentials that she couldn't produce herself. No money changed hands. The back of Brady's travelling shop was a genuine market, the only essential kind we would recognize if we knew what was good for us.

The point of money is to facilitate the exchange of products and services. To believe that money itself is the valuable thing is not merely to lose the economic plot, but to misunderstand human existence. To 'trade' not in things that humans need and desire, but in the tokens by which they have arranged to exchange these quantities, is to make inevitable the enormous distortions that now cripple our country. Debt is merely the expression of human desire exceeding human capacity to generate human needs. We have natural inclinations to seek more than we need or can afford, but in a localized, truly rational economy, these tendencies are carefully policed. If, any Saturday evening, my grandmother had only one tray of eggs, she would have had to do without sugar or salt for the coming week. She accepted this and lived with it. Unless this principle is reflected in the money system, it is only a matter of time before disaster strikes.

The biggest problem in our economic world now is that almost all those who explain what is happening have by definition a vested interest in the delusional system that places money at the centre of everything. Thus, we are rarely permitted to see events in essential terms. By definition, economists are expert in money, but know nothing about keeping hens or making country butter. So, when economists talk about 'the markets', they add to both the confusion and the problem: mesmerizing us with jargon, but also distracting our attention from the basic connections that need to pertain between what we produce and what we expect. Journalists, bedazzled by anything smacking of 'science', treat these constructions as holy writ.

Economics is not a science, and never was. Neither is it an ethical programme. It is merely a lurching system of half-understanding that needs to remain aware always of the unpredictable behaviours, uncontainable needs and unquantifiable freedom of humanity. Money is merely a collection of counters and tokens, which fulfil a mechanical function in society. The debt problem is a technocratic matter arising from a malfunctioning of a system that was at best only crudely adapted to human needs.

There is no recession in Europe. There has been no scarcity of essential items, no decline in human needs. The conditions for a functioning economy are as present now as they were a decade ago. The present crisis has nothing to do with a failure of human productivity. To the extent that demand is affected, this is a function of the artificial conditions arising from the malfunctioning of the system.

What is happening in Europe is very simply stated. The failed project of economic integration has created massive imbalances in balance-sheet terms, which are almost precisely matched by an inverted calculus of means. In other words, the countries which appear to have frittered away the most money have the least to show for their experiences of what they assumed to be prosperity. This arose not because of any moral defects but because the system was constructed in such a way as to make this inevitable.

In a hyper-aware culture, once what is called 'confidence' starts to haemorrhage, it becomes difficult for what is known to be forgotten. What distinguishes the present crisis from that of the 1930s is this quality of hyper-awareness, which prevents a clotting of the collective memory. Such clotting, as John Kenneth Galbraith pointed out, runs the risk of eventually leading to a recurrence of the problematic behaviours, but it is also a necessary element of the initial recovery.

Now, there is a further – and possibly lethal – problem. Because the system operates around a gaming table, and depends on the mood and emotion of the players, there is now the possibility that the shock of what has occurred can never be forgotten. For an economic system to be rebooted after such an upheaval requires a certain degree of amnesia. This is the only way that what is called 'market sentiment' can be appeased into something resembling confidence. However, the moralistic discussion provoked at a political level demands the precise opposite: a crystal-clear remembering so that 'this can never happen again'.

This confusion is mirrored in the above-ground discussion of the present crisis. Politicians talk about cutbacks, bond issues, quantitative easing and raising the debt ceilings, but such measures smack of relining the brakes when the driveshaft is broken. A system that is plugged into a gambling casino is at the whim of the most volatile and ruthless of human emotions: respectively, fear and greed. Speculation, borrowing, lending – but also, to a large extent, consumerism – are largely virtual activities, divorced from everyday human necessity. They have real effects in the real world, but are not themselves real in the same way. They are games played around the necessities of human existence, but upon these games depends the security and welfare of the entire community of real people. In many ways, it is quite mad, although very little of the commentary draws attention to its insane aspects. On the contrary, the great 'hope' underlying much of our present commentary is that we will soon be able to reboot the consumer mechanism for one more spin around the block.

To perpetuate its operating logic and to survive for a time in the hope that the markets will 'settle down', the European Union, which had already borrowed insanely from the future, now insists on these borrowings being paid back even as it forces its member economies to borrow yet more to pay off the loans. Austerity programmes designed to 'punish' profligacy and reassure the markets are throttling weaker economies, which lack the instruments – interest rate manipulation, devaluation – by which to jockey their way out of difficulty. These policies sentence already heavily indebted countries to years of deflation and ever-growing indebtedness. For most of the past four years, Ireland has been in a depression, and soon the economists may be flittering through their textbooks in search of a new term to describe our condition. But, as we are beginning to observe, the bigger European economies are in reality no better off, because of the interdependence of the world economies and because they, too, are in debt up to their chinny-chin-chins.

For the past three years, the broad media treatment of what is called 'the financial crisis' has implied that there is, at the heart of these events, a suffering community understanding itself in some way as equating to 'Ireland'. Virtually all such discussion has assumed that we are all, more or less, in a shared boat – that 'our' country has been grievously damaged by events and the actions of politicians, bankers etc. In all such commentary, there has been a continuous sense of a moral convocation: outrage on behalf of Ireland and her people about what has happened to 'us'. But the thought seems unavoidable that among those paying most careful attention to such discussions are people who can tell an inflection point from a hole in the ground and have benefited significantly from such familiarity with concepts that cause other people's brains to melt.

Perhaps, after all, there is no longer a 'we' worth talking about. Perhaps the persistence of such concepts of collective endeavour is a residual fiction based on a nostalgic sense of reality. Perhaps it is not just that a moral convocation is impossible in a country which has turned itself over to the global economy, but that it no longer makes sense to speak of such an entity as a 'country' at all. In the economic sense, there are nowadays only the warring interests of players who seek to become winners in a game which just happens also to govern the real fates of real people living real lives. Perhaps it is nonsensical to appeal to the patriotism and restraint of a community calling itself a nation, when really Ireland is just a business, and not a particularly successful one at that.

But, although, in literal terms, there may no longer be any entity of Ireland to be called 'we', it is in some ways instructive to reflect on the collective drift of things as resulting from a coherent single impetus. In seeking to describe the dominant wave of the past four years, you would perhaps identify a pattern of intense public rage, followed by frantic conjecturing, followed by hoping and resolve – coming in the end to precisely nothing. For four years, we listened, almost constantly, to discussions about options encompassing every conceivable possibility. We moaned and groaned and foamed at the mouth. We went to the core of our economic condition and concluded that it arose from obvious and fundamental mistakes, from greed or corruption. Judging from media-hosted discussions at least, it seemed many times that anything might happen – indeed might be about to happen at any moment – as we discussed burning bondholders, withdrawing from the euro zone, refloating the punt and going it alone. In this discussion, the most radical voices appeared to be the most listened to and respected. The books we bought and presumably read were the ones pointing fingers of blame and offering the most sweeping proposals for a solution. And yet, like Beckett's Unnamable, we go on, although we can't, because we must.

Perhaps things have not yet grown sufficiently bad for us to discover in ourselves the courage that history suggests lies somewhere deep in whatever remains of our collective consciousness. Or perhaps it comes down to the quality of our faith, by which I mean our capacity to envisage possibilities that are not yet present or visible. True change involves a leap into the unknown, and this is only possible if there exists both an overwhelming motivation and a shared belief in some greater force that cares and protects. In the absence of such a confluence, it seems, we cling to what we have, and yet remain puzzled as to why nothing ever changes.

And yet there persists, underneath, this longing for something completely new, as we observed in the 2011 presidential election, when we gazed into the eyes of a previously uncontemplated figure and briefly toyed with the idea of electing him as our moral and symbolic leader. But then, sensing something – or sensing nothing – we lost courage. It is, I suppose, reassuring that, no matter how jaded or weary we become, we remain open to seduction by the possibilities of new beginnings. But always such possibilities are hijacked by the political time-servers, or twisted by the machinations of politics operating independently of the supposedly sovereign people.

There is a music in the soul of Ireland that can still be heard, except that nobody knows they are hearing it because there is so much other noise. 'The harp that once through Tara's halls' does not hang mute, as in Thomas Moore's famous song, but plays softly in the background, its music creating dissonances against the conflicting tunes of the new ideologies which have infected the public realm. On the surface, yes, it is indeed as if the soul of Ireland has fled. The pride of former days undoubtedly sleeps. The hearts that once 'beat high for praise' now appear to beat only for transient things, like sporting success or material gain.

But, sometimes, through the fog of prejudice and irony and rage and self-hating, we hear the music and are moved by it in spite of ourselves. We hear again of the unconditional bravery of some great patriot and not even the collective efforts of the legions of revisionists can talk us out of seeing it for what it is. Mostly, though, we hear the music only in the manner of subliminal advertising – slipping beneath the consciousness, leaving the surface undisturbed. But even then, in these communications with our unconscious, it conveys to us through the ages messages that find their harmony in our DNA, enabling the soul of the nation to breathe feebly on but without self-awareness.

It is hard to speak of such things without being drowned under an ocean of ridicule, and yet many people, in the quietude of their hearts, still hear those chords faintly in the distance – almost tauntingly speaking of what might have been. In the plaintive contrast they evoke between what is and what might be, they bespeak the ruined dreaming of people, our own ancestors, who suffered far more than we can imagine – but gladly, in the hope that their children's children might possibly be free. This music of the Irish ages has been inherited by the present generations whether they know it or not, and mostly they don't. From time to time, as Moore's song essays, it breaks forth in unpredictable and unexpected ways to show that Ireland still lives.

Perhaps Seán Gallagher, in deciding to run for the presidency, sensed or perceived this barely detectable music, and realized that, in spite of themselves, other Irish people might be hearing it too, causing them to hunger without knowing what they were hungering for. Perhaps never before in Irish political history had an electorate wanted something with an intensity equal to its lack of clarity as to what it wanted. Gallagher talked around this desire, in the modern parlance of business opportunities, effort and initiative, and somehow this translated itself beneath the surfaces of public thinking and talking as a correspondence for the deeper felt desires of a people lost without knowing just how lost they were.

In this regard, the extent to which he was an unknown became for him an advantage. Analysts who sought to understand Gallagher's seemingly miraculous trajectory were naturally inclined to look at his qualities, experience and vision. They were not to know that, on this occasion, this was to miss the point. It was the blanks, the vagueness, his inscrutability and absence of clarity that made Gallagher such an attractive candidate.

Martin McGuinness broke the spell, not so much by kicking up mud as by making things literal. His intervention reminded people that they were not writing a screenplay but electing a functionary to live in Áras an Uachtaráin. The man they would choose, however much in keeping with their fantasizing, would have a reality also, and they would have to live with this, perhaps even take responsibility for it if things emerged later. We woke up, and the rest is history.

One way or another, it seems that we are governed by, above all, inertia. The crucial moment in the general election of February 2011 occurred before the campaign started, when a number of high-profile journalists, having feinted a radical alternative, decided not to proceed with the proposed new political movement, named in advance of its not happening as Democracy Now. In the two years up to that moment, we had observed the growth of what might be called a crisis sensibility, whereby it became possible that the outrage being expressed in the extra-political context might be imported into the system. But the revolutionaries, having occupied the public square and monopolized the balcony, suddenly vacated the platform, casting us back upon the standard options. We lurched to the opposite end of the civil war spectrum and embraced an unconvincing coalition of Fine Gael and Labour.

If you consider together the outcomes of the 2011 general and presidential elections, you perhaps begin to perceive a pattern. The sudden surge towards Seán Gallagher, followed by the on-the-rebound embrace of Michael D., is exactly the same process that occurred in the general election. In both cases, we briefly contemplated kicking over the traces before clinging doggedly to Nurse.

But there approaches a day of reckoning when we may have to think the so-far unthinkable, a gloomy Monday morning when Ireland will have to struggle out of its bed, comb its hair, and face the fact that almost everything it has done for nearly four decades has been wrong, and that now it has to start over from the beginning to build its own future. It's a scary thought for anyone, but especially for our leaders, who are expert in nothing but managing our relationship with the EU, on which they – we – have depended, in one form or another, for forty years.

Way back then, when I was a teenager, I became aware that our leaders had taken an ominous fork in the road, committing themselves to a particular way of running Ireland's national affairs. There was, as I often heard my father say, another option: they might have decided to take us on a precarious, courageous and somewhat scary path to self-sufficiency. They took the easier, softer way, and by and large, the people supported them in this. This path to survival meant essentially signing away certain of our rights and resources, in return for the means to build our society in accordance with a more modern blueprint. We signed away most of our fisheries, and accepted subsidies in return for surrendering the right to control our own productive capacities. We agreed to accept all kinds of rules and limits concerning all manner of things, great and small. In return we were given the means of running our society in a way that didn't involve much thought or imagination or courage.

As time moved on, we agreed to go deeper into the bed. Bit by bit, the deal was refined and amended until eventually we began to get used to the idea that, actually, Ireland had been doing itself no favours in insisting upon becoming an independent, sovereign nation. There was more to be had in developing our relationship with 'Europe', and this indeed was the 'modern' way of seeing things. Bigger was better; Independence was for the blinkered and insular-minded. We observed the culmination of this thinking in November 2010, when 'The Troika' came knocking on the national door. Was it for this? No, it wasn't, but what did we expect when we started to dishonour our patriot dead and the sacrifices they had made so that we could live freely?

On the face of things, it was one heck of an achievement to persuade a nation that had spent several centuries fighting for its independence to give it away salami-style, slice by slice, in return for motorways and flyovers, but that's essentially what we did to ourselves. A country that might, for example, by its own lights have become the breadbasket of the world, was reduced to an ecological wilderness dependent on chemical industries and tax dodges. If you think this an exaggeration, count the ploughed fields between Dublin and any major population centre in any direction. Actually, it's not all that surprising. Because we never took the time to truly examine the nature of the toxic relationship we emerged from nine decades ago, we have been doomed to repeat the experience at the first available opportunity.

One way of putting the problem with the European Union would be to say that it is not a union but a dictatorship of the strong over the weak. A decade ago, when the euro currency was introduced, this dictatorship effected a kind of benign manipulation of small European nations using cheap money to inflate human desires with a view to long-term profit. Now, the process works in reverse, with these small nations (and some not so small) being compelled to pay back horrendously engorged debts arising from the hyper-inflation created by an unbalanced and dysfunctional currency and a poorly organized banking apparatus. These circumstances were rendered inevitable by two factors: one, the lack of economic cohesion into which a functional currency might have been bedded down; and two, the requirements of German reunification, which provoked a sluggishness in the German economy, and resulted in interest rates for the whole of the union being set at a level that destroyed the integrity of smaller economies which had never previously been subjected to such an explosion of available credit.

But far worse than any of this is the denials which followed. Instead of admitting what has occurred, a generation of European politicians, and their contemporaries here in Ireland, sought to pretend that the real problem was the unruliness of these decimated small nations. And these small nations, partly through powerlessness, and partly arising from a misplaced guilt provoked by their recent experiences of the inevitable effects of untrammelled credit on their cultures and peoples, engaged in what looked like a half-hearted acquiescence in this characterization – hoping, perhaps, that the shattered fuselage of the Euro-project can be patched up for another flight or two.

On both sides, the necessity for the perpetuation of this humongous lie arises from the self-serving blindness of recent generations of European politicians who cannot bear to contemplate the absolute failure of their guiding ideas and set about leading their peoples back to the beginning at the very time when they expected to be taking a lap of honour.

This is the meaning and purpose of the fiscal compact treaty, about to be considered by the Irish electorate as this book goes to press. Following an uncertain period in which it seemed that the very nature of the euro might come under review, a new climate of normalization is asserting itself, with the compact at its cutting edge. Once in place, this measure will confirm that the problems in the euro zone have arisen solely from the recklessness and profligacy of small nations. The true problem has long been so obvious that the imposition of this fictitious analysis will amount to a miraculous achievement of public indoctrination.

The fiscal compact is analogous to the conjurer's act of misdirection, by which he distracts the audience from the workings of his trick. In practice the compact will be toothless, since it is illogical to threaten struggling economies – as a way of keeping them in line – with massive financial penalties which can only make their situations worse. But the act of misdirection is vital to ensure widespread acquiescence in the idea that the core nations of the EU should suffer minimal consequences for the failure of the euro zone project, while citizens of other EU member-countries pay the full price. Germany and France have achieved this impressive outcome on their own behalf by appropriating the levers of the EU and suspending its already weakened democratic instruments, utilizing their new-found hegemony to insinuate that the EU is entirely the creature of German and French philanthropy. Having hijacked the key EU institutions, they have proceeded to bully and intimidate the feeble leaderships of peripheral countries, and where necessary replaced them. This Franco-German initiative has been assisted by the fears and inadequacies of the leaderships of the aforementioned peripheral nations, and also by inevitable political dynamics governing such democracies, whereby party political rivalry and citizen rage against domestic politicians served to occlude the true and complete nature of the problem. It has been tempting for citizens to place the blame on their own leaders, and this interpretation has been propelled by a short-sighted journalism which contrived to downplay broader, deeper analyses in favour of a cynical populism.

In Ireland, the early signs were that our contemplation of these weighty matters through the medium of referendum would, as usual, be dominated by emotions – mainly fear and rage – driven by misrepresentations and manipulation. The Yes tactic would be to scare people while accusing the other side of scaring people, hoping that our European 'partners' might weigh in with some minor concession on the debt burden to enable them to buy off the electorate once again. The early catch-cry of the Yes side related to the desirability of avoiding 'becoming bogged down in peripheral issues'. But the way things had been going, it was difficult so see how anything could be regarded as peripheral. In this referendum, Ireland faced the most fundamental questions to have confronted an Irish electorate since 1992, when we signed up to the Maastricht Treaty – if not indeed 1972, when we agreed to join what was then known as 'The Common Market'.

But the truth of it is that none of the major Dáil parties is able to envisage ever again participating in an Irish government other than in a relationship with our 'partners' in the EU. The thought of being required to wake up one Monday morning and lead the Irish people away to start over from the beginning causes them to break out in cold sweats.

A No vote would not just be a thumbs-down to our continued membership of the euro, but a verdict on the spineless behaviour of Irish politicians in the teeth of an almost total breakdown in the democratic façade that hitherto characterized the EU. The referendum therefore comes down to whether or not Ireland is prepared to cede the entrails of its sovereignty in exchange for a few more penny rolls and another lump of hairy bacon, or whether we might finally be prepared to think the hitherto unthinkable: that our salvation resides in reclaiming our independence and starting over.

The clearest way of seeing to the root of Ireland's continuing problems is to view us as a nation that exhibits some of the key symptoms of what psychoanalysts call co-dependency. The relevant symptoms include low self-esteem, an excessive tendency towards compliance, inverted narcissism and an inability to function outside of some liaison that by definition becomes unhealthy.

The co-dependent individual seeks out a stronger, more powerful person to become dependent on, and to obtain from that person approval, sustenance and even opinions about the world and everything in it. A psychoanalyst of nations would have to conclude that these characteristics describe Ireland exactly. Just as there are some people who function well on their own, and others who need always to be involved in a relationship, so there are countries which thrive on their own energies and resources and some which need to nestle up to a bigger beast for warmth and security. Ireland is one of these latter types. Our history is best understood as that of a battered spouse who, having escaped from one dysfunctional relationship, immediately began to look for another. Fifty years after breaking free from the clutches of the British Empire, we snuggled up to an even more powerful and – ultimately – more destructive entity. This is where we now awake to find ourselves.

These conditions are underpinned by the ubiquitous generational problem, whereby the natural flow of succession has been interrupted by the failure of the middle-aged and older to devolve power downwards, to integrate the energies and enthusiasms of youth in the creation of a society that will soon belong to this new generation, whether we of the older generations agree to it or not. Thus, every prescription that is offered tends to come from the perspectives forged in the era of failure, and dissent in general tends to be of the impotent and frustrated kind.

We need to go back to the beginning. We need to open our eyes and look at everything as though we were seeing it for the first time. Where such clarity might come from now, and how it might be communicated to the greater number, is hard to say.

But hope lies in believing that something will happen, something unexpected and unpredictable. The Celtic Tiger boom from the mid-1990s onwards, for all its damaging consequences, offers us now at least the memory of something happening that we did not plan, that was not the obvious result of human preparation and scheming: it merely manifested itself as the outcome of a confluence of circumstances which nobody had really remarked upon. We can be certain that a new confluence will soon occur in a similar way, perhaps one involving a realization at the heart of Europe that the failures of the recent past cannot be undone by repeating the same policy mistakes that unleashed disaster, and listening to the same voices that advocated those policies.

We are in the midst of events the equal of Independence, or the Easter Rising, if not, in a certain context, the Great Famine of the 1840s. I mean this not in the sense that the putative collapse of Europe's money system might equal the heroic dignity of these events, but that this moment is equally significant as a milestone in our collective journey. Finally, we have had our illusions about materialism stripped away. The moment when radical government action became necessary to save the Irish banking system was the moment when, for the first time in our history, we came face to face with the fact that all human endeavour, seen purely on its own terms, is eventually futile, that our sense of what sustains us is deluded, that nothing is as it seems. Unless man understands what he is, the world goes nowhere rather than somewhere and then stops in the middle of a sentence, a thought or a cup of tea.

It is easy in our society to forget oneself, to be sucked into a common way of thinking. From early morning until after midnight we are bombarded with a menu of subjects and ways of thinking about them. This is a crucial element of democracy. But, precisely because of the communal dimension of this process, it is easy to overlook the extent to which it tends to fashion our thinking along certain fixed and narrow lines. We imagine we are absorbing an unlimited range of possibilities, but in reality we are offering our intellects and imaginations for all kinds of ideologues and agenda-setters to inhabit rent-free. This has been particularly noticeable over the past four years, since the onset of the present economic crisis, when broadcasters in particular appeared to follow the same relentless path, seemingly in response to a public mood, recycling the same responses day after day and freeze-framing the public mood at a particular pitch of frenzy and hopelessness.

To put it another way: there are different levels of human thinking. At any given moment, I can be trapped within the common mentality created by public conversation, or I can be free to think and feel for myself. Or I can flit between the two, now absorbing the content of a public discussion, then drawing it into myself to judge what it really means for my humanity. Unless I have some way of reminding myself, I will not be aware even of the existence of these different possibilities, never mind knowing which of them applies to me right now. Unaware, I can be swept along by a communal rage or outrage, convinced that a particular event is the most significant of the hour, persuaded that there is only one correct way of seeing it.

Ultimately my citizenship is a communal thing. But it begins in the heart that is mine alone. And just as there is a part of the heart that the transplant surgeon cannot find, the part that opens back into the origin of knowing and being, so there is a part of the citizen's democratic heart that keeps itself detached from what everyone else thinks. Yes, that space needs to be informed by what has been said and done, by the 'facts' of the present as much as the passions and deeds of the past. But there comes a moment when it must retreat into itself to understand things beyond the sway of ideology and manifesto and self-interest.

There is a human dimension to politics that does not find itself in the arguments, the policies, the personalities or the opinion polls. You could, for want of a better word, call it instinct. It is the ultimate human response to another human being, the spark out of which a relationship might grow. It is based on trust and hope and, ultimately, the desire to love and be loved: to be parented in the public domain.

Fundamentally, what has happened is that, for the first time in our history, we have no sense of an elder generation that, though necessarily grey, dull, pedantic, plodding, boring, anal-retentive and somewhat embarrassing, was also driven by a fierce and to us simplistic idealism which burned like a pilot light at the heart of national life. There is now no one of whom we can think, 'They're in charge.' There is no one of whom we can say, as we fall asleep in our lazy, disengaged and feckless beds: 'Those bastards will be on our backs again tomorrow, demanding that we evince and demonstrate a love of country to match their own.' When tomorrow comes, there is something missing: the sense of an elder generation that cares enough to make demands of us. My own generation, now, is that elder generation, and we lack the words to issue such demands.

The result is that, if you listen hard, you notice something missing: the faint heartbeat of a driving idealism, a cohesive sincerity, a slightly ridiculous seriousness of purpose. There is no one to laugh at in the knowledge that, though ridiculed, they still do what they have always done in acting out Ireland's sense of its own importance. And because they don't, Ireland has no importance, and neither do its people, so confused by where they've arrived at that they are no longer able to remember why they were so anxious to forget where they came from.

# Bibliography

Bewes, Timothy, *Cynicism and Postmodernity*, Verso, 1997

Bly, Robert, *The Sibling Society*, Addison-Wesley, 1997

Bohn, Willard Eugene, *Apollinaire and the Faceless Man*, Fairleigh Dickinson University Press, 1991

Caulfield, Max, *The Easter Rebellion*, Roberts Rinehart Publishers, 1964

Crotty, Raymond, *Ireland in Crisis*, Brandon, 1986

Galbraith, John Kenneth, *The Great Crash 1929*, 1955

Havel, Václav, *The Power of the Powerless*, Hutchinson, 1985

Houellebecq, Michel and Lévy, Bernard-Henry, *Public Enemies*, Atlantic Books, 2011

Kundera, Milan, *The Joke*, English translation Coward-McCann, New York, 1969

Lloyd, John, *What the Media Are Doing to Our Politics*, Constable and Robinson, 2004

McDonagh, Martin, *Plays 1*, Methuen Drama, 1999

Mitscherlich, Alexander, *Society Without the Father: A Contribution to Social Psychology* (with a Foreword by Robert Bly), Harper Perennial, 1993

Morozov, Evgeny, *The Net Delusion: How Not to Liberate the World*, Public Affairs, 2011

Patel, Raj, *The Value of Nothing*, Picador, 2009

Pearse, P.H., *Collected Works*, The Phoenix Publishing Company, 1917

Stephens, James, *The Insurrection in Dublin*, The Macmillan Company, 1917

Waters, John, *Jiving at the Crossroads*, Blackstaff Press, 1991; reissue Transworld Ireland, 2011

Waters, John, *Long Black Coat* (with David Byrne), New Island, 1995

Waters, John, *Every Day Like Sunday?*, Poolbeg, 1995

Waters, John, *Lapsed Agnostic*, Continuum, 2007

# About the Author

John Waters has been a columnist with *The Irish Times* for over twenty years. As well as *Jiving at the Crossroads* (Blackstaff, 1991; reissue Transworld Ireland, 2011) his books include *Race of Angels: Ireland and the Genesis of U2* (Blackstaff/Fourth Estate, 1994); *An Intelligent Person's Guide to Modern Ireland* (Duckworth, 1997); *Beyond Consolation: On How We Became Too Clever for God . . . and Our Own Good* (Continuum, 2010); and *Feckers: 50 People Who Fecked Up Ireland* (Constable and Robinson, 2010).